Interviewing and Representation in Qualitative Research

Series Editor: Harry Torrance, Manchester Metropolitan University

This series is aimed at research students in education and those undertaking related professional, vocational and social research. It takes current methodological debates seriously and offers well-informed advice to students on how to respond to such debates. Books in the series review and engage with current methodological issues, while relating such issues to the sorts of decisions which research students have to make when designing, conducting and writing up research. Thus the series both contributes to methodological debate and has practical orientation by providing students with advice on how to engage with such debate and use particular methods in their work. Series authors are experienced researcher and supervisors. Each book provides students with insights into a different form of educational research while also providing them with the critical tools and knowledge necessary to make informed judgements about the strengths and weaknesses of different approaches.

Current titles:
Tony Brown and Liz Jones: *Action, Research and Postmodernism*
Mairead Dunne, John Pryor and Paul Yates: *Becoming a Researcher*
Stephen Gorard with Chris Taylor: *Combining Methods in Educational and Social Research*
Joe Kincheloe and Kathleen Berry: *Rigour and Complexity in Educational Research*
Richard Pring and Gary Thomas: *Evidence-Based Practice in Education*
Maggie MacLure: *Discourse in Educational and Social Research*
John Schostak: *Interviewing and Representation in Qualitative Research*
John Schostak: *Understanding, Designing and Conducting Qualitative Research in Education*
Lyn Yates: *What Does Good Educational Research Look Like?*

Interviewing and Representation in Qualitative Research

John Schostak

Open University Press

Open University Press
McGraw-Hill Education
McGraw-Hill House
Shoppenhangers Road
Maidenhead
Berkshire
England
SL6 2QL

email: enquiries@openup.co.uk
world wide web: www.openup.co.uk

and Two Penn Plaza, New York, NY 10121-2289, USA

First published 2006

A catalogue record of this book is available from the British Library

ISBN-10: 0 335 21240 9 (pb) 0 335 21241 7 (hb)
ISBN-13: 978 0335 21240 8 (pb) 978 0335 21241 5 (hb)

Library of Congress Cataloging-in-Publication Data
CIP data applied for

Typeset by YHT Ltd
Printed in the UK by Bell & Bain Ltd., Glasgow

Contents

Introduction

Don't be misled. The interview is not a simple tool with which to mine information. It is a place where views may clash, deceive, seduce, enchant. It is the inter-view. It is as much about seeing a world – mine, yours, ours, theirs – as about hearing accounts, opinions, arguments, reasons, declarations: words with views into different worlds.

Listening to the lives of others, then, is a curious kind of voyeurism. It is like having many lives by proxy. Vicariously the interviewer lives the memories told through anecdotes. Momentarily there is the thrill of being other than myself as the images, the personas, the actions of others fill my imagination with lives I might have led had I been luckier or less fortunate. There is a kind of pleasure there. But also more than that. There is the hope that somehow by listening enough, something might be learnt and something might be changed.

There's something very familiar about the interview. We submit to them when going for a job, or a place in a college, membership of a club, or as respondents to a street survey. We watch professional journalists attempt to wheedle statements from politicians who dodge and weave. We are entertained by fictional accounts of detectives and spies interrogating suspects. We are drawn into the accounts of the lives of 'stars' or of 'exotic' strangers from other cultures. In each case we know its purpose is to uncover 'truth', reveal 'realities', provide 'information'. We know too that people can lie, provide misleading impressions, or refuse to say anything. So we marvel at the skills of professional and fictional interviewers who seduce, trick, bully or as if by some magic 'empathy' ease the truth from their interviewees. No one can claim the innocence of 'just asking', 'just conversing', or even 'just following the rules of professional or scientific procedure'. Yet, what else do we do but ask questions, allow people to respond and glimpse their worlds? So, interviewing a 50 year old ex-police inspector for a project (Schostak and

Walker 2003), I ask him to tell me about his experience of school. He was:

> a very poor student. I left school with woodwork O level, which was for the (Grammar School) very poor, bottom set. Um education wise I then did most of my things with GCEs through evening classes, maths English and several others. (at the Further Education College) That was after I got married, then started to study for my promotion exams and passed both of those. And then did a couple of A levels because I enjoyed studying. And I realized I wasn't really thick and I could achieve those. And the last one I did funnily enough was during the miners' dispute which would be about 18 years ago now. My daughter came up from school and uh talking about computers. I knew nothing so I went and did a GCE in computer studies. And in the miners' dispute I did all the work in the transit van (brief chuckle).

Just like that, he starts talking, staging his life, his experiences, the settings, the characters, the events that are called out by my earlier statement of the project purpose.

His words tug at my prejudices, my social attitudes, my values. I cannot just be 'objective' – an attitude that will be progressively dismantled throughout this book – yet I do not interrogate him about his role in one of the major events of UK social and political history during the last 50 years, the miners' strike of the early 1980s, a battle with the then Conservative Government led by Margaret Thatcher. It destroyed entire communities, broke families and left a legacy of bitterness that lives still.

Suspending my own interest at this point left the historical conflict as an incidental background to his own day-to-day agendas of 'getting on with the job', advancing his career, bringing up his children. The ways in which conflicts are foregrounded and backgrounded either by the speaker-as-interviewee or the listener-as-researcher create the theoretical and practical tensions through which contemporary issues can be explored and so a project developed as a course of reflection upon everyday experiences. The notion of the project as a course of critical reflection is developed in the earlier companion book to this, Schostak 2002. Here, the inter-view creates the conditions to see what is at stake for individuals, communities, societies as a project evolves. It goes beyond introductory approaches to methodologies by revealing the fragility and ambiguities inherent in apparent generalities, systems of categories, knowledge, facts, identities, structures and processes. As such it identifies the points of challenge to taken for granted views and draws out the implications for political and ethical struggles.

Although the project purpose was to explore what in the biography of each individual led them to their decision to change from one career to that of teaching, it also provided unexpected insights into the memories of those who had been participants or witnesses of the historical drama of the miners' strike. Thus, this snippet is not inconsequential. It has the power to position the speaker (as well as myself as listener, and the readers of this book) on one side or another politically. An attitude is struck for or against the speaker, the writer, or some commentator who reads this account and then speaks about it. How is such an attitude constructed, personally, socially, politically, philosophically, historically ...? What does it say about contemporary ways of living? How does it relate to the specific project purpose? To deal with these questions requires an exploration – see Chapter 5 – of what is at stake in recognizing how one is positioned by adopting attitudes towards others, their actions and their ways of thinking.

But this seems a long way from the routine and the practical needs of collecting, processing and analysing piles of interview transcripts. How this is done is the subject of hundreds of introductory textbooks each providing the survey or 'in-depth' rituals of academic research practice. Yet, the experience of gaining access to people, doing the interview, dealing with the scripts that pile up, and reflecting on the meanings in many ways un-do the how-to-do prescriptions and invite deceits that cover up the gaps, the short-cuts, the appeals to authorities only partly read and understood. Repressing these problems undermines understanding, the facilitation of change, and engagement in action. Homing in on the underlying social and personal conflicts of contemporary life, and on the methodological and theoretical paradoxes, conflicts, contradictions generates a different kind of practice to that of the ritualized performances of textbook research. The practice pursued in this book is embedded in the nexus of problems animating the debates of competing philosophical traditions with their very different implications for 'knowledge', personal, social, political and historical 'meaning', ethical behaviour and hope for the future. I adopt a position crudely describable as an anti-totalitarian humanism, that is, a position focusing on the experience of individuals living their lives which seeks to dismantle authoritarian and totalitarian threats to their existence.

The practice that follows from this I call the inter-view. A simple hyphen that splits the word – a textual sleight of hand that disrupts, puns and opens alternative readings – enables a change of focus. This textual play has been done before, many times, for similar purposes. What it does is allow a suspension to take place, its meaning unfolding through practice, taking on the meanings of particular project purposes and experiences rather than imposing a dictionary definition. It does not key into a ready-made toolkit to allow novice researchers to go out and ask scripted questions. It creates the basis for engagement with others, the openings for dialogue, the modes of drawing out views, the strategies for forming and framing questioning, the critical approaches to analysis, the strategies for representation politically, ethically and textually, and an approach to writing views. To say the inter-view is a way of seeing as a condition of asking and hearing is at this stage misleading. But it will have to do. It has a resonance with two other key terms, inter-subjectivity, and intertextuality. Like them it refers to a process extending beyond the given instance, individual, utterance and text. One subject, one text, one view connects complexly to others, transforming the given instance, the particular, as a way to explore contemporary circumstances and debates.

So, continuing the example, a year earlier, by chance – and chance or contingency or the accidental is what the research project both struggles with and evolves through – I interviewed a young man, an ex-miner:

> (...) I was 16 after I left (school). I worked for an engineering firm for about 3 months, three or four months they kept offering me an apprenticeship and then it turned into a YTS scheme, so I left. (...) So I chucked it. Basically I was offered a job in the mines. Um, I come from a mining family, a mining village. It was always said you were guaranteed a job in the mines. As I got in it wasn't entirely true but it was almost. There were people with no common sense at all working in the mines so if you ended up working with them you ended up training them. (lists various jobs he had in the mines, ventilation systems, haulage train driving ...). I went on the development side but I was still being pulled back to train these people up in these other jobs I've already done. Um when they closed the mine I left and went travelling but about a year before, and I did steel erecting, brick work, carpentry anything basically you can always work, there's always someone who works for someone who has, who needed a spare pair of hands. I did all sorts of stuff. So a bit of a jack of all trades and master of none.

There is now a juxtaposition of anecdotes, snippets from personal histories that become rhetorically powerful because of the miners' strike, an event in common with the police inspector which led in 18 June 1984 to the notorious Battle of Orgreave. It was posed in the language of war, summed up in Thatcher's statement in July 1984 'We had to fight the enemy without in the Falklands. We always have to be aware of the enemy within, which is more difficult to fight and more dangerous to liberty' (quoted in: Schostak 1993). The two transcripts are now intertextually connected not only with each other but with all the texts produced during and after the miners' strike. One can imagine the young man, his friends, his family on the picket lines while the then young police officer was in the transit van. The historical event is dramatized in personal terms. The one was fighting for his job, the other just doing his job, planning for his future. Each were members of distinct communities – intersubjectively entwined in struggle – sharing common experiences, facing common problems, applying common solutions. As such they represent *anyone* who was either a miner or a police officer at that time.

Both were elements in a larger political drama concerning the demands of labour, the demands of employers and the demands of government. There is a sense also in which science in its quest for knowledge and for control desires to reduce the uniqueness of the individual to the status of 'anyone'. So, as individuals they were marshalled into position, one employee set against another. Both were from similar working class backgrounds, just wanting a job in order to earn money and get on with their lives.

In this simple juxtaposition is an image of the deep social divisions which impact on individuals who seek simply to live out their lives. Philosophies of various kinds have sought either to reconcile or to manage in some way such perceived divisions in their theoretical, practical and existential forms. An approach to exploring and handling divisions will be discussed throughout the book as a way of employing the inter-view as the process through which the multiplicities of views are drawn into expression and debate to create the conditions for creative change. A guiding question is: How can one gain a view of each other's lives that somehow opens the way to understanding their personal experiences and the complex connections these have with the multiplicities of alternative perspectives, subjective interests and circumstances of the world about? And thus, how can one draw from the analysis of personal accounts the socially and historically significant themes, issues and questions that shape/structure interests as personally and politically significant motives for action and change?

Methodological and philosophical debates that question claims to 'knowledge', 'understanding', and the validity of representations of data derived from interviews, observations and the collection of various artefacts are essential to maintaining an openness to the views of the other and to 'otherness' as the seeds through which creative change can be fostered. Careers, social status, and economic rewards are typically dependent upon how the report of a research project is received by those whose interests may be quite different, who may wish to focus on control rather than emancipation. Funders, for example, may not like the findings of a project. They may be inconvenient for policy makers who want to claim success for a particular strategy or blame a particular group in a given organization for all the problems. Powerful bodies may attempt to control and even suppress reports. Thus, the findings of a particular report may be 'unpopular', showing an aspect of society that the majority (or the powerful elites able to control or manipulate news media) would prefer not to see. The research enterprise is therefore riven by conflicts or splits at personal, methodological and social levels. Hence, as a political enterprise researchers may weave the views and interests of different groups to gain the maximum support as explored in Chapters 5 to 9.

It would be so simple if there were a theory of interviewing to be applied, and a set of methods that incorporate well defined procedures and techniques resolving splits and conflicts and hence reducing the sense of the researcher's political and ethical angst. Increasingly, there are calls to develop research training courses at masters, doctoral and post-doctoral levels. The emphasis is on 'training', ensuring the researchers of the future have a proper grounding in the methodological practices that have become accepted as 'scientific method' so that research is directed towards the needs of policy makers and 'users'. The danger in this is that the courses produce 'competent' and boring research that reproduces the accepted research designs that never fundamentally questions the basis of the practice that is presented as 'good practice'. As Rabaté (2002) complained of the boring theses produced by students who have learnt how to produce literary Theory through a technicization of the complex writings of people like Barthes, Kristeva, Irigary, Derrida, Foucault, Deleuze as they are represented for the purposes of university courses and examinations, so social research degrees are in a similar danger of becoming boring by being reduced to 'training'. The function of the 'boring' is to cause no ripples, no critical thinking, no innovation, no challenge, no surprise. When such trainees are let loose on the world they are safe, compliant, useful to policy makers and other 'users' – that is, they are boring. To counter such policy driven trends in research training and the myriad of methodological textbooks that feed them research, like Rabaté's Theory, should 'move, seduce, entrance, keep desire in motion, in other words be "sexy"' (2002: 16). Research too often abstracts, squeezes the personal life out of the accounts provided by people thus ridding the 'findings' of the ambiguities, paradoxes, existential dilemmas, deceptions, lures and lusts of the actors involved. How to be 'sexy', retain the 'jouissance', the pleasure of doing research, creating theory, discovering the accounts of people's lives will be a key thread throughout the chapters of this book.

It starts in Chapter 1 by embedding the process of interviewing for project purposes within the context of the complexities and deep divisions pervading intellectual, individual and social life. It sets up strategies through which an inter-view strategy can be developed as a basis for an emancipatory project.

Chapter 2 addresses the questions raised in Chapter 1 through a discussion of what has been called the 'linguistic turn' in academic approaches to studies of cultural production, society and the individual. It explores the play of the signifier – underscoring the body – the role of language in the inter-view as a model through which social life is organized, identities constructed, subject positions identified and action framed and justified and the process of reading and writing the politics and ethics through which views are articulated. It presents an approach to the inter-view by which a field of struggle for meaning can be represented.

The experience of accomplishing an interview is discussed in Chapter 3, as a creative, conflictual, lived experience set alongside the earlier discussions of language to develop the inter-view as a strategy for mapping, representing and exploring the world as a network of 'addresses' where people are 'criss-crossed' with subject positions calling out different interests and responses during interviews.

Chapter 4 directly addresses the question of the interpretation of given transcripts in terms of their transposition from the context of the speaker and listener to that of debates in other contexts, places and times. As a subject of interpretation, the individual is always placed into the position of asserting, clarifying, elaborating and defending his or her intentions. It raises the question of whether it is possible to read innocently.

Chapter 5 provides a discussion of the ways in which subject positions are constructed, enacted and frame the identities of self and others, how they relate to each other and how they respond to, organize and use the world of 'others' and 'things'. The chapter explores the value and use of the interview for the political representation of relationships that both augment and constrain the powers of individuals occupying particular positions or ranges of positions within networks of relationships.

Chapter 6 develops the political implications of subject positions and the impact of intersecting subject positions on individuals and social life. It explores in detail the processes of constructing and dissolving alliances between people whose interests are shaped by multiple subject positions. By focusing closely on interview transcripts, the structures of desire, reasons and perceived causes can be mapped that generate the political games through which people strive to win access to opportunities, resources and rewards. In the process of analysing the transcripts and exploring the implicit political structures, processes and issues the chapter provides a way of 'growing' the research project to represent the emergent themes and issues. However, the project may also be 'grown' through exploration of the ethical issues implicit in the ways subjects are positioned. This leads then to the themes of the next chapter.

As politics is one side of the face explored through interviewing, so ethics is the other. Chapter 7 focuses attention on witnessing, judgement, value and truth in making choices between different interests and courses of action. In the inter-view difference is experienced, explored, judged and represented in ways that can be positive or negative in their impact on the individual and on relations between individuals. Opening out to or closing off from the views of others, is an ethical as well as a political choice.

Chapter 8 makes explicit the role of the anecdote in the interview for the development of projects and the production of narrative case records as a means of representing the political, ethical and everyday experiences and interests of individuals. And Chapter 9 continues this process of representing experiences, realities, interests in the relation between the interview and 'writing' as a mutual process of multiple readings and writings. The inter-view is at the very inter-face of what can be thought, what can be represented and what *is*, in terms of what is experienced, is the case, is in existence. The one face turned towards the ideal, the conceptual, the theoretical has to do with reason, logic the necessary – the universal. The other has to do with what actually happens that is, the chancy, the contingent, the uncertain – the particular. Writing the play between the particular and the universal has both mimetic and poetic dimensions. The mimetic draws upon the rhetoric of realism, the production of valid copies of the real. The poetic opens towards the 'truth' talked about by people that cannot be reduced to propositional logic, the correspondence between a statement and a brute observable 'fact'. Finally, to generate the conditions for emancipatory strategies for writing the play between the mimetic organization of the real and the poetic is subjected to what Rabaté (2002) calls, following Lacan, hystericization. In brief, by hystericization is meant the continual subjecting of authorized knowledge, expertise and any notion of an Absolute and thus any totalitarian tendency to questioning. All forms of authority are thereby relentlessly undermined. We all ask questions, all the time. However, how we ask questions and how we reflect upon the answers provided will determine what we say we 'know' and 'believe', will influence our relations with others, the world and our actions and thus determine the possibility for emancipatory writing and action.

The Interview in the Project Context

Here's a challenge:

> I was really looking forward to Tom starting school 'cos it had been like 10 years I'd been you know, all the time taken up with the children which I adored but I had a real crisis, I was so looking forward to it, as I say I didn't want to get shot of them I just thought I'd have some bit of me back um and I just completely lost it and I cried for a fortnight I completely and utterly lost it and uh Stephen wasn't having any of that so he said you need a job, you need to get out and do something, you know. I think it's just like self esteem 'cos you just feel like you've, all you've done (...) I was 35 and I'd got three children, they're great and I'm Stephen's wife and that's great and then where's me uh you know, I just felt like I didn't have an identity.
>
> (Schostak and Walker 2002)

Listening to people's lives, recording their experiences, their moments of crisis, their frailties, their intimacies, these are the challenges to the researcher. What is this moment of listening? And how does it 'translate' into the text of the transcript? How is the text then to be read? By focusing upon that moment of engagement between people where each attends to and addresses the other, this moment of engagement is critical for every dimension of what it means to be human. It sounds like a grand statement. But here an emancipatory project either stands or falls.

In this moment, my interviewee, call her Maggie, described being 'utterly lost'. She had been looking forward to the freedom of her children growing up and becoming less reliant on her. However, the sense of freedom did not materialize. Her whole being had been caught up in her family. Her sense of identity as founded in a relation to others provides a way of describing how her world is structured and how that structure either enables or disables action. The structure is rather like a knot. Knotted together in her identity are the interests and needs of her children, and her husband. It is this knotting that constitutes the social ground of her existence. Freedom, or emancipation, within the context of this structure is thus threatening to her existence since it involves a 'letting go' or 'cutting ties' with others. When the ties were felt to be cut, her husband witnessed the collapse and in her words as she developed the story, 'took charge' in order to re-connect her, to fix her identity in relation to a job able to reconstruct her 'self esteem,' re-tie her back into a recognizable social role, that is, re-ground her in the social. Now, what in the life-drama that this extract has described may be considered as pointing to an emancipatory project, if any, for the individual concerned? Thinking this through will require an exploration of the role of the interview in opening up views through which the conditions enabling both the possibility for emancipation and its opposite can be described. That is the object of the following sections.

Theorizing the Interview

Crudely, the interview can be described in terms of individuals directing their attention towards each other with the purpose of opening up the possibility of gaining an insight into the experiences, concerns, interests, beliefs, values, knowledge and ways of seeing, thinking and acting of the other. In the extract above, Maggie is open to questions that might seem intrusive, impertinent, too nosey within the context of polite conversation. However, this is not to say that an interview only occurs where it is explicitly said, 'this is an interview ...'. Rather, it points to certain conditions under which an interview is possible, conditions where a degree of openness is brought about. But what is meant by openness?

By openness I refer to a relationship between the participants of an interview where each as addressee of the other contains the mark of the other at least as possibility within themselves. Addressing another, that other must already have available within themselves a category, like an empty waiting room, where what I say as originating from a point external to their own thoughts and feelings can arrive and fill that category with views recognizable as 'other'. The category I refer to has no content other than saying whatever content arrives is 'other'. So, in order to address another and be addressed by another, a given subject must already hold within, the place of arrival of the other as a possibility. That is to say, a subject as a human being is always in relation, which means, in a state of 'being towards' something outside itself (or in the case of reflection, is capable of making a difference within itself in order to hold itself as an object) and thus makes available within itself a place of arrival for that which is other than itself. If this were not the case, no subject could ever change or be influenced by anything outside itself or indeed be capable of self reflection. Such a subject could not change. Metaphorically, the subject would be like a perfect circle, fully enclosed admitting nothing in and letting nothing out. There could be no 'waiting room' able to accept some content external to the circle. This circle is fully saturated with itself. Think of the yin and yang of Taoism: a circle composed of black and white flows. The white contains within it the seed of the black as the black contains within it the seed of the white. Each seed grows but cannot fully saturate the space in which it grows because as it grows the seed of the other emerges within it. And so the process continues. More formally, Gasché (1999: 1–13) describes the general structure of the concept of relation as a 'minimal thing', the essence of which is being-toward. The subject of a relation always tends towards the other as the other (as object of, address of, target of the relation) 'lets the subject come into a relation to it', thus '(t)here is no relation, then, without a prior opening of the possibility of the being-toward-another by which the subject is allowed to arrive "in" the place of the other. Without this gift of an opening for a subject to turn toward the other, no relation would ever be able to occur' (1999: 9). This difficult concept of relation as being-toward, and in particular, the nature of being human as being in relationship, is implicit in the examples explored in each chapter. It is fundamental to the concept of the interview that I will develop.

Returning to Maggie's interview extract it can be theorized as a relationship, a mutually constructed being-towards-the-other accepted by myself and Maggie. As interviewer, my 'gift' was to create a space within myself for her to talk and so address something of herself towards me. This was a space without prior content signifying nothing other than a place where otherness could arrive. What I mean by this is: in asking and in listening, the content that I received was recognized as other to my own interests and internal processes of constructing meanings and construing relevances. There is a similarity here with the phenomenological strategy of 'bracketing', that is, taking no position either for or against the truth, being or existence of a phenomenon or object. But only a similarity. A recognition of otherness is more than a suspension of one's taken for granted values, beliefs and knowledge. Such a suspension cannot take place without a recognition of the otherness of what is being suspended, nor without recognizing that this very otherness constitutes myself as a subject. That is, how can I know myself as a subject without there being something other than myself as subject? Without an other there would be no possible way of making a demarcation. Yet, to know this is also to harbour the other as an other in waiting (Gasché 1999: 8). The interview, then, is a particular case of being towards the other, recognizing the otherness of the other and in so doing not reducing this otherness to a sense of 'the same'. By this I mean: if the other is truly other, then there is no place where the otherness of the other can be simply reduced to being 'just the same as me' at some fundamental level. A religion might want to say we are 'all God's children', or a western Enlightenment philosopher might want to say we are 'all rational creatures'. The power – and indeed the tyranny – of this 'all' is to reduce all difference, all essential otherness, to an homogenous base. Once so reduced, then sweeping statements can be made about what is in the best interests of 'all'; and more dangerously, acted upon. So, the gift that is made is to recognize the particularity, the uniqueness and thus the otherness of the other.

Her gift to me was to open a space within herself where the otherness of my questions, my curiosities, my concerns, my interests, could arrive and be the focus for her self reflections. The notion of 'gift' in relation to otherness is essential to the emergence of the interview as a space/place, a kind of perpetual waiting room, where otherness is expected and awaited but never assimilated. Furthermore, the 'gift' signifies something that does not belong within the market place of exchange where all is reduced to exchange value, property rights and competitive struggle to gain the upper hand. Having said this, 'gift' and 'market exchange' signify different conditions under which relationships can emerge. They are not polar opposites in the sense of parcelling up the universe of all possible relationships into either gifts or market exchange. Rather, without the gift pre-existing market exchange (together with the market produced concept of a 'free gift', or the gift of a market bought product or service at Christmas) no market could exist. In this particular use of the word 'gift', the world is presupposed as existing, as being there in its otherness. However, in market exchange terms this otherness is reduced to being simply raw materials open to work, to use, to exploitation, to appropriation. Gift then refers to a prior condition that must exist if the world of market exchange is to be possible. Crudely, the substance of the world pre-exists (that is as gift) any appropriation of it by people who establish property laws, monetary systems and rules of market competition.

It is this condition of gift that makes possible the interview as a space/place where otherness is not reduced to being but an aspect of some common or homogeneous underlying substance that can be fully categorized, explained, interpreted, theorized, controlled and exploited. It is the difference that enriches the encounter by expanding the field of experience. However, rather than the excitement, the creative challenge of otherness there is the reductive possibility where otherness is marginalized, and differences erased in order to maintain a sense of all being a part of the same underlying substance or framework or structure. Here, for example, market exchange transforms relations between others into a scene of struggle for control, for mastery, for ownership of meanings, positions, objects and territories (see Chapters 4, 5, 6 and 7 for further development of these themes). This does not mean that reductive strategies like market exchange necessarily and fully supplant or overcome, negate or saturate the space/place of the gift. The gift always remains as a possibility through which reductive strategies such as market exchange are open to deconstruction. Methodologically, this means that the interview has to be approached in a double fashion: in terms of the possibilities of its constitution (whether as arrangements of gift giving; or as reductive arrangements like market exchange) and in terms of its deconstruction towards an infinitely expanding, fluid, field of differences. It is because of the double fashioning that the research project takes shape as a way of articulating either an emancipatory project, or as a reductive project of mastery over limited aspects of the world, or as totalitarian control over all. The emancipatory project is essentially open ended seeking to explore open systems where as the reductive project seeks closure and thus to formulate the conditions for closed systems of control (cf. Bhaskar 1975 and 1978).

This double fashioning has an echo in the word 'interview' itself which can be broken up into 'inter' and 'view' on the one hand or articulated as the closed unity of the 'interview' on the other. Taking 'inter-view' first, this initial splitting of the word places a grid – or matrix – over the terrain of the apparent unity of the 'interview' whether conceived of as 'event', 'block of text' or as a 'classifying set of interactions'. In one part of the grid, as it were, the 'inter' implies some space between, or some relationship that is taking place between two or more 'elements', 'particles', or in someway definable entities existing in definable spaces. This inter generates a sense of priorness to relationship, a betweenness which must exist if there are to be relationships. The betweenness is as real as the physical distance between New York, Hong Kong and London. Yet, the betweenness cannot be pointed to separately from the physical distance. Nor can the betweenness be simply reduced to this physical distance. It cannot be picked up and separated out except conceptually. However, the betweenness does not just exist conceptually as an intramental phenomenon. It has an external reality in the sense of being a real, discoverable phenomenon that is a particular quality of an external (as well as an internal) world. In this sense, it is what Gasché calls a minimal 'thing'. This 'thingness' of the inter means that there is a real, if minimal, separation that both makes a relationship possible but also creates a sense of uncertainty while in the state of betweenness. Flying to New York, will the plane arrive on time, will I be ill as a consequence of the flight, will it be hijacked, will the pilot be able to land safely ... and so on. The space between two or more people who are conscious of each other (or indeed, the betweenness that separates me from the five year old child that I recall being to the adult I now am) is more complex still given that unlike the aeroplane I can never arrive in a place called 'you' (or 'me-then'). Yet, as a conscious being I can look towards, listen, converse, touch and go along with the other and so build a view, or multiple views of this being-with and this being towards, and this betweenness that characterizes our relationships with others (and indeed, reflections upon who we were and who we might become).

Thus the 'view' suggests that located in some determinate space a 'seeing' is taking place, or a scene exists *here and now* that can be *observed* by some witness, or had existed *there and then*. The role of the witness is vital. Without the mediation of the witness the correspondence between what is said and the reality of what is being talked about cannot be ascertained in anyway. The articulated view of the witness is thus critical. This notion of the articulation of a view by a witness and its importance for theory can be elaborated in terms of the ancient Greek connection between theory – *theoria* – and witnessing.

There were certain accredited individuals who were on special occasions to witness events and to attest to the fact that they had indeed taken place:

> The structure of the functioning of the Greek *theoria* is as follows then: between the event and its entry into public discourse, there is a mediating instance invested with undeniable authority by the polity. This authority effects the passage from the seen to the told, it puts into socially acceptable and reliable language what it apprehends. This authority, the *theoria*, has to use language itself though, and its language is not yet covered by the guarantees it brings to the polity. In fact, it must construct that guarantee within itself, although the *theoria* is alone socially recognized as capable of wielding such language. The structure of such a language must be of a nature to permit the following, admittedly awkward paraphrase: 'We who now address you here, were there then, and we witnessed there then what we are about to tell you here now in order that you here and we here may all talk here now and in the future about how what happened there then affects us here.'
>
> (Godzich, p. xv in: de Man 1986)

Similarly, the interview sets two witnesses side by side, as it were, each attesting to their views *here and now* complexly in relation to various *theres and thens*. However, in the matrix of heres and nows, theres and thens subjects are continually shifting positions over time without ever being able to hang onto an experience except in memory and without ever drawing close one to another. The interview thus existentially places individuals in relationship to others and their worlds at the same time as it is a recognition of the radical separation between individuals. No individual can step 'inside' the experience of another. Bataille had another way of putting it!

Each being is distinct from all others. His birth, his death, the events of his life may have an interest for others, but he alone is directly concerned in them. He is born alone. He dies alone. Between one being and another, there is a gulf, a discontinuity.

    This gulf exists, for instance, between you, listening to me, and me, speaking to you. We are attempting to communicate, but no communication between us can abolish our fundamental difference. If you die, it is not my death. You and I are discontinuous beings.

(Bataille 1987: 12)

That is to say, the interview is not a tool but an encounter, an event amongst other events in the lives of people. Each encounter involves negotiations, calculations, interpretations. If we knew what others were going to say, presumably we would not bother to ask them. And if we could trust their words, and if we could ensure ourselves of the neutrality and comprehensibility of their accounts, just asking and just listening would be the simplest of acts. At the heart of the interview, therefore, there are essential (or necessary) discrepancies, differences between views, a continual postponement of certitude and comprehensibility, or, a lack that can never be filled except in fantasy. Each interview is a partial (both incomplete and biased) view of particular states of affairs or events. Any move one person makes to or away from another involves a degree of risk, a risk of misunderstanding, of misjudgement, of misadventure. It also involves an opportunity to enrich experience through increasing the field of difference, where new things to see, feel, think about multiply. This process makes possible new articulations of experience. That is to say, new ways of combining or knotting together differences into syntheses. In the extract from Maggie's interview she claimed that her husband opened the way to explore different, previously unthought of ways of re-forming her identity. In the process she 'knotted together' activities and experiences of which she had no previous acquaintance or indeed access: studying for a foundation course and then a degree and teacher training qualification. As a result her sense of identity underwent changes. The object of my interview with her was to explore her accounts of these experiences and changes. In that sense, she was the witness to her own experiences. To what extent was she a reliable witness?

    As with the Greek *theoria* the role of witnessing in the interview slides towards a role of representing what is seen, felt, heard, experienced, thought about. How can eye-witness accounts be trusted? The Greeks decided on selecting those who could be socially recognized as wielding authority, who could use appropriate language and thus be masters of a given situation. Through such a witness the complexity of the witnessed events becomes reduced to a legitimized closed unity bearing a one-to-one relationship between 'what happened' and 'this account of what happened'. Likewise, contemporary approaches seeking to master the messiness of reality and achieve the security of the closed unity of the account and the event, and the trustworthiness of witnesses, formulate various procedures to standardize interviews to reduce interviewer bias and create the basis for comparison and quantification. It is, as it was for the ancient Greeks, a search for legitimation, for trustworthiness, to inform judgements, decisions and action. However, language as a medium for the representation of personal and social experience and of symbolic phenomena and processes is not that easy to control. Nor is there any simple relationship between account and event. Indeed, such attempts to control add to the sources of distortion and bias by reducing the complexity of what is being witnessed into pre-ordained, or limited frameworks of categorization. Maggie's way of describing, interpreting, explaining and naming the event is just one amongst many once the privileged authority of the speaker-as-author is under question.

There is then, something of a dilemma. The interview as inter-view generates an ever expanding field of difference and otherness which can be mapped and explored but at the cost of uncertainty and thus the risk of misinterpretation. The interview as a closed unity mastered by a legitimated witness, or a legitimated procedure produces texts capable of comparisons, measurement and generalization at the cost of over-simplification and hence distortion. Any validity achieved is thus more technical than real. Is there a solution? The answer, or at least the seeds of an answer, will be more fully discussed in relation to language and signifying systems in the next chapter. For now, the dilemma can be seen to motivate debate: that is, a multiplicity of views concerning issues of witnessing, legitimation, otherness. This in itself is a clue as to the resolution (or rather, for reasons to be discussed in the next chapter, a quasi-resolution). The many voices of many views are drawn out in the interview. The existence of such multiplicity generates effects. The next section will provide an introductory illustration of these effects and the practical implications of the theoretical developments made so far.

From Theory to Practice

Already, it can be seen that the interview is much more than a simple tool to be neutrally applied in undertaking a given project within some chosen perspective such as Marxism, phenomenology, or indeed some poststructuralist or postmodern anti-perspective through which professional or student researchers claim to frame 'pure' or 'applied' research while undertaking their cultural studies, ethnographies, case studies, action researches, or evaluations. The implications for a particular research project, whether funded or otherwise, whether personal or professional, whether novice or experienced can now be drawn out, not exhaustively, nor definitively, but suggestively and provisionally at this stage. To recap:

1. The interview is an encounter by individuals who:
   a. Stand in a relationship of being-towards each other;
   b. Are fundamentally discontinuous from each other – the gulf that separates them cannot be closed;
   c. Experience each other as *other*;
   d. Adopt the role of witness and of giving accounts of what is witnessed, that is, the 'observed' real, mimetically represented.
2. The condition of 'gift' makes possible the interview as a space/place of relations between differences, between othernesses.
3. The mutual recognition of subject and other founds an essentially human relationship, creating the conditions both for identity (as *this* rather than, or as distinct from, *that*) and for change since *this* has within it the seeds of *that*. That is, the constitution of identities-in-action; or, the performance of identities through the medium of the interview.
4. Any lack of mutuality founds the other as object capable of being fixed, manipulated, controlled, and for example exchanged under market conditions.
5. Differences are articulated to produce syntheses, or quasi-unities which create the sense of substance of a world and of a subject.

The practice of the inter-view, whether as closed unity or open field of ever-expanding differences, begins in the encounter. What follows can only be mapped but not predicted by an emergent theory of the inter-view.

Imagine three scenarios of encountering the other. The first is being alone, wandering through the countryside. Suddenly you see someone far in the distance. It is difficult to know whether this person is moving towards you or moving parallel to you. Gradually you realize the individual is approaching you. How do you read the situation? Will the stranger pass by quietly? You look for clues. What sort of clues? If you are a woman and the stranger is a man will your search for clues differ than if it were two men, or two women who were approaching each other?

Now imagine another case. You are walking along a busy street, you barely notice the strangers that pass by. Suddenly a hand holding a bowl rises up towards you from someone seated cross legged on the pavement. How do you react? Do you pass by barely registering the fact? Or, do you drop a coin in the bowl?

Finally, the third scenario: you enter a shop in search of some item. The salesperson greets you with the words "Good morning, and how are you today?" Do you respond with a detailed account of your aches and pains, your financial worries, or how well you're doing in your present job?

There is a potential danger in the first scenario that can be ignored in the other two. However, what if in the second scenario the scene had been a darkened, empty back alley? Or, what if in the third scenario the location was not a shop but the consulting room of a surgeon you had visited because of serious fears for your health? In each case the responses to the words and actions of the other would change. It is not just that the context makes a difference. It is that in coming face to face with another their potential intentions have to be taken into account. I cannot treat the other who is conscious, like I would the thing that is not conscious. The other makes judgements, has intentions, desires, feelings and can act upon them towards me.

In each of these scenarios of meeting, the subject analyses the possible intentions and courses of action of the other just as in a game of poker or chess each player continually assesses and reassesses the state of play. If I do this will the other do that? If the other does this, then I will have to respond by doing that. There is a continual calculation of possibilities, consequences and responses. The relation between subject and other bears no relation to elements subject to the physical laws of cause and effect. If a lit match touches the gunpowder it will explode (unless there are intervening conditions such as water preventing the gunpowder from lighting). However, thinking, emotional, ethical or deceitful beings can respond in ways that are surprising, inconsistent, not in their best interests just as much as they might respond in ways that are entirely predictable if they choose to follow clear rules of logic in circumstances that are amenable to such rules. Hence, the interviewer – just as much as the interviewee – will assess the relationship that is taking place: what is at stake in the interview? What is at stake will impact on the kind of relationship that is in play. To explore this point a little further here is another extract from the same project as the opening extract from Maggie.

Frank is a successful businessman who had decided to retire early and then retrain as a school teacher. He described his early school experience:

> It was a Catholic grammar school um where discipline was, you know, the first and the last um, knowledge wasn't dispensed for for joy or for or um self improvement. Knowledge was dispensed to pass exams and that was it you know. You'd sit mock exams again and again and again until you got it right and then you were good enough to take the exam and then you'd move onto the next one. It wasn't the case of oh isn't this a wonderful book to read, you know, isn't maths fun you know, it was just constant um just the old style um old style keep repeatin' it until you get it right and um and a hard stick round the back of the head now and again just to make you concentrate (mark 10). It wasn't a very

pleasant experience. Couldn't look back and say any teachers were alright. Even at the age of um 47 there's there's some that if I met in the street now, 'cos they must be you know in their 70s, I'd I'd willingly walk up and punch them in the mouth because it was ... well, the world's moved on. The way they behaved was acceptable then um t' to inflict pain on, on little kids but um I don't, no compunction but to pu' punch 'em in the mouth (laughs) for what they did to me. (...) There were specific things that you know, will always live with you and you have to come to terms with them or else you'll go mad um I mean, I came home from school once with my my face all all all bruised completely blue from bruisin' round there and my parents said what happened to you and I said you know (XXX) who was my form master decided it would be good fun to grab hold of my chin and lift me up off the floor by my chin and, they said oh well you must have you know 'cos they were they were good good Catholics and they couldn't believe that anything that um happened at school by the masters or the monks could possibly be um in any way sinister or sadistic it was just all good education. Yeah and I mean the same ... the same teacher ... gave me ... six of the best with a cricket bat once, you know and I couldn't sit down for for for a few days.

(Schostak and Walker 2003)

As a child, face to face with teachers and parents, he expressed in this extract an underlying conflict, feelings of alienation, betrayal, disappointment. Like the imagined encounters, there is the pervasive sense of potential danger. The child, however, is trapped in the encounters; and in many ways, the adult who is recalling them for me is still trapped. His anger resonated in his voice, flushed his face, and tensed his fists. Close attention to the detail of the extract enables the identification of a range of relationships between subjects and their others/objects. For example:

a. The reference to 'a Catholic grammar school' presupposes an education system deliberately divided according to religious affiliation as well as selection according to some ability and/or other social and economic criteria. Thus the structural relationships of the system are hierarchical according to ability and also split according to whether one is a member of one religious group or another.

b. Teaching discipline is very clearly perceived as being set apart from, indeed more important than, the value of knowledge. Discipline, following instructions, negates the need for direct knowledge of a situation, if it is presumed that the instructions emanate from a 'good', 'rational' or 'legal' source. 'I'm only doing my duty', or 'I'm only following orders', or 'you only need to know on a need to know basis' absolve an individual from, or even prohibit, an individual from having knowledge in order to inform their own judgement and make their own decisions. Many organizations are based upon variants and combinations of these kinds of principles: military, police, government, commercial organizations. For people like Maggie, this is what makes school attractive. There is a lack of mutuality between the children and the adults which at an extreme creates the conditions for the acceptance of exploitation, manipulation. Teachers through discipline master the children. The powerlessness of the child face-to-face with the power of adults is institutionalized in law (cf. Holt 1974; Freeman 1983).

c. Fun and wonder as educational goods in themselves are seen as being negated by an emphasis on prescribed examination work. Work and fun have long been separated, particularly in relation to what has been called the protestant work ethic and is picked up in such sayings as 'all work and no play makes Jack a dull boy . . .'. The function of schooling to prepare children for boring forms of work, doing as one's told, waiting in queues and so on has long been argued (cf. Jackson 1968). The relation underlying schooling thus is not a gift as between individuals educationally opening up their experiences one to another but rather an element in the market exchange system where exchange value is attributed through pass marks.

d. Within the family itself, the essential division that articulates schooling divides the child and the parent. In Frank's mind it was articulated as: parent as believer in child v. parent as believer in 'good Catholic' teachers. The desired relationship 'parent as believer in child' defines for Frank the absent ideal of the family as a mutually protective and supportive unity. Unfortunately for Frank as a child, the parents sided with the teachers creating another kind of synthesis. This unity composed of parent, church, teacher knotted family, state and church into a powerful structure of authority over the child not just as an individual but as a member of and therefore subject to, a category. Both the uniqueness and the agency of Frank as a child has been erased.

Each point provides possible directions to pursue in formulating strategies to develop the project and identify themes that can be the basis for later interview questions. The last point, 'd', which in many ways is a culmination of the others goes straight to the heart of an emancipatory project. How does one unknot the dominant syntheses of interests – for example parent, church, state – in order to bring about some unity such as Frank's ideal family that is considered more desirable? Of course, this was from Frank's point of view as a hurt child. Nevertheless, the essence of the project is there: how does one generate a more satisfactory way of life?

Moving On

What I have described as the method of the inter-view is not the reduced form of the interview so revered by survey designers but involves engaging with the otherness of others and thus the necessity of the act of the gift (that constitutes a 'view') as well as the possibility of deceit, misdirection and mistake. A view is 'given' under conditions of equality between subject and other, an observation is 'made' under conditions of inequality between subject as master and other as object of control. It is not a matter of either/or, it is a matter of exploring the conditions under which each is possible and thus impossible. The shift then is towards the ways in which social life is articulated, that is, knotted into complexes of relationships and how these articulations can shift, or be made to shift, or seduced into shifting. This opens the possibility that an emancipatory project can never be completed or tied down in some final conception of 'reality', or totalitarian mastery over the social.

To move on, taking steps to design an interview methodology whether for a case study, an ethnography, for action research, or an evaluation, thus requires an alertness to otherness, to the relations that this generates and the ways in which relations knot or fall apart. Thus drawing upon the discussions so far in terms of otherness, difference, being towards (relation), gift and knot an inter-view strategy can be sketched for projects in the following ways:

Case Study

A case study is typically defined as a 'a bounded system', a single instance (cf. Simons 1980; Torrance 2005). But, can the individual instances be connected to each other and organized as a 'larger' system? This is the essential problem of a case study conceived as in any way singular or bounded – how are generalizations, or comparisons, or connections with some larger or other case to be formed? In formal philosophical terms this has been explored by Laclau (1996) and Butler, Laclau and Zizek (2000) in relation to a radical pluralist democratic project. Broadly, the issue focuses on the problematic of the particular and the universal. If, as Postmodern adherents assert there is a scepticism towards grand Theory or grand narratives (Lyotard 1984) that explain everything, then the response is to rush towards the particular, the little local narratives, the concrete single instances of everyday life. However, as Laclau points out even if we agree there is nothing else but particular narratives there is an implicit universal. Indeed, in order to overcome, or master, issues of particularization and the difficulties of generalization, case study approaches have included the strategy of multi-site case studies. The multiple sites imply some totality of such sites and a ground that is sufficiently common for comparisons and contrasts to be made. Similarly, if one group in, say a multicultural society, both asserts its difference and complains of an injustice in relation to a concept of human rights to equal treatment, these rights already point to a universal that subsume all the different multicultural groups. Even if each particular group lives in such a way that the one never comes into conflict with another there is an implicit totality of these particulars organized in such a way that there is no conflict. Furthermore, to be considered different each member is defined as being different from all the other members and thus belongs as such to a system of differences – this is the definition that Saussure employed to define the relations between the elements that comprised language (see Chapter 2). The case study, then, cannot simplistically be reduced to being a single instance without reference either to others from which it is different or to a whole/totality/universal to which it has some generalizable relation.

It is insufficient therefore to conceive of the 'case' as a mental construct thrown for some reason over some aspect of social reality (because it seems like a good 'unit' to focus on, like a school, a pub, a supermarket). As a construct it mentally limits ways of thinking by creating a non-necessary category into which to fit a rather messy, knotty, slippery reality. In Schostak 2002 I argued for a different approach to the case study founded upon the tracing of relationships. So, starting from my interview with Frank, an arbitrary starting point, a mapping of relationships can begin that reveals the implication, imbrication, or woven and knotted strands of relationship as between people and things of the world as well as the boundaries that they erect between each other and things. Each individual provides a point of view that takes the other and otherness into account. Each view as a directedness towards an other carries also its sense of limit or boundary between subject and other. That is to say, with every view directed by a subject towards another there is an inter-view, a space between views. It is this betweenness that ensures no single view can fully saturate the views of others. There is in every view always a difference, a 'betweenness' that cannot be crossed as a subject looks towards, or reaches towards the other. The interview, in this sense, is constructive and de-constructive of cases not as singular instances, nor as bounded systems but as infinitely extensible, richly connectable plays or weavings of ever expanding horizons of differences.

Ethnography

Definitions of ethnography tend to focus on the lived experiences of social actors in a given location (e.g. Hammersley 1984; Pole and Morrison 2003). Following inter-view methodology, however, the ethnographer does not begin with a definition of the location but rather an invitation to the otherness of those who have views regarding what constitutes an 'insideness' to a way of life and thus an 'outsideness'. These views become the basis of an ethnography – a writing about/of the people who together are witness for, and thus constitute, an 'insideness' whether for a moment or for an eternity (cf. Schostak 1999a). To build the ethnographic case requires collecting data on the capacity for difference and for knotting differences into unities through which the social and personal life of individuals can be made to be ordered yet creative and thus evolving as a way of life. In Maggie's interview, an ethnographic case can be composed by taking each of the participants – the husband, Maggie's children, and in later parts of the interview the other characters who became important in her development as an undergraduate, a post graduate student teacher and then a qualified teacher – and beginning the job of taking their eye-witness accounts of 'what happened', their feelings about this, their interpretations of what it all meant, their judgements of each other, the values that they brought to bear and so on. Each view describes a difference which then is 'knotted' into a unity which structures the way in which they act and interact: as husband and wife, as mother and children, as student with other students, as teacher with other teachers, as teacher with class. There is a sense in which at each stage in her career as wife, as mother, as student, as teacher she was constituted with others as a 'temporary people' with an identity of being insiders to a given mutually recognized 'event', set of events, 'stage' of life. It is thus an ethnography of a connected set or sequence, or temporary synthesis of events, and so on, and those who peopled it. This then is the work of the ethnographer to identify those fluidly occurring and dissolving unities through which individuals generate a sense of sociality and identity that Berman (1982) has described as characteristic of modernity and that Bauman has described as 'liquid' (2001). In the case study and the ethnography there is an implication of 'telling it like it is', of being a true, honest witness of 'what happened' – a view challenged by, for example, Geertz (1988) in his studies of the writings of anthropologists. An alternative is to explore the multiple possible readings, a view developed in later chapters, particularly Chapter 9 in relation to writing up.

Action Research

Action research is typically defined in terms of systematic reflection on a social context in order to improve the quality of action therein (cf. Elliott 1991; Noffke and Somekh 2005). The difference then from the ethnographic approach described above is the focus on 'improving' action. There is an ethical and political dimension in the word 'improving' in the sense that from some point of view the action research is carried out with the intent to make changes that from that point of view is considered an 'improvement'. The danger, of course, is that what is improvement from one point of view can be denounced as a totalitarian imposition from another. Inter-view methodology can be employed as a means of sub-verting such authoritarian views by counterposing them with alternative views. There then remains the issue of how to generate conditions of improvement that do not also suppress or repress other viewpoints regarding what counts as 'improvement'. In discussing Frank's interview the problematic of an emancipatory project was raised around his ideal notion of the family as one that would side with the child against the power of the school to abuse him under the guise of legitimate authority. Implicit in this problematic is a notion that one cannot be emancipated if there is a fundamental sense of lack together with real impediments to being able to resolve this sense of lack. In Frank's case this lack involved a sense of injustice, a sense of not being trusted as a witness on his own behalf, and a sense of not being cared for. The impediments I have described in terms of a knotting together of the interests of parents, church and state. This synthesis is, of course, a crucial structure of social power more generally. A fuller description of its articulation will have to await further discussions in Chapters 2, 5, 6 and 7 which explore how language, subjects, political action and ethics are mutually constituted. A young child, as indeed any adult, when confronted with such a structure is likely to feel up against a brick wall. How can such a brick wall be dismantled? Action research is just as likely to be co-opted into building and reinforcing such brick walls as in dismantling them (Schostak 1999b). Unless action research adopts an emancipatory strategy then 'improvement' can just as easily be defined in terms of increasing the efficiency of controls over children as in enhancing their agency for decision making in a democratic environment (see Schostak 1988, 1989, 1990). Fundamental to an emancipatory strategy therefore is the act of engaging with the otherness of the other, enabling that otherness to be expressed through acts of witnessing.

Evaluation

Evaluations, in very broad terms, inform decision makers about the state of play of a current or intended programme of action. Often they are commissioned for innovations or systems under the pressure of change. The purposes vary from the attempts to improve performance and accountability through to social critique and transformation (cf. Abma and Schwandt 2005). MacDonald (1987) made a useful distinc-tion between three kinds of evaluation. The *autocratic* style involves independent evaluators who make their assessments and tell the funders/commissioners what they should do whether or not the funders/

commissioners want this. The *bureaucratic* style places the evaluators under the control of the funders/commissioners of the evaluation who define what should be done. The *democratic* style acts as a broker of information to inform all decision makers at all levels in the organization or system being evaluated. This latter approach suspends the hierarchies of information that are essential to the autocratic and bureaucratic styles. The methodology of the inter-view by addressing otherness and difference in the constitution of multiple views subverts hierarchy and opens the possibility of change and in an evaluation context raises the question of the appropriate political forms required to bring about change in ways that accept rather than suppress otherness and difference. Again in Chapter 6 the political implications will be drawn out both for debate and for their implications for the design of emancipatory projects.

But how to get started? The theoretical dimensions of the inter-view have begun to be crudely outlined. They can be elaborated in more detail by exploring how language mediates experience both for self and for others in creating views.

Language as Method, As Model, As World

An ex-military officer, Jane, talked about her experience of school:

> I went to a grammar school, all girls grammar school and so I look back
> on that and remember um and I was always in the top sets as well so I
> always look back at that and remember well behaved children um
> teachers who most of the time were respected and listened to and we did
> exactly as we were told and if anything bad happened, it would happen
> in another set in another part of the school and that one person was the
> one bad person for that entire year. Um I remember school assemblies,
> and prayer and kneeling and school uniforms and they are my out-
> standing memories of school.
>   I liked it yes (. . .) I suppose I like rules and regulations, suppose I like
> to know where I fit in. I like a system, an organization. I'd probably be
> no good in a sort of very um egalitarian, flexible, no structure organi-
> zation that some of these modern organizations are. I probably wouldn't
> be any good because I quite like to have a pecking order, I don't mean I
> want to be at the top of it, I just like to know who's where, who slots in
> where, who belongs to who, who's responsible for who and, and that
> probably appealed to me in school.
>
> (Schostak and Walker 2002)

Without language no account of our experiences, nor any sense of a
'world' could be made. In the extract, Jane's account of her world begins
by reference to an 'all girls grammar school'. Her account indicates some
of the 'dramatis personae', the key actors, who together created the
dramas, the narratives, the stories that underlie her anecdotes of school.
We also get some hazy images of the practices (doing as you're told,
prayer, kneeling, school assemblies), a sense of there being a system
(composed of rules, regulations, pecking order), together with a location
(school). However, we do not see in our minds the same school as seen
by Jane. Nor do we see the same 'well behaved children', or teachers, nor

recall to mind her images of school assemblies, praying and kneeling. However, we can recall our own school experiences.

Although I did not go to a grammar school, nor to a church school, I know enough to be able to locate the secondary school I went to alongside memories of people talking about the grammar school that 'took all the bright children'. Alongside this there are the newspaper accounts, books and films that I have read and seen and, of course, much later when I became a teacher and later still a lecturer and a researcher I can lock it all into memories of classes I have taught and students I have supervised on teaching practice and research undertaken in the UK and abroad. From these memories I can perhaps fill out some of the gaps in terms of the key people, the dramatis personae – the head teacher, the deputy head teacher, the hard teachers, the soft teachers, the bullies (teachers as well as pupils), the pupils who were swots, who were clowns, who were tough, and then there were the caretakers, the kitchen staff and so on. I can review in my mind the system that pervaded the schools of my memories, the rules employed and how different classes would have different approaches to the application of rules, indeed, how pupils and teachers would in effect struggle with each other over what rules, what kind of order should apply. Then there were the daily rituals, the lining up outside of class, then the orderly walk to pre-assigned desks or the unceremonious clamour for the best desks and to sit next to friends or away from enemies, or far from the sight of the teacher. There were then the little everyday practices like shielding one's work (or rather doodles) from the prying eyes of neighbours or the teacher, the raising of hands to answer a question or request to leave the room to go to the toilet. There were the little ways of attracting each other's attention and communicating judgements, jokes, insults, by a raising of the eyebrow, a glance towards the ceiling. And of course, there was the stage – the classroom, the playground, the assembly hall, the corridors, the stairways, the toilets, the library, the dinner hall and so on – where people were drawn together, by design, by accident, into relationships. Each stage had its backdrop framing the action, its fixtures and fittings, its resources. The shape of a room, the way it was decorated, its entrances and exits, its cupboards, its shelves, its windows all created a frame that was either too small and cramped, too large and full of echoes or just right and comfortable. And there was the way the furniture was arranged and whether the chairs and desks scraped on the bare floor or were softened by carpet. There was the equipment, the resources to hand or out of reach which necessitated getting up and fetching them or could be easily brought into reach. All this can be filled in from memory. But no matter the richness of my experience I cannot call up any of the specific memories of Jane's school. For that, I have to ask questions and keep on asking questions until a picture begins to emerge.

As in the following diagram I can organize my questions to get her to tell anecdotes of the characters from the school that she remembers, the way in which the school was organized, its daily routines, the practices engaged in by children and adults in order to get what they want and avoid what they don't want, the design of the school, what it looked like in every location of the school together with what resources were to be found. Each anecdote is a weaving of each of these structural features – dramatis personae, system, practices, material elements – into an event structure, the things that happened to who, when, where, why framed by the particular stage or location where it took place. Through the anecdote the experience re-lives. Of course, an interview schedule of questions could be constructed that asks for factual statements regarding each of the 'headings' in the diagram. My preference is for the anecdotes to be the focus of questions that gently ask for concrete elaboration until the picture is filled as far as memory allows.

Each anecdote can be further woven into more encompassing narratives or stories of 'Jane's Schooling' – a process to be further explored through each chapter and in particular, Chapters 8 and 9. However, no matter how good Jane's memory, nor however good my ability to represent her account, something is left out. In this case, it was not possible to go and see the school, it was a 'school' of some 20 years ago, a

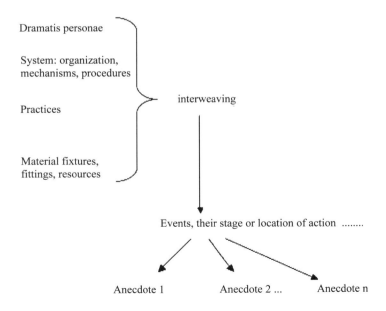

Diagram 1: Anecdotes and the location of action

school remembered. In other circumstances, her story could be checked by going and seeing, so providing a *triangulation*, a correlation between what is said and what is seen. Triangulation involves the general process of taking multiple perspectives on the same thing, or the thing that is allegedly 'real', 'objective', 'true', or defined in meaning and is the same under a variety of circumstances. Thus triangulation can be performed during an interview and between interviews. Each question provides a different view, a different angle, a different approach to the 'thing' in question. How does the other elaborate this 'thing' in response to each question – are there differences, are there inconsistencies?

The power of language is not that there is a one to one match between a word and a specific object but that a given word refers to the concept of a school and thus can be used to indicate any school real or imaginary. Hence, through the use of language views can be constructed that can then be compared and contrasted – triangulated – with each other. So, when Jane talked about her school, her teachers, her friends none of these were physically present in the room with us. Language is a way of talking about things whether or not they are present to be pointed out as *this* school, not that one, real or imaginary. This power to talk about absent things, real or imaginary, is what enables individuals both to describe and to go beyond their immediate experience. Even in this brief interview extract the processes that make generalization possible are taking place, tying her particular uses of words into a more universal language framework that enables others to read the words being used to produce meanings that are open to further readings. Particular readings may be contested or supported by other readings. When I read the words 'grammar school' I lock them into a context of formal schooling that reinforces social divisions by applying limited and highly problematic tests that are supposed to represent 'ability'. Others will have counter readings.

'Ability', unlike 'school building', does not refer to a solid physical entity that can be touched. It can however be defined. How it is defined is when it starts to be open to contestation and the politics of manipulation. In the case of the British grammar school ability became associated with an intelligence test that children took at the age of about 11 years old. Hence it became known as the 11 plus. This test crucially determined the future lives of millions of children. Hence, it was a powerful political and social tool serving interests that went well beyond the immediate needs and interests of children and their parents. Comprehensive schooling, where all children of all abilities would be taught together became a counter political tool as debates about wider definitions of ability and of the purposes of schooling and of education took place. At a further extreme were the 'free schools' of the 1970s which in various ways experimented with greater degrees of democracy as between teachers and children (Kozol 1967; Kohl 1971; Neill 1973; Richmond 1982) or the notion of education as cultural action for freedom of Freire (1970, 1973) or indeed, the de-schooling arguments of Illich (1971). Jane makes her preference known: 'I like rules and regulations'.

Language, it seems, does not provide a simple way of accounting for the world of experience, but affects worlds of experience by creating contestable ways of talking about experiences, needs, desires and interests. The following sections will explore the characteristics of language that make this possible in connection with the articulation of views and the development of emancipatory projects.

Language as a System of Differences

By disconnecting a particular word from a particular thing, language as a way of talking about things that are absent becomes possible. It is a kind of emancipation from the givenness of particular circumstances. It is also a condition for the sharing of views. If I accept and understand that a given word – school – can refer not only to many possible schools but also to many ways of defining and experiencing schools, then there is the possibility that I can be open to another way of 'seeing' school, both *my* school and some more conceptual way of perceiving school as an 'idea', through the ways another person talks about it. That is, I can free myself from my own view of school. School, in this sense, is best defined in terms of what it is not. School as a word becomes meaningful to me in a general sense because it does not relate to any given real school. Moreover, the sound I make when speaking the word 'school' is arbitrary in the sense that there is no necessary relation between the sound and the concept or thing it designates. In French, the sound is 'école'. The use of these sounds in these ways is due to historical, social circumstances. Such considerations led Saussure (1966) to propose his view of language as a system of differences that could be analysed according to sounds or marks and the content that those sounds or marks designated. Sounds or marks of various kinds were called signifiers and the content that attached to them, signifieds. These two orders may be visualized as floating over each other, distinct from each other. Language does not so much designate, but creates the conditions for the designation of contents and thus meaningfulness or signification to take place. In that sense, it is like an infrastructure, but an infrastructure that is entirely negative in the sense that it concerns relations of difference, that is, the signifier 'school' has no positive content but is defined as different from every other signifier in the system. When Jane talks about her school, I know it is not my school. I cannot draw upon any predetermined contents of the word 'school' in order to conjure up the school as she sees it or experienced it. Rather, I have to play a game of differences – the school is not a nursery school, nor a primary school, but a grammar school not a secondary, not a boys' school, and it is not the part of the school where the bad things happened, and so on – to enable something of the contents that she wishes to occupy the empty space of the category 'school' to emerge. However, the image I construct in my mind will never equal hers. I know that her experience of school is different from mine and I know she is interpreting it differently. To refer to these differences in interpretation, the idea of a discourse can be used. The notion of discourse that I will employ is informed by the dialogues between Laclau, Mouffe, Butler, Derrida, Rorty, Zizek and others. It is to be distinguished from those approaches, like Habermas, that try to reduce it to a process underpinned by consensus. However, each have a focus on discourse being 'a relational ensemble of signifying sequences' (Torfing 1999: 91), that is, each element (signifier, signified, or word, phrase, sentence and so on) is marshalled into relationships to produce significance, meaning, a way of unifying the disparate elements of life into frameworks, into identities, into categories that can be communicated to others, that can be made open to contestation or concealed. To illustrate this, consider the following diagram:

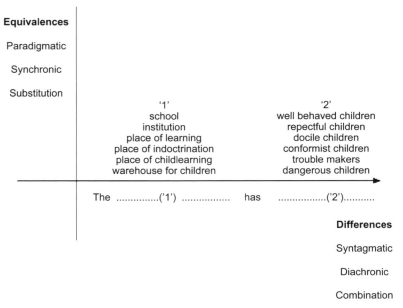

Diagram 2: Articulating experience as discourse

From the diagram different articulations of experience can be constructed. In trying to describe something I can choose from a wide range of words and combinations of words, phrases and so on. The meaning units stacked under '1' refer to a building. In that sense they are equivalent in being possible names or ways of referring to that building. Similarly, the meaning units of '2' are substitutable for each other in the sense that they are ways of referring to the behaviour of children. The meaning units of '1' can now be combined with those of '2' in order to express particular meanings, for example, the blank spaces '1' and '2' can be filled in to read:

a. the school has well behaved children;
b. the institution has respectful children;
c. the place of learning has docile children;
d. the place of indoctrination has conformist children;
e. the place of childrearing has trouble makers;
f. the warehouse for children has dangerous children.

And, of course, there can be any combination between each member of '1' and '2'. In each case the sense of what is being talked about changes. To refer to a school as an institution draws in a number of connotations that school does not have. Lunatic asylums and prisons are often designated as institutions thus giving the word a negative, pejorative tone, that the words school and 'place of learning' do not have. Certainly, 'place of learning' seems to carry a positive tone that school does not have and place of indoctrination is clearly negative in intent. When speaking we can choose our words to convey these differences in sense and tone. This temporal dimension to speaking and selecting words to fill out different slots in the form of a sentence or statement or some other utterance is designated the diachronic axis. Each meaning unit or syntagm is chosen from a list of possible substitutions. Instead of 'the' starting the statement, alternatives could have been 'a', 'one', 'some', 'all', 'this', 'that'. Such 'stacks of alternatives' are available for every slot in a sentence. In a sense the stack is available all at once, a-temporally, synchronically. The stack defines the list of substitutable terms – called the paradigm, a set of lexical items, like a menu, from which choices are made that can be combined with others to form syntagms. How and why we choose one from the stack rather than another is significant for the nuances of meaning that we wish to convey. These nuances play subtly with the minimal differences that are jostled into relationship between one term and another in the overall speech, text or dialogue taking place. Where Jane talks of her grammar school in warm tones of being a place of well behaved children who were respectful, I might choose different terms to say the school was part of a divisive elitist system where historically the children of the lowest classes were warehoused because they were thought dangerous and those of the higher classes were schooled to conform in order to maintain an essentially unjust system. In short, Jane and I construct different discourses concerning school and the role or function of school in producing social order. These discourses may be found to be common amongst different professional, occupational, political groupings in a given society. If so, we may find it useful to talk about different communities of discourse who through their language strategies construct particular views of society and the world.

Each given discourse constructs views of the world positioning subjects in relation to others in three broad ways: as raw material to be worked upon to produce the exploitable furniture of the world; as the brute givenness of the world; and as conscious others whose intentions must in some way be taken into account. These three dimensions of the world-view of a given discourse can be illustrated when Jane described her experiences of being a student on teaching practice. Principally, she categorized the 'conscious others' – the dramatis personae – into the 'good' and the 'bad' just as she had in her memories of her own childhood school experiences:

> in my two teaching practices I had three sets of year 10 and to be quite frank two of them I disliked intensely, thought they were foul. (. . .) They were just rude and just disrespectful, uncaring and ungrateful teenagers. I picked up though this particular group, halfway through the academic year, they were trouble makers, they, they were poor ability, both groups um and I found them quite hard work. And because I had a natural time limit to teaching them um I quickly lost interest, I have to say, and I concentrated on the groups that I I did like. And I just got through them as a matter of having to for the course's sake.

The classes she disliked, are described as: foul, rude, disrespectful, uncaring, ungrateful, troublemakers, poor ability, in contrast to the classes she likes:

> those kids that just listen um, ones that ask questions and trust you that you'll be able to help them further. Ones that are eager to please. Um ones that put their hands up and say miss miss, you know. Guess what and tell you a little story. Um I quite like having a banter with the kids as well and so I like all that side of things. And I find that the brighter the children the more articulate they are and the more you can do that. When they're poor ability their inarticulate manner prohibits that sort of interaction.

Where the one class is foul and of low ability, the other is eager to please and bright. In the first class otherness is recognized and rejected. In the second, similarity to herself is recognized and accepted. In each case, differences are collected together and organized oppositionally. In one 'stack' are piled all the values regarded by her as positive and in the other all those regarded as negative. Each element in each stack is, of course, different from all other elements. However, each is counterposed to the elements of the other stack. In that sense, there is a relation of equivalence between the members 'inside' a given stack. They are equivalent in the sense of being on the same side. Hence, in creating a statement 'One class . . .' a number of terms can be equivalently substituted for each other and still refer to the particular designated class. Thus, one class has a 'lack of ability', is 'disrespectful' and so on. In calling this the bad class, 'bad' then implicitly has as its content all of the elements in the stack as in the diagram below:

The diagram is a simplification of a complex process of selection and

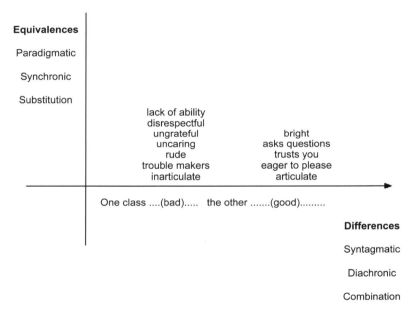

Diagram 3: Articulating equivalence by opposition

ordering. At a formal level there is no reason why, for example, rude and lack of ability should go together or be substitutes for each other. These elements are placed together in a relation of equivalence only because Jane has articulated them as such by placing them oppositionally to those of the 'good' class. This process of articulating together (or knotting together) diverse elements into structures of equivalence will be explored a little further in this chapter but in more detail for its importance in exploring political organization in Chapter 6. As an intimation of the political importance of such a process of articulation, the following extracts show that this categorization into polar opposites can be continued and indeed can be extended well beyond the school gates:

Society's attitude to children needs to change. I think that kids have a lack of respect across the board I think and it generates an awful lot of time in the home (...) I think adults, parents um are disrespectful towards any form of authority, within the home, authority outside but within the home they're disrespectful of it and that rubs off on children.

In her image of society, authority plays a pivotal role dividing the people of the world into those who have respect for authority (the 'good') and those that don't (the 'bad'). Without authority there is disorder as in the classes she considered 'foul'. How can this be solved, in her view? To explain, she tells a story:

I was quite shocked a few weeks ago, a year 7 group, so 11 and 12 year old girls and boys are in it the classroom and a supply teacher came in, he'd retired and he was just uh a supply covering and he'd popped into the classroom because there's a student teacher and the proper teacher should always be around and he was coming to say look I'm the supply do I need to be here and I said, no I'm OK. Fine, but in the introduction to that and he was messing around with them and he said which of them are naughty and which ones do you want me to hit. And so I said that one there and that one there. And he went up to them and he went shht (as a swipe) but he was only pretending, he went like that and he didn't touch th', didn't lay a finger on them. Nothing. I watched it with my own eyes. About 10 minutes after he'd gone one of the kids put up his hand and said, miss who was that man there and I said Oh Mr so and so. Right well I'm going to tell my mum about him because he hit me. Now to me, well I had words with him about it 'cos I just thought I'm going to stamp this on the head right now 'cos he's lying and that's all there is to it. I thought what this guy did was a bit strange anyway I certainly wouldn't have done that but some old teachers have got funny methods. And um but I was quite surprised at this 11 year old who effectively said I'm going to tell my mum, my mum'll sort you out, I know my rights and I think that, that cuts across society. It cuts across everything, attitudes towards NHS staff, police, teachers, councils, you name it anything. It's an impatient um I want my money's worth, and if you don't I'll sue attitude and for anybody working in the public sector I think they suffer as a result of it. And I think that's got to change in order for teachers' lot in life to change because kids now are not only rude to their parents but they're rude to all sorts of people so of course they're going to be rude to their teachers.

JFS: Is there a way of bringing it about?

I suppose the only way of doing it is. You see you can't have everything you can't have this wonderful capitalist society with potential rewards with everybody who works hard in the private industry and great standards of living and everything you could possibly want in life and on TV and magazines so it's all there to be achieved if you've prepared for it, and at the same time expect everyone to have these exceptionally high moral standards because the two don't go hand in hand in my opinion. And so I think that, the further we go down the line towards being materialistic and wanting things and always trying to pull a fast one on someone else and they sue I'm going to sue you for this, that and the other I think that, the further we'll get away from being having a communal attitude toward our fellow human beings. And I think it's more natural nowadays to assume everyone's bad until you know better as opposed to the other way around. And I don't know how you ever change that. I think you need something, it sounds horrendous but for something really awful to happen to bring everyone together, for some community spirit um not a war but do you know what I mean something so drastic that everyone just realizes what the benefits are of life and what's important and to get together and have some community spirit. And whether that's, however that could happen in a modern equivalent without anybody dying I don't know what, how it could happen but I think we're all so self centred um and demanding nowadays I think that it's long gone.

Her image is of a society pervaded by an inner sense of contradiction: capitalism promoting a lack of morality versus high moral standards. The paradigmatic case of this lack of high moral standards is condensed in the anecdote of the child who 'knew his rights'. The materialistic desire for things is in her mind associated with the manipulation of rights to create a culture of litigation across society. Opposing this materialistic society is the ordered sense of community she associates with the military. It is a powerful 'imaginary' which discursively structures her experience into good and bad from the day to day incidents in the classroom to looking at the general state of the world about her. In this imaginary is constructed a conflictual world without respect for some controlling authority – or more generally, some master discourse assuring political order – where only something dreadful happening will bring back some sense of to-getherness. This 'something dreadful' has a powerful role to play. Its function is to transcend differences and thus be the condition for a new unity, a new social imaginary. What is missing is a constructive encounter with the many voices of children, parents and others in society and how they talk about the experiences of their own lives. Her discourse is premised upon a single dominant view through which the world as a totality is imagined. The wished for unity is to be built not upon a dialogue of differences, but through a fear of 'something dreadful'. The fear of chaos, barbarism and bloody revolution has long been the motive behind the acceptance of political compromises where conflicts are resolved without bloodshed.

Language and the Rational Community

In Jane's social imaginary of a rationally ordered community, there are rules and regulations and these in turn define subject positions, identities and relations between identities so that each knows from whom to take orders. This is not to say that everyone is identical to everyone else, far from it, just that all the differences are subsumed in an orderly fashion under the imagined system. As a model, it is beguiling.

Its underlying imaginary of an essential order can be seen throughout the ages in various guises and with various implications for the nature of reality and relations between people, each version providing an interpretative view of the world. Taylor (1975: 4–5) describes the pre-modern approach to understanding the world as the expression of a fundamental 'order of Ideas or archetypes, as manifesting the rhythm of divine life, or the foundational acts of the gods, or the will of God; seeing the world as a text, or the universe as a book'. The world as book is open to be read, assuming one is qualified to read it; that is, knows the language within which it is written. For those who know how to read: '(t)he idea of a meaningful order is inseparably bound up with that of final causes since it posits that the furniture of the universe is as it is and develops as it does in order to embody these Ideas; the order is the ultimate explanation' (1975: 5). If it is the case that science is founded on such a vision of meaningful order, then it is a matter of reading the world for significant correspondences. The example Taylor gives (1975: 4) is of a critic of Galileo's who refuted the discovery of Jupiter's moons because animals have seven 'windows' through which to experience the world: 'two nostrils, two eyes, two ears and, a mouth' thus linking this to other examples of the significance of seven – like seven metals – then the number of planets was 'necessarily seven'. Obviously, this is not the world of contemporary science. For the world of science to come into view required a revolution in thinking that would enable new ways of talking about the world. It required an emancipation from the book, from the world as constructed through meaningful correspondences as described by Taylor. In the Europe of the seventeenth century, that revolution in thinking is linked to the names of Descartes, Galileo and Bacon.

Through his method of doubt, Descartes emancipated his own thinking and laid the foundations of contemporary scientific methodology for discovering 'order', 'facts':

> So, because our senses sometimes play us false, I decided to suppose that there was nothing at all which was as such as they cause us to imagine it; and because there are men who make mistakes in reasoning, even with the simplest geometrical matters, and make paralogisms, judging

that I was liable to error as anyone else, I rejected as being false all the reasonings I had hitherto accepted as proofs. And finally, considering that all the same thoughts that we have when we are awake can also come to us when we are asleep, without anyone of them being truer than the illusions of my dreams. But immediately afterwards I became aware that, while I decided thus to think that everything was false, it followed necessarily that I who thought thus must be something; and observing that this truth: *I think, therefore I am,* was so certain and so evident that all the most extravagant suppositions of the sceptics were not capable of shaking it, I judged that I could accept it without scruple as the first principle of the philosophy I was seeking.

(Descartes 2001: 53-4)

The procedure of placing all into doubt has secured for the I-think, the cogito, reason, a privileged role. It is an inaugural step of a methodology that has shaped the Western imaginary, its philosophy, politics and science in the search for knowledge that is *certain,* and social order that is rational. Descartes' methodology was consciously modelled on geometry because the results of its rigorous proofs could be applied in the material world, the mathematization of the world as Husserl called it. Mathematics is a language, a system of differences that for many is the ideal language by which to explore the physical and social worlds. It is a language that appears to be capable of precise definition in a way that the words of a spoken language like English, French or any other 'natural' language seem not to be.

If only it were possible to construct an objective language, or a way of framing language stripped of all its ambiguities, its connotations of values, so that a given statement or proposition could clearly and distinctly correspond to 'facts' in the world. Such approaches have often been labelled positivistic. They tend to privilege measurement, observation and statements that can be operationalized or expressed in a manner capable of proof. To say, for example that all swans are white means that there is a way of proving this to be false: by finding a swan that is not white – a single black swan falsifies the statement. In order to operationalize something is to give the precise conditions under which something will work. For example, the behaviourism of Skinner (1953) is operationalized in terms of specifying in minute detail the conditions under which rewards are to be delivered so that the behaviour of a dog or human is modified in some desired direction. Both falsification and operationalization are powerful methods for control. However, for what reasons is such control to be exercised? Through what language can these reasons be expressed? If it is the language of common sense, whose common sense counts? Common sense is highly contested and varies according to different cultural and linguistic communities.

Even if it were possible to construct an objective non ambiguous, non-value laden language it could not help with the fundamental questions of what society to build, how to live one's life and what kind of future could be hoped for. Why, for example, should rational as distinct from value driven discourse be considered preferable in deciding what kind of society to build? To decide to have a rational as opposed to say a need or a desire driven society presupposes some set of values that enables this decision to be made. Is a neutral language, like mathematics, capable of deciding upon value based issues? In economics value is decided through the mechanisms of the market. In classical economics the conditions for perfect competition were theorized to ensure that no single person or group could control the market. Hence, in theory, goods and services could be fairly allocated to meet needs and interests; in practice, such conditions have never existed. Furthermore, the definition of demand in economics is not the same as in ordinary speech. Demand is defined in terms of being both willing and able to purchase something. I may demand something but not have the money (or other resource) to buy it, hence this cannot be registered through the market. Furthermore, such demands are not necessarily ethical, nor indeed wise. In the market place, demands for a particular commodity may lead to illness or death as in smoking or massive pollution in the use of petrol. Trying to construct an objective calculus of benefits then hits the difficulty of defining 'benefit' in any clear and distinct manner that could be applied across all communities, in all individual cases, in all contexts at all times. Indeed, in its extreme, the greatest number may consider that the greatest benefit is to exterminate the few as in the various 'ethnic cleansings' that have taken place over the last century. Rather than searching for a language stripped of values, the power of natural languages is that they are able to express, evoke and construct values, desires, needs, feelings in a way that mathematics is not. That is, the focus is not the construction of language as a neutral or objective representation of things but as a means of expressing, evoking and constructing the meaning and value of human life. Meaning involves addressing the consciousness of others and hence the views of others as a step towards the inauguration of a dialogue capable of formulating a politics and an ethics that does not reduce all to homogeneity under some absolute view or absolute reason.

In the quest for a rational model to describe, explain and control the world, the search for an objective language tried to exclude the need for conscious, subjective viewpoints from its formulations. But in doing so, the human is sacrificed to the mechanical, the abstract. In this sense, the method was flawed as an approach to encompass All. From the start, Descartes was unable to prove the existence of other consciousnesses without the postulation of God – a kind of supplement – to fill the gap. Kant sought to remove God from the equation in his exploration of the limits of reason by declaring that what could be known could only be whatever appears to consciousness (the phenomenon) as distinct from the nature of the thing in itself (the noumenon). The nature of the thing in itself could never be known. Hence in privileging the I-think and the ways in which it was able to process information provided by the phenomena that appeared to consciousness the other was thereby reduced to its appearances to that consciousness. The I-think, or reason, therefore became the privileged centre of the system of knowledge which reduced the other to an inferior position, a point that is encapsulated in this exchange:

> BRUNSCHVICG: The idea that I have of his consciousness is a component in the system of my judgements about existence.
> CRESSON: I cannot accept that I might be reduced to a judgement in Mr Brunschvicg's consciousness, and I doubt whether those present, for their part, would be prepared to accept this either. Moreover, to be consistent, Mr Brunschvicg ought to declare that his is the only consciousness, and that the sole aim of knowledge is to draw up a harmonious table of its representations for the purposes of his solitary ego.
>
> (Bulletin de la Societé Française de philosophie (1921), source
> Descombes 1980: 21)

There is a demand to be recognized as an independent source of consciousness, and hence of judgement, that the idealist (Brunschvicg) is unwilling to acknowledge. In the Cartesian framework of methodological doubt, – or indeed the Kantian system – privileging the I-think above the object of the conscious act meant that the other could only ever be, as Brunschvicg put it, reduced to a component in his system of judgements. Different ways of reading the other give different views of reality which in turn give different powers to act, organize and manipulate the world about. Descartes opened the scientific world to the view of the solitary ego and provided a method which he claimed would provide certainty of judgement. The world could be read mathematically, rationally and the accomplishments of the rational vision of modernity are everywhere to be seen – including its disasters. The reduction to the rational had its consequences on diminishing the status of the other. The other was simply an object to be manipulated according to the designs of reason as in the policy and planning rationales to sweep aside the lives of ordinary people to make way for the progress of science, cities and commerce (cf. Berman 1982).

The Subject of Language and the Field of Struggle

The dissatisfaction with the Cartesian/Kantian view of the world and of the self that many on the French intellectual scene of the 1920s and 1930s felt, opened them to the Hegelian interpretation of the world, reason and the self that was brought to them variously by Koyré, Kojève (1969) Wahl and Hyppolite (1974). These readings produced a version – referred to as the French Hegel (Baugh 2003) – which seemed to offer a better reading of the historical, political realities of a world riven with conflicts, yet offered the hope of an end to such conflicts under the rule of reason as exemplified by the State. A story was told positioning Modernity as the final stage of history, separating us decisively from the middle ages and antiquity. It is a seductive story which many, like Habermas (1987) still sought to save from its wrong turnings. In the Modern imaginary, forms of belief, ways of behaving and frameworks for knowing were not to be borrowed from earlier epochs but created from within itself. The Hegelian story – as the emancipation from slavery – thus posed an ideal end of history where through the self reflective actions of the Moderns all divisions could be overcome. Kojève drama-tized this in his retelling of the Hegelian master–slave relationship. This drama has a critical importance for thinking about the nature of the inter-view and will be taken up again in Chapter 6 for its political implications. For this section, its impact is in a reworking of Saussure's structuralist approach to language in relation not only to Hegel but also to existential and psychoanalytic readings. In common with others, Sartre, writing about language stressed the centrality of the human act of speech:

> This thing without man is at the same time matter worked by man, bearing the trace of man ... If you admit the existence [of structure], you must also admit that language exists only as spoken, in other words, in act. Each element of this system refers to a whole, but this whole is dead if nobody takes it up for his purposes, makes it work ... In the system of language there is something that the inert cannot provide by itself, the trace of a practice. Structure imposes itself upon us only to the extent that it is made by others,
> (Sartre 1966: 88; cited in Fox 2003: 62)

As a further critical and far reaching move, Lacan, who along with others such as Bataille and other surrealists attended the lectures of Kojève, took the drama of the master–slave conflict and reread it alongside Saussure's concept of language as a system of differences as well as Freud's psychoanalytic theories of the unconscious. Lacan's re-interpretation of the relation between the signifier and the signified is indeed a precondition of post-structuralist and de-constructionist devel-opments. For Saussure the signified dominated the role of the signifier. For Lacan this was reversed in order to stress the materiality of the sig-nifier as sound impression, or more generally, sense impression, rather than as simply the sound of a given word being spoken (Grosz 1990: 93). That is, there is a material impact of the signifier on the body. This becomes particularly significant in Lacan's description of the unconscious as being structured like a language – it consists of signifiers that have been repressed. The body can show (or be the site of inscription of) the effects of repressed signifiers symptomatically. According to Lacan the network of the signifier is 'the synchronic structure of the language material in so far as in that structure each element assumes its precise function by being different from the others' and that of the signified:

> is the diachronic set of concretely pronounced discourses, which react historically on the first, just as the structure of the first governs the pathways of the second. The dominant fact here is the unity of sig-nification, which proves never to be resolved into a pure indication of the real, but always refers back to another signification. That is to say, the signification is realized only on the basis of a grasp of things in their totality.
>
> (Lacan 1977a: 126)

The concrete, pronounced discourses are in effect the conversations, speeches, texts of particular individuals through which the continual drift of signifiers is historically frozen into systems of signifiers (say, the material trace, the impression on a body, the memory of a given con-versation in time, or a particular book and transcription of a speech). The signified, in this reading then, is composed of signifiers. The order of the signified is defined simply by its position as a system of historically (diachronically) composed signifiers 'under' a separate drifting network of signifiers whose only form of regulation is that each signifier is defined by being different from every other signifier (Grosz 1990: 97). The sig-nified is simply a particular historical composition inscribed on some surface (brain neurones, rock, paper, computer hard drive and so on) which is a record of how that drift was articulated into a given pattern of relationships. That historical form can then act to influence future compositions just as the continual drifting enables changes in meaning, alternative readings, alternative re-compositions, and new meanings by ensuring that new combinations can always be made.

However, where is the subject in this system? Classically, it is the subject who speaks, who is the author of what is said. The subject is the master of what he or she intends to say. In Sartre's words, 'language only exists as spoken'. However, in Lacan's reading of Freud, there is no longer a conscious subject who speaks, but rather a subject who comes into existence through his or her position in the relational system of differences that underlies language. Yes, speaking takes place as the condition of a living language but language predates the birth of a child. That child becomes a subject not because the *child* speaks but because the

child is *positioned* by the ways others draw upon the language that predates their own existence to name and refer to him or her:

> Long before a child is born a place is prepared for it in its parents'
> linguistic universe: the parents speak of the child yet to be born, try to
> select the perfect name for it, prepare a room for it, and begin imagining
> what their lives will be like with an additional member of the house-
> hold. The words they use to talk about the child have often been in use
> for decades, if not centuries, and the parents have generally neither
> defined nor redefined them despite many years of use. Those words are
> handed down to them by centuries of tradition: they constitute the
> Other of language, as Lacan can call it in French (L'Autre du langage),
> but which we may try to render as the linguistic Other, or the Other *as*
> language.
>
> (Fink 1995: 5)

In Lacan's words '(t)he subject is born insofar as the signifier emerges in
the field of the other' (1977a: 199). With every act of naming the
newborn baby emerges as a subject, and solidifies as a signifier of all
historical acts directed towards him or her. Rather than being the master
of speech, we are spoken by the language of the Other, our subjecthood
is shaped and positioned by the Other. There is the possibility of a
struggle here between how others define who I am and what I feel as
against how *I* struggle to define myself and what *I* feel. There is the
possibility of a mismatch between the categories available for use and the
complexity, the messiness, the inexpressibility of what is felt. The impact
on the sense of self is to split it between the I as defined in language and
the I that linguistic categories cannot capture and thus remain unexpressed, or rather, incapable of expression. In this sense, the self is
alienated in and through language. In the one dimension the self is a
subject defined only in terms of its difference from every other signifier in
the system; in the other, the self is this existential flesh-body that feels,
that cries, that reaches out to touch that is somehow more than, different
from the 'language-body' of signifiers and yet is both, not as an homogeneous unity, but as a split being, each side at war or perhaps in an
uneasy truce.

This evokes Hegel's drama of the Master and the Slave which begins in
the struggle between two warrior consciousness' each wanting to be
recognized as winner by the other. It is thus a drama of aggression and a
struggle for mastery that Lacan read alongside Freud's and Saussure's
theories to produce his own theory of the role of the master signifier and
the discourse of the master whereby the subject in submitting to the
Other is mastered by the Other. Recalling Jane's memories of her
schooling and of being in the military it is clear that there is a closeness of
fit between her sense of being a subject at ease in the system and the
system's clear rules and regulations. She knows who she is in this system

and how she relates to others. In not struggling against the system, she has found a home within it which provides a number of pleasures and satisfactions. However, she recognizes that there are those who struggle against it, labelled the 'bad' children, the troublesome, the inarticulate and so on. The language with which she describes the children is the language as defined by the master discourse through which she herself and her preferred organization of the world is defined. This 'master discourse' may well be the language of schooling, the military and government but it does not have total dominion as in Hegel's Absolute Reason. She is aware that society itself is riven by conflict as between a high moral order and the desire for wealth at any cost. If a master signifier is to emerge, and a master discourse is to prevail in the lives of individuals then, it is only because the individual, *for some reason*, submits to it. Such reasons may be lost in the historical biography of the individual, or due to some traumatic experience, or some crisis or some sense of fear of the power of the other and the weakness of the self and so on. Whatever is the case, the subject emerges in a field of struggle complexly structured like a language.

It is this sense of struggle for meaning that underpins for example, Barthes' proclamation of the death of the Author (1977), Kristeva's theories of intertextuality (1984), Derrida's deconstruction (1974) or Lyotard's (1984) scepticism towards master narratives of science, history and religion. In each case, the authority of the text and of the author of the text is undermined and thus a multiplicity of readings struggle for recognition. If there is no longer one view that counts as the master view through which to read or produce the world, then the way is open for a contest of views. It is this contest of views that forms the basis for inter-view methodology as a pre-condition for any emancipatory project.

Next Moves: Articulating the Project

Inter-view methodology draws upon the multiplicities of views of individuals, their struggles for meaning, identity and recognition. It does so by exploring the impact and role of language in the articulation of subject positions and experiences as a sense of self, other and views of the world are constructed.

Case Study

The case can be construed as a field of difference, struggle, contestation. Its dramatis personae identified through accounts of people's lives defined through the struggle for meanings, identities and boundaries. The case then emerges from the ways in which individuals and groups articulate – or knot together – their different needs, desires and interests – how they join forces, struggle against each other, or keep separate from each other. In the emergence of a case, then, the researcher can ask:

1. Is there a gelling, knotting, articulation of signifiers so that an organized social space emerges to view? If so, what are the key factors involved in that 'gelling'? What are the key categories that members of the dramatis personae employ to organize their worlds?
2. If an organized social space emerges for one or more groups, does this create boundaries, or is it threatened by the total field of struggle?
3. In the relationship between any organized space and a field of struggle are there particular locations which can be said to physically define the 'case'?
4. As a historical construction, does the case have 'phases' and a beginning and an end? Are there case events that can be distinguished from non-case events?
5. Is the case a legacy of the modernist quest for containing and controlling in order to create a rational universe, a community of reason? What, then, is the role of the researcher in the production of the case? Does the case only exist in his or her mind as the organizing principle for the production of a text or some other form of 'case' representation that contributes to the historical legacy of 'cases' which together comprise what is 'known' about such cases? To what purposes is such 'knowledge' put?

If the privileged position is not that of the researcher but of the people, then can an approach to the case be drawn from an ethnographic point of view that escapes a modernist desire to produce research for the purposes of imposing rational control and development? For this it is necessary to consider the concept of 'people', how people produce and maintain that concept or image of themselves as belonging to a 'people' and how they organize themselves.

Ethnography

If ethnography is a 'writing of/about the people' in a field of difference, struggle, contestation:

1. How does one present oneself (as researcher) to others? and in the context of the Other/People? Chapter 3 begins this discussion.
2. If a 'people' is constituted, what is the range of subject positions that are available to an individual? And how are these 'allocated'? Can individuals change subject positions? If so, how? This is discussed in particular in Chapters 5 and 6.
3. In being present to the People, that is, adopting a recognized subject

position in the universe of discourse(s) of the People, how does the researcher engage with others in the articulation of the ethnography? If the subject is spoken by the Other, who writes the case of the People? Is it possible to let the People write through the researcher? Or is this just mystification, self delusion? These questions are developed in Chapters 4, 8 and 9.

4. Where are the points of resistance to and struggle against the view of the People? Do these points of resistance and struggle announce alternative lines of development and ways of becoming? If so, as witness, is there a role of the researcher in announcing these? What is the politics and ethics of either doing so, or keeping quiet? These questions are addressed in Chapters 6 and 7.

Like it or not, the researcher may be positioned as an agent of change. All claims of being neutral, of being merely an observer, of being a 'fly on the wall' may just be self-deluding fantasies. In carrying out an inter-view strategy, performing a given interview, these issues hover like ghosts. If action cannot be wished away, then perhaps it should be given a central role in the research design?

Action Research

If action research is concerned with improving the quality of action in a social situation then, as described in Chapter 1, this can be reduced to one subject imposing on another, or opened out to a dialogue between subjects as the basis of an emancipatory struggle. In each case, action has to be contemplated to bring about a change in the state of affairs. This is suggestive of the Hegelian Master–Slave struggle the political implications of which will be discussed in Chapter 6 and the ethical implications in Chapter 7. If action is either desired, or unavoidable, then:

1. What are the points of difference and conflict which articulate alternative forms of possible action? What are the rationales through which a struggle is articulated?
2. What kinds of envisaged 'community' result from alternative forms of action? Is there an implicit idea of a People that is constitutive of each 'community'?
3. How are decisions about actions to be made?
4. How are actions to be implemented?
5. What are the consequences of actions implemented by an action researcher and on whom do they impact? How are consequences to be handled?

Action research is consequential, impacting on the lives of others, perhaps others not initially included in the sphere of action. Each other makes decisions based upon the circumstances they interpret themselves as being within. Hence, the action of the action researcher is likely to set in train a series, fanning out, of further actions across (a) network(s) of decision makers (cf. Schostak 2002). This then may return the debate to issues of the 'case' interpreted now as the field of consequential actions within which a specified action research project takes place and which become the basis upon which the quality of the action research is evaluated.

Evaluation

If evaluation raises the question of the appropriate political forms required to bring about change, then the field of impact of any change, intended or otherwise, and its implications for the production of difference, conflict and struggle is the primary focus. The evaluation 'case' is thus defined in terms of all those subjects whose identities, forms of practice, life circumstances and sense of being a People, however constituted, are affected by change, intended or otherwise.

1. In whose interests is the change?
2. Who is threatened by the change?
3. How, if at all, is the constitution of 'subjects' and the relations between subjects altered by the change?
4. Does the change seek to master all circumstances and subjects within its sphere of impact? If so, what are the political implications for emergence of a 'community' or other form of social order? How is difference, conflict and struggle to be treated?
5. If evaluation, as a framework through which change is interpreted and managed, has implications for the political order underpinning any community or particular social order, then to what extent, if any, is it implicit in any emancipatory project?

Such questions arise throughout the book and are very much taken up in Chapters 6 and 7 as the conditions for an emancipatory project are explored.

3

Doing the Inter-view

After asking a colleague to make notes on his first experiences of doing interviews for a funded project, he wrote:

> I travelled across country to meet and interview four respondents at a large former poly in the region. I had previously visited another institution with a colleague, and we had undertaken three interviews there. The purpose of the fieldwork was to gather data for a project which was broadly aimed at getting universities to contribute more directly to, mainly, commercial innovation in the region. I had arranged to meet: the senior Pro-Vice-Chancellor responsible for outreach/innovation; a Computer Sciences lecturer who was in the process of raising funds for a new university-supported business; the course leader of a new MA in Entrepreneurship; and the manager of the institution's Business Partnership Office.
>
> I knew they would have different levels of familiarity with my project. I wanted to understand better how/if a university can successfully address the policy agenda of 'commercialisation'. Can this be successfully managed alongside a commitment to the 'core businesses' of teaching and research? How does it feel to be engaged in this kind of work? How far is the institution really committed to it? What sort of evidence of this commitment can be identified? I was aware of not wanting to influence responses by disclosing my own somewhat cynical position. Indeed I had come to this particular institution hoping it would turn out to provide examples of real commitment and achievement.
>
> These were some of the general thoughts I had in mind as I approached the campus. Unusually for me, I arrived in time to have a coffee in the canteen, and to arrange my questions, or themes for enquiry, in a way that seemed to be reasonably progressive and coherent. I scripted a couple of sentences by way of general introduction. These identified overlapping themes: what, in the respondent's view, was it important

for the project to achieve? (this was supposed to be a question about values); and what would need to change to enable the project to succeed? (assuming that the project sought to bring about a change, or improvement in existing practice, this was a question about the cultural and operational constraints on change which would need to be recognized and addressed).

I then listed four questions, roughly equally spaced on a page of an A4 pad, allowing myself space to scribble notes (which I didn't do). I assembled my tape recorder with its remote microphone; somewhat self-consciously announced into it the date, location and name and job-title of my first respondent; and played it back to ensure the machine was functional.

What is it about meeting someone for the first time? A touch of excitement, maybe anxieties, or at least just a frisson of apprehension: Who are they? What will they think of me? How should I present myself? Will I look silly? Should I be early? How early? What will I say? An interview formally set up for a project adds another layer of expectation – how informed should I be? Will my questions betray my lack of expertise? Do they know about the project? And why should they care about it anyway?

Although a highly experienced lecturer with a background in a marketing agency, my colleague still considered himself a relative beginner as a researcher. In a previous interview carried out together, I recall rehearsing with him the possible themes. Even now, after hundreds of interviews over 30 years during around 50 projects, this is something I still do. Why?

It is maybe a cliché to say that every meeting, every interview is new, different. There is an element of that: the cliché *and* the newness. However, what compels the rehearsal, the quasi-simulation of the interview in the mind, is the sense of an engagement with an other who is fully capable of playing games and creating deceptions just as they are able to be open, honest and self critical. The trouble is, you never quite know which is the case. The initial scene setting moments are crucial. This is the period of getting to know each other, settling down. My colleague ran through his mind what little he knew about each interviewee, recalling to himself the purpose of the project, scripting introductory questions, organizing them for ease of note making. He checked his tape recorder and readied it with basic information about the first interviewee. Then what happened?

We had asked the respondents for between 30 and 45 minutes of their time. In all cases, these interviewees had a lot to say. My four questions stimulated enthusiastic discussions in which I participated as an interested party, almost a co-practitioner in fact. This meant that supplementary, or follow-up questions suggested by initial responses turned the 'interview' into something more like a discussion. I was conscious of offering opinions and experiences to reflect, and compare with, and sometimes confirm those of my respondents. For me, this sort of personal engagement feels like a better way of generating spontaneous (and honest) interaction, than a more formal or structured approach. (Listening to some other interviews conducted for this project, I was aware of rather a stilted interaction, as the interviewer sounded as if he was referring back to a checklist of questions at the end of each response. The responses themselves are thoughtful and considered, but the encounter sounds rather hesitant, almost suspicious compared to my experience.)

A space opened up. The interview transformed from its expected course of question followed by answer into 'something more like a discussion'. To my colleague this seemed 'better' than other interviews carried out more formally, stilted. The spontaneity seemed 'honest' not 'suspicious'. As a performance, or rather an unfolding relation between conscious beings who are not necessarily fully aware of their affects on each other, the emergent form of the interview can be surprising and stimulating. These effects are created by the positions adopted by each member of the interview as well as the manner of the performance and as such are a part of the data of the interview. However, such data is rarely provided and if it is, is barely theorized.

Each interview can be seen as a project having as its aim the exploration of the projects – real, potential, imagined – held by others. In this way, the interview is the means to educate (that is, draw out), elucidate and evaluate what is at stake and also to elaborate and effect projects of one's own making. In this sense, the 'discussion' strategy that emerged created a sense of interchange where ideas amongst co-equals could be tested out. Almost as a co-practitioner, my colleague adopted a subject position that was recognizable to the other, a position from which he was able to offer 'valid' (that is recognizable and comparable) opinions and experiences whether or not they were agreed with. The exchanges thus called out responses, views that were continually checkable against each other's experiences. As quasi-co-practitioners, each could be expected to be able to check the clarity, reasonableness and sense of reality of the views of the other. Clearly, alongside the impressions of the interviewer, it is necessary to have the record of the interview itself. Hence the importance of the form of recording:

> One of my respondents (the Pro-Vice-Chancellor) was initially reluctant to be taped, but I improvised a rationale based on the need to make the transcript available to a multi-institution team of analysts, and I detected no sign of inhibition in his subsequent responses.

People do not always feel comfortable with a tape recorder. Hence, my colleague had prepared his notepad. However, in this case he succumbed to exerting some pressure, calling upon the imagined authority of a 'multi-institutional team of analysts'. His ploy worked. It is an instance of 'gamesmanship'. The politics and ethics of the interview as a contested field of action cannot be overlooked. The ethics of the form of recording is not necessarily a simple matter to decide. 'Data' as the trace of an interview (or observation) is the product of the means of recording. To refuse a form of recording is as much a political/ethical act affecting the nature of the data as is the coercion (however nicely accomplished) employed to obtain it. It is vital to the quality of insight to be gleaned from each interview:

> One of the most useful insights for me from these interviews/discussions was a finding from the lecturer involved in a business start-up. He described a situation where at some levels the institution had been very supportive of his undertaking. He cited individuals from whom he had had enormous help, and the university had committed itself financially to the project in order to buy him out of teaching and research duties for a year. But he had still met local resistance (from an academic manager to whom his project was either inconvenient, or inappropriate, or both); and local incompetence, in administrative departments with little or no experience of the legal, financial and Human Resource issues associated with business start-up. This 'hassle factor' was powerful, despite the generally supportive environment. The individual needed to be highly motivated and persistent to create and sustain the opportunity. This finding – that institutional competence is often missing, and that this can contribute to a lack of confidence in individual academics – was reflected widely in this work, and should be central to our thinking about this as a change management project.

> It has been this finding, however, which has been most resisted by some colleagues involved in the project. Because it is problematic, and reflects the complex relationship of institutional, cultural and psychological issues which will support or inhibit engagement in commercialisation agendas, senior colleagues seem reluctant to accept this account. So a challenge which we have not yet met is how to 'sell' these findings to some of the key stakeholders in the project.

The project's purpose was to engage universities in stimulating and supporting business innovation. My colleague and I interviewed key players in the region to map the issues as seen from their different perspectives. The emergent insights – such as 'institutional competence' and the 'hassle factor' – had identified key points of resistance, potential conflict and hence struggle which could be translated into the challenge to 'sell' the findings to those who, if persuaded, could ensure the greatest impact.

This description of interviewing written by my colleague has neatly illustrated many of the important features of the interview process as they emerge within a project context. His final reference to a particular anecdote which illustrates what he considered to be a more general finding acts as not just a simple illustration: it is an organizing structure given in the interview. This structure acts like a map, although not a comprehensive map, but a way of generating a network of addresses by which members of a case or a People can communicate, locate and find their way to each other in order to co-ordinate activities and engage in courses of action.

Addressing the Case

Language can be thought of as a process through which individuals address each other, transforming each other and the world about into 'addresses'. In the simple model of the transmission of a message, addresses are assumed to be precisely identifiable within a stable system. Something is conveyed, just like the freight train and truck conveys material goods from one address to another. To address and be addressed is to be transformed into a location in the system of addresses of the Other. From each address a particular view can be adopted and relationships (connections real or imaginary), positions and directions formulated. Without an address, there is no 'way' to go.

Language, as previously discussed, provides a powerful approach to conceptualizing case studies as a fundamental unit of analysis for the qualitative sciences. It can do this by regarding a case as a nexus of addresses defined through an historical tracing of relationships between subjects and things in a world. Each subject and object is defined within a complex system of differences composed of a drifting network of signifiers and the articulated texts or more generally 'works' through which a world and a People may be composed. An address is a means of directing and co-ordinating attention and effort within this complex system of relationships. Consider the following transcript extract:

> JFS I mean one of the things that has already come up from inter-views, particularly when you are interviewing people, say in [Smoke City], or some other institutions in the [Green County] area, that don't see themselves as part of the high tech anything. They're basically saying 'What's in it for us?', and I guess parti-cularly with your [Regional Development] hat on, rather than your University hat on ... How does one, I suppose, spread innovative potential mechanisms and so forth that gets things working? We can almost take it for granted, I suppose that the [Elite City/Aspiring City], there's going to be a powerful line

there ... How does it then move, to say, [Smoke City ... Slow-town] ... (laughter)

EE Well this is, this is, do you know what I mean, you're actually talking about what is a significant [Regional Development] strategic thrust, which is a combination of things ... one is to try and reduce the barriers to the growth in [Elite City] and the other is to spread that growth outwards (unclear 070) not a lot of point (unclear 071) The [Aspiring City] development is perhaps the first (unclear 072) of that number, and we've eventually sketched out, I think they're called 'Corridors', that causes lots of people to get upset, then because you, they sort of feel (unclear 073) They're more, sort of trying to get people linking up and thinking about things, and the principle apart from (unclear 075) and see if you can persuade people to get involved The principle thing we are doing from an [Regional Development] point of view is building Innovation Centres ...

Transcribing is typically frustrating. Recordings are never perfect. No matter how many times you listen to a word or phrase it remains unclear – its address in the system is as yet unknown. Here, the interview had been transcribed by a secretary who placed into round brackets the locations on the tape where she found the words impossible to decipher. I have further placed into square brackets fictionalized names of towns and a simplified name of an organization charged with supporting development across regions in the UK. Although I have left my own initials, I have changed those of the interviewee to EE. Work has already begun, therefore, to domesticate the interview, anonymizing some of its addresses, targeting those to be clarified and fictionalizing those where the more general indication is of more importance (for the purposes of the project, the thesis or the publication) than the particular. Here, the changes are made as much for illustrative purposes than for need. Prior to the interview, I and my colleague who was present as co-interviewer, established the conditions under which the data would be used: first for the report for the project and second for publications such as this book. Clearly, due to the seniority of the person being interviewed, anonymization within the project would not be possible. Describing the role would be enough for identification purposes. But, EE was not concerned about anonymization since what was said was part of public policy for the region. Nevertheless, there are ethical protocols to run through, defining how each interviewee, each observation, each case, each project is to be addressed. Generally speaking they involve:

1. *Anonymization* or fictionalization of those unique identifiers which define the address of the individual, role and location.
2. *Confidentiality*, which is partly handled by '1'. However, confidentiality

may also imply being party to information that cannot be made public even in anonymized or fictionalized form. Sometimes an interviewee asks for the tape reorder to be switched off. Nevertheless, it is clear that the interviewer is going to be influenced by what is heard. There is a double bind here: use the information and the ethical agreement is broken, don't use the information and either the general report is subtly coloured by the repressed information, or it is misleading because the repressed information was not used. Making clear the double bind may prevent the other from using the strategy. However, there is yet another double bind in that the repressed viewpoint is often key to understanding a complex situation.

3. *Negotiation of access* to people and places relevant to the research is vital if a mapping of all views from all individuals and locations (addresses in the network of interrelationships) is to be constructed.

4. *Right to say no,* means that people, areas and sources of information remain closed to the researcher. Hence a full mapping is not possible. The negotiation of access as a principle means that access can either be granted or denied or conditions given which reduce the ability of the interviewer to record or represent what is seen and heard.

5. *Independence,* of the researcher to report what is said and seen. That is to say, that there should be no external right or power to veto.

6. *Representation,* of the range of views in ways that do not privilege one or more over others. The object is to represent a view in such a way that it gets a fair hearing.

These are not easy to adopt and sustain. Sometimes, they may be impossible, even dangerous, to make explicit – particularly in covert research where for example a researcher may become a member of a dangerous gang (e.g. Patrick 1973). If, however, principles of openness and a concern for fairness and accuracy underlies the research strategy, then it is arguable that interviewees should have a right to review and comment on transcripts and accounts. However, is such a negotiation of accounts carried out in the interests of fairness, accuracy or censorship? Rather than an ethical principle this may be of more use as a political strategy to get as much as possible of the views that would otherwise be unexpressed into the public domain.

EE having agreed to an interview which essentially could not be anonymized within the context of the project or the region, provided accounts of what was essentially in the public domain. Of what value was this? For some there was the suspicion that there was something EE was not saying, a hidden view concerning the real thoughts, values and opinions. Perhaps 'beneath' the public discourse were alternative dis-courses held in private which if known would provide insight into hidden agendas. Such is always possible. If so, then a struggle emerges

between the interviewee and the interviewer where one seeks to dominate the other (Ball 1994: 113). In such cases of 'power imbalance'
various strategies may be adopted. Puwar (1997) describes a number in
her study of women members of parliament in the UK. In a review of the
literatures she contrasted approaches to elites with those of feminists.
Elite interviewing tended to discuss issues of gaining control over the
interview while feminist literatures discussed how to give control to
interviewees. There was an assumption typical of Oakley (1982) and
Finch (1984) that a greater rapport would develop if the interviewer and
the interviewee shared the same gender, ethnicity and so on. A woman
interviewing a woman 'share a subordinate structural position by virtue
of their gender' (Finch: 76, quoted by Puwar). However, in her own
studies Puwar (1997) found that a rapport developing due to such
identification was not always the case because 'I was often considered an
outsider, because I did not share the occupational identity of my interviewees.' Instead:

> I found that experiences other than class, gender, race or sexuality
> became unexpectedly important in establishing rapport. For instance,
> one Labour woman was rather detached upon meeting me and told me
> that she was tired of requests for interviews on women in politics. But as
> we went through her life trajectory and she mentioned her first con-
> stituency in Coventry I told her that I was brought up in Coventry and
> she immediately became much more open, relaxed and warm in her
> approach to me. Another MP was describing her constituency to me and
> when I informed her that I had actually lived in that part of London for a
> few years she also thawed out a bit. When one female MP mentioned
> that she had taught sociology in a comprehensive school in Coventry I
> reminded her of my nephew whom she had taught. She remembered
> him and talked of him and I think this created a close link between our
> worlds. In the last correspondence I had with her she says 'hello' to my
> nephew. Being a constituent of one of the MPs interviewed, we shared
> something very important to her existence as an MP. So my own MP
> treated the interview seriously and seemed to talk quite frankly about
> the House of Commons as a gentleman's club. Another MP has a degree
> in anthropology which gave her some insight into my way of seeing that
> enabled us to share a common intellectual language in the interview.
> She joked, for example, that the House of Commons was a good place
> for fieldwork into a tribal culture.

An interview is, in a sense, addressed towards something that one may
want to call 'the truth', 'an honest account', 'the reality', 'the hidden'.
Finding the key to that address is not at all easy, yet may appear in
unexpected ways. What Puwar discovered is that individuals do not, as
Oakley and Finch appeared to assume, construct their identities
according to a single structural position constructed by gender, or race, or

sexuality alone. Rather their identities are criss-crossed with a range of possible connections to a multiplicity of categories for identification. Rather than an open clear pathway connecting one identity or subject position with another the course to be followed may be more labyrinthine, a zig zag, a kind of dance, or a game of hide and seek. As Laclau and Mouffe (1985) point out, an oppressed worker does not simply identify with some grand category 'the working class' but will perceive many differences along the lines perhaps of gender, race, age, church affiliations, language, neighbourhood – even identifications built through supporting a team in a sport like football. If, as Laclau and Mouffe argue, identities are defined analogously with Saussurian linguistics, within a system of differences, then identities are not constructed by reference to some positive content (I am male therefore I identify with males) but negatively in terms of being different from all other categories. Hence an impoverished worker may construct his or her identity not according to class as a positive content that speaks for all oppressed individuals no matter their race, gender, or the sports team supported – but may see a considerable range of differences which override the apparent class similarity and so construct his or her identity as a particular articulation that knots together church allegiance, hatred of scroungers, idolization of the self-made man/woman, fear of immigrants and thus see more in common with those who have right wing rather than left wing political visions.

Instead of a rapport based upon identification, the interview with EE could better be defined in terms of a play of addresses (defining people, things, places, organizations, systems and so on) where subject positions are articulated in relation to a range of discourses (class based, gender, religious, professional and so on) and identities are constructed historically within given concrete contexts (like an interview, a family argument, a conversation during a train ride). Furthermore, taking the Lacanian view of language as Other, as discussed in the previous chapter, it can then be held that rather than speaking, EE is being spoken by a given discourse. Who composes the community invoked by that discourse – a particular power elite? Who are its members, how can they be contacted and interviewed in order to map the complex intertwinings of influence? The articulations – or knotting together – of differences into some kind of unity or identity may not be just a matter of simple, rational, conscious construction and manipulation. If this is the case, then the interview recording is likely to reveal more than the interviewee and the interviewer had intended. In any case, it will point to the discourse communities (as that Other discourse) that provide it its structuring categories, its addresses and its bearings:

> Well the Elite City/Aspiring City Corridor, we got that ... I was having

breakfast with Andrew Leader one day and I said 'Look this is what you ought to be doing' and then he stopped and pondered over it for a while coz the idea of a proud town like Aspiring City, not only linking its name with Elite City, but putting Elite City first was bit of a shock to the system but he thought about it a bit and he went with it.

While people in Old City sort of think about it a bit, but they don't go with it, they feel somehow Old City is the superior city and so there is an issue, so from a marketing point of view. However the launch of the (unclear 095) Centre, which is part [regionally] financed, Innovation Centre of the Old City research park, is one step in that, that is part of the launch. A number of Elite City scientists actually visited Old City, which is one of the difficulties, and so again this is a question of getting people up here.

I have chosen the names 'Elite City' and so forth deliberately. They refer to key dimensions by which these cities can be described. Of course, choosing just one such category artificially reduces the complexity of the city. However, the corridor to which EE refers calls into play the perceived eliteness of the one in relation to the aspirations and the pride of the other. The sense of the interview is that pride had to be swallowed in order to take advantage of the technical expertise and potential commercial benefits that a linkage would bring. Old City, by contrast, is implicitly criticized for its sense of superiority, its pride – the implication being that this sense is somewhat false as well as self defeating. In order to make something happen, the discourses that construct identities and attitudes have to be taken into account. The corridor that is made to connect two addresses and thus enable communication and commerce is not a simple matter of geography but is a complex matter of articulation. This is illustrated in the anecdote as conversations between powerful people. Where Old City people 'sort of think about it a bit' but do nothing, the key player at Aspiring City thinks about it and does it. The anecdote positions EE as the provider/broker of ideas or catalyst and the others as people who either follow advice or do not. If they do not, then it is a matter of marketing. Implicit in this anecdote then are distinct discourses that structure the different decisions made by those who are in a position to act. EE's discourse positions these other discourses in relation to the broad regional vision. Outside of this set of discourses are those of other cities and towns like Smoke City and Slowtown where no corridors are envisaged. If there is to be a benefit for them EE later indicates that this will either be due to the spread of wealth (a kind of 'trickle down') from the key corridor cities or to an enhancement of some of the old skills and industries of those cities and towns. The plans are not as grand nor as exciting as the sense of the 'corridor'.

Something of the network of relations through which a regional case study can be made is beginning to emerge. Starting with the extracts so far given a number of addresses to locate and explore have been identified:

1. Physical locations: the named cities, Innovation Centre of Old City Research Park, other innovation centres, the Region;
2. Key connections: the 'Corridor';
3. Key individuals: EE and the regional development people, Andrew Leader, the 'people' at Old City, the Elite City scientists;
4. Discourses: those located in relation to each physical location, the regional development organization to which EE belongs, the Elite scientists.

The full interview provides considerable further detail so that the list can be greatly expanded and specified. Nevertheless, for illustrative purposes the four kinds of address identified provide a way of mapping a case analogously to Saussure's conception of a language as a system of differences. Since identity is negatively defined as being different from all others, then each difference is also an address within the system. A discourse, being similarly defined in terms of its difference from all other discourses, is also a unique address: an address of addresses. A given individual as a social actor is intersected by a multiplicity of discourses (professional, family, cultural, religious and so on) and thus articulates (or is articulated by) them according to historical context. Each articulation can be explored for the ways in which differences are knotted together, or indeed, excluded. Each such knotting (or exclusion) can be examined for their historical construction, their implications for identity formation and social action across a range of occupational, personal and other public domains.

EE has articulated together within the regional vision only a few of the key cities and towns. There is little mention of rural needs nor any sense of dealing with a range of social issues. These exclusions are critical. If resources are to be allocated, then only those that are within the field of the vision will obtain them. Where are the discourses, if any, that articulate these other needs or interests? Any discourse implies its Other. Hence, the address of this other is already postulated by its absence. Where in the named cities or outside the cities is it to be found and what needs or interests are to be articulated? One possible source are the 'people' of Old City. Questions can be posed as to who they are and where they can be found. Another source are the people of Green County who I mentioned but EE ignored in the following discussions. Who are they, what have they to say? Each of these will mention others who in turn can be tracked down and interviewed. Each will provide insights into the ranges of interests that are being articulated by those who hold power, and those who do not have the power to allocate resources to their needs and interests. Who is it, indeed, that has the power to create a high technology/business 'corridor' between Elite City and Aspiring City but not between say Elite City and Slowtown? EE clearly remarked that the very mention of 'Corridor' upsets a lot of people. Who are these people who are upset? What is the nature of their discourse and its key articulations of needs and interests? By asking such questions a case can slowly and painstakingly be elaborated increasingly to include the different discourses through which needs and interests are differently and conflictually articulated throughout the Region. The Region as a case begins to be physically and socially defined through the complex of discourses that articulate it. The Region then is the address of addresses that composes the case as a field of differences, conflicts and struggles.

Addressing the People

What constitutes a people? What are the implications of a *category* named the people? In a discussion of the Region as in the previous section, what is the relation of the powerful to the people as individuals, as communities, as the People? Is whatever constitutes the emergent case of the Region in conflict with some more general, more universal concept of the People? What do the people want and what is the nature of their lives? And in what sense do they see themselves as a People? In Pierre Bourdieu's (1993) monumental study of poverty, the opening sentence reads: 'Here we deliver the eye witness accounts men and women have confided in us concerning their existence and their difficulties in existing.'[1] The tone is quite different to that of the extracts concerning the project in the previous section. The tone of a project is significant. The project carries the burden of representing eye witness accounts, accounts that have been *confided*. Thus, he too is concerned about the *right* way to interview in order to elicit the confided eye witness accounts. His core principle is to:

> reduce to the maximum the symbolic violence that can be exercised through it [the interview]. One thus tried to bring about a relation of active, methodical listening, as far from the pure laisser-faire of the non-directive interview as from the dirigisme of the questionnaire. It is an apparently contradictory posture that is not easy to keep to in practice. In effect, the total availability/openness to the person questioned – submitting to the singularity of their particular history which can lead, by a kind of more or less mastered mimicry, to the adoption of their language and entering into their views, feelings, thoughts – is to be

---

[1] My translation of: 'Nous livrons ici les témoignages que des hommes et des femmes nous ont confiés à propos de leur existence et de leur difficulté d'exister.'

associated with a methodical construction that is strong in knowledge of the objective conditions common to an entire category [of people].[2]

(my translation, Bourdieu 1993 :1393–4)

What is being addressed to the other is a 'listening'. If a subject is listening for the message of another then there is an address, a confidential address, marked as a waiting room for the arrival of the other's message within the listener. And there is in the speaker a recognition of this listening that is like a waiting room, expecting the arrival of the message. If there is this recognition and an acceptance on both sides, then the interview creates a space, a listening space where a message may be heard. This listening space is formally empty, like a waiting room. Bourdieu writes of symbolic violence. It would be a violence for the interviewer to compel what should appear in the listening space, it is a space made for the telling by the interviewee. This Jill Schostak (Schostak, J.R. 2004) calls the telling space. It would be a violence for the interviewer as listener to disabuse what is confided in those spaces by selective interpretation, by imposing desired meanings that suit a particular case, by omitting aspects of what is told and privileging others. However, if it is the case that a subject is spoken by the Other, then the subject speaks more than he or she knows. *That* is another kind of violence.

Bourdieu seeks to reduce the symbolic violence exercisable by the interview. There is a sense of a boundary between the maximal reduction and zero violence. Violence, then, is inevitable in Bourdieu's view. It is inherent in the essential relation of conflict or struggle that is described in terms of submission and mastery. This Hegelian style framework involves the interviewer 'submitting to the singularity' of the interviewee's 'particular history' which leads to a 'mastered mimicry' of the interviewee's language, views, feelings, thoughts. This mastered mimicry of the particular is then associated with 'a methodical construction that is strong in knowledge of the objective conditions common to an entire category' of people. What is the nature of that association? If it relates a particular with an entire category, that is, a universal, then the particular is read as a subject under the universal category, the people. Is the individuality, the particularity, subsumed, submitted, erased under the general? This

---

[2] My transalation of: *'réduire au maximum la violence symbolique qui peut s'exercer à travers elle.* On a donc essayé d'instaurer une relation d'*écoute active et méthodique*, aussi éloignée du pur laisser-faire de l'entretien non directif que du dirigisme du questionnaire. Posture d'apparence contradictoire à laquelle il n'est pas facile de se tenir en pratique. En effet, elle associe la disponibilité totale à l'égard de la personne interrogé la soumission à la singularité de son historie particulière, qui peut conduire, par une sorte de mimetisme plus ou moins maitrisé, à adopter son langage et à entrer dans ses vues, dans ses sentiments, dans ses pensées, avec la construction méthodique, forte de la connaissance des conditions objectives, communes à toutes une catégorie.

would be a violence if there were not 'objective conditions' that could be relied upon, as given, as incontrovertible, as foundational, as Truth. If there are such conditions, then representation is easy. It is a matter of attaching a name, a signifier of a particular objective condition that exists as a real referent that cannot be disputed in the world. However, a natural language itself is not neutral nor objective in the sense of a mathematical language as discussed in Chapter 2. All is mediated by language, or as Derrida more controversially put it 'there is nothing outside the text'. This implies that any 'objective conditions' will be subjected to the rules and processes of language, to a symbolic violence, as it were, in the production of linguistic categories. Thus any 'objective conditions' are already linguistically constructed.

In submitting to the singularity of the interviewee's particular history (assuming that history is something tellable, fully, without gloss, without loss – not his-story nor her-story) the interviewer duplicitously masters it to produce a category of the People. Such categories can be used for many purposes. Norval (1996) described the darker purposes in her history and political analysis of South African Apartheid. In doing so, she rejected any conception of some foundational, objective reality 'underneath' that could explain a particular account. Instead:

> Rather than trying to penetrate below the surface of apartheid, this study takes as its object of investigation the discourse of apartheid; the multifarious practices and rituals, verbal and non-verbal, through which a certain sense of reality and understanding of the nature of society were constituted and maintained. This analysis of the political grammar shaping and informing the construction of apartheid hegemony does not seek to uncover some dimension of activity covered over by ordinary language and practices. This is not to say, however, that since these practices are already in plain view, no investigation of them is needed. Quite the contrary. Any attempt to come to an understanding of the political grammar of a particular discourse presupposes that there is a context to be explained, and logics to be made visible. In so doing, it is important that the account provided adheres to two central principles, namely that the discourse analysed be taken seriously, and that the theoretical tools utilised in such an analysis do not prejudge, in an a priori fashion, what is to be found.
>
> (Norval 1996: 2)

Taking the discourse of the other seriously seems to provide an alternative to a notion of submitting to the particular history of another. It is taken seriously because it has real effects in the way the world of people (not as yet, the People) is organized and how resources are allocated. In apartheid discourse the category of the People is employed to marshal the concrete histories, the needs, the interests, the concerns, the fears of individuals defined by the characteristic of 'whiteness' (not principally

language community, class, gender, wealth, church and so on) to produce a political ordering of a State favouring the interests of the People as
against those of the Native. The political grammar and how it may be
analysed in terms of the inter-view methodology will be taken up in
Chapter 6. The theoretical tools referred to by Norval are essentially a
post-structuralist interpretation of Saussure's concept of language
developed by Laclau and Mouffe (1985) and Laclau (1990). In this
approach, described in Chapter 2, the system of differences has no
positive content, each element (signifier) being defined only in terms of
its differences from all other signifiers in the system. Hence, the tools
utilized do not prejudge what is to be found, since there is nothing in the
system that presupposes any content. The content to be found is that of
the concrete discourses, discoverable in speeches, publications, interviews and so on as well as practices. What then becomes of interest is
how universal categories such as the People are produced and employed
through discourses and for what effects. In this way, an ethnography (a
writing of the People, about people) is essential to any social analysis
revealing the connections between the particular (as my story, my
experiences) and the universal category (as all people's history, story,
experiences).

Addressing Action

At the back of studies such as Bourdieu's (1993) and Norval's (1996) is
the desire to understand in order to change. But change in whose
interests? It is at this point that research can be drawn into a politics of
control as much as one of emancipation. These are scary words: control,
emancipation. They are used to justify all kinds of action. What is
emancipation for one group is control for another. In developing a
research design, therefore, it is how views are to be incorporated that is
decisive in terms of how a given change will be perceived.

Years ago in the Talking and Listening project (1988–9) for example, I
was interested to see whether a particular approach to working with very
young children could be exported to another school. This was interesting
to me because it seemed to take the views of young children very seriously. It started in a school with a very charismatic teacher. Was it the
charisma of the teacher, or the method that made it appear to work?

> *scene*: it is a first school classroom, there are just under 60 children in a
> large room which has been used as two classrooms. There are two
> teachers and one welfare assistant. It is nearly dinner time and the
> children have just cleared up their work. One of the teachers has just
> praised them and the excellence of their work and clearing up their
> work quickly and neatly. She goes on to say:

T: Before we have our lunch ... could I just speak to you for a moment ...?

p: yes

T: Um ... Quite a few people have come and said that other -people are bothering them. I think people came and said me that Alan was bothering them and people came and said to me that Mary was bothering them. What do you think you should do in that situation? What do you think is the best thing to do, Jill?

Jill: Go on the carpet.

T: Go on the carpet and sort it out. You can just say to the person 'You are bothering me, please come with me on the carpet and we can sort it out.' Now, what are you going to do if you can't sort it out, it's too hard? What do you think you could do then? Jane?

Jane: Come and fetch you.

T: Yes, come and fetch some help and then we'll, we'll help. There's no point in coming and saying to me 'Alan did this and Mary did that', because I'm not going to sort it out for you. .... OK? So, let's try that and see how it goes. Alright?

(Schostak 1988)

This kind of approach intrigued me at the time. If seemed to fit my rather anarchist approaches to education which privileged the freedom of the individual (at whatever age) to engage in decision making on their own behalf in a climate of mutual aid. These children were 5 to 6 years old. The school took children from nursery age (about 3 years old) to 7 years old. The rationale was that children could sort out their own problems for themselves without the teacher always being the 'judge', the final 'Authority'. It was not limited to just that kind of situation but extended to curriculum matters and other matters of social organization. Indeed, if teachers had issues with each other or with the children, they too would 'sort it out' in a similar manner – in front of the children. Amongst the benefits claimed were that the school became less aggressive and the work quality increased and the lives of the teachers became less stressful. But was it the charismatic nature of the lead teacher that made it work? A critical – and self critical – history of this approach in the school can be seen in Coathup (1997).

The Talking and Listening Project (1988–9) was born to test this out. It was conceived as an Action Research project. In brief: a school was chosen that was considered by the local education authority, as well as the school itself, to be fairly good, but rather dull. Many of the children were considered to have behavioural problems. At the beginning of the project I asked all the staff to consider whether they wanted to do the project. It had, I said, to be a whole school approach. They agreed. I asked them then to say what they really wanted for the education of the children – what their values were. Although each member of staff expressed their views differently, there were commonly expressed desires such as wanting the children to be more self responsible; a friendly atmosphere where children were happy. Simple aspirations, but not ones that had been easy to achieve. Following this, I asked each teacher to make an observation of some activity of their choice, by video or by note-taking. Examples are discussed on the ELU website (Schostak 1988, 1989, 1990 – http://www.enquirylearning.net/ELU/SubFrame.html). The action research approach, and particularly the use of video to record and feedback the recordings enabled the teachers to reflect on what they had taken for granted and rarely noticed. They discussed with each other everyday incidents where they caught themselves undermining their own stated values. In one staffroom conversation I heard two teachers discussing the simple routine of getting children to move from the classroom to the hall for assembly. One teacher said that she had told two children to be quiet and walk quietly. She then said 'But this is not allowing them to act self responsibly.' She wanted to know what she could have done instead. Such conversations led to a radical change in the school structure to enable children greater freedom of movement about the school. Similar conversations based upon video analysis led the teachers to reconceive how the curriculum could develop and how classroom learning could be organized in order to maximize the decision making of the children. A space had emerged that enabled the views of children to be heard. As the behaviour of the children changed, so the behaviour of the teachers changed – each contributing to the changes in the other. The methodology underlying the change was what I now call inter-view; each view engaging the other in a serious quest to value the different experiences, the feelings, the ideas of the other.

Combining Moves

The approach developed in the Teaching and Learning project sowed the seeds for the methodologies I developed with colleagues for later projects concerned with the evaluation of innovations and programmes of action. What changed in the later evaluation projects was the scale of the research. The school case study of change in progress provided in-depth insights into face-to-face processes. The evaluations however demanded national coverage, not just the in-depth study of one relatively small institution. In a sense, there is a return to the issues discussed in relation to the regional innovation project discussed at the beginning of this chapter and the discussion of the particular and the People. Action Research and case studies seem to privilege the particular actions of individuals in relation to others. Here inter-view methodology opens decisions about action to the multiple views of others who together reach decisions. Each view as a particular is constituted also in relation to its Other. Hence the general, or the universal cannot be excluded. Evaluation concerns the general implementation of policy either in a given location in a system in order to inform policy makers about whether or not to roll it out across a system; or the impact of policy that has been implemented across a system. However, policy is always implemented in particular ways, in particular circumstances, by particular individuals. In the following funded example (Schostak and Phillips 1997), we combined the in-depth dimension with that of the need for 'coverage' through an interview based survey conducted nationally. We argued that the project:

> is designed to (a) ensure key issues are identified through the comprehensive study of a *full range* of practice environments and (b) enable assessment practices to be investigated *in-depth* in selected cases. The proposed methodology combines the strengths of survey with those of case-study. The aim is to build an accurate and representative picture of key issues in a short space of time, and to construct context-related case studies giving insights into the affects of the issues over a longer period. This methodology combines fast, detailed coverage of institutions, practice areas and courses with close analysis of student and staff experiences and perceptions.

We divided the project into 4 phases:

> **Phase 1** will be conducted by a team of senior researchers and a highly experienced clinically qualified Senior Research Associate (SRA). This team will be advised by a Support Team comprised of clinically qualified nurse educators from each branch of nursing and a senior midwife consultant, and from time to time by an A&E Consultant.[3] The Senior Research Team are able to work in concentrated time periods, meet short deadlines and apply their experience to produce highly analysed and detailed accounts following surveys and intensive ethnographies. With this approach they will be able to provide the essential baseline and strategy indicators on which subsequent in-depth evaluation of the assessment of practice processes and outcomes will be founded. Essentially, their task will be to ensure coverage during the initial year of the project.

> In **Phase 2** in-depth case studies will be carried out by a smaller research team who will follow up key issues through longer term contact with the subjects of the research. This team will consist of the co-directors,

---

[3] The senior medic who will take on this role is a Consultant in A&E at a District General Hospital. She will provide advice on matters to do with (a) the primary/secondary interface and (b) multi-professional teamwork.

the clinically qualified SRA, the RA, the midwife consultant and one or more Senior Team member(s) where appropriate to the case being studied.

The **Third Phase** will again address the issue of coverage by checking the findings from the in-depth case studies with the fullest possible range of institutions, courses and practice areas.

The summative evaluation report written during the **Final Phase** will offer the Board answers to the questions raised in the invitation to bid. In particular it will provide an evaluation of *'the effectiveness/outcomes of the assessment of the professional knowledge and competence of students at different levels within the practice area'* in ways that conceptualise and manage political and practical realities.

The design combined case study, ethnography and evaluation. The missing dimension is action research. It was however implicit in the possible recommendations discussed in the final report which indicated that implementation requires interpretation through action tailored to circumstances. The broad strategy involves adopting a mapping of issues derived from views gained in interviews across a range of contexts, institutions and professionals nationally. This is the survey phase which generated a sense of the kinds of discourses that were in existence and how they seemed to relate to each other. Each viewpoint expressed pointed not only to the key categories through which experience was being organized and rationalized but indicated particular instances as illustrations. From this we were able to identify a range of institutions and concrete settings (wards, community contexts) which would provide in-depth access to the kinds of discourses identified and to the ways that these operated and interacted in everyday practice. From the in-depth analyses we again developed insights which had not been discovered in the survey. Hence, we needed to see to what extent these particular views had a more general resonance around the country. Thus there was built into the design a complex relationship, like an interweaving, of the particular and the general (or, indeed, universal). This complex inter-weaving of the general and the particular is the focus of the next chapter's discussion of the issues involved in interpretation.

4

Interpreting, Understanding, Explaining

Is it possible ever to read a text innocently?

Anonymized name: Jack

TAPE ONE: Side A

Int   This is Regional Infrastructure for Innovation Project, first interview with Jack, Deputy Chief Executive and Pro-Vice Chancellor at the University of Toytown, recorded on 28 May 2002.

So my start point really is with this agenda – the Third Strategic Priority for (unclear) Education and when that was announced sort of three to four years ago, how did you respond as an institution to that explicit statement to the new strategic aim?

J   I guess we responded like most people did in that we first of all looked at the definition of that third leg funding, er third leg activity and identified what areas we were currently undertaking that actually lay within that third level funding region. And like most of us, I guess, we were quite surprised at how much we are actually doing already, (unclear) because it is quite a broad definition all the way from CPD to spin out companies. So the research especially for us (unclear). So it is actually quite a broad field of activity. So taking the sort of broad spectrum of third leg funding, we then looked at areas of strength, areas where we could facilitate growth, but also areas of void, because we have areas of void. (unclear) institutions have areas of void. We really tried to evaluate whether it was worthwhile trying to penetrate those markets or not, because it's quite tempting, isn't it, here at the university, (unclear) to do everything? We tried to take a fairly objective view about which departments we should be focusing on this activity. Which departments really it's a low priority. We had to be quite strong in that. When it first evolved, it was really a

> process of (unclear) and then identification of strengths, weaknesses and gaps–

This, of course, is not the interview and never will be. Like the transcript extract commencing Chapter 3 it is the product of transcription by a secretary who did her best to make out the words from the recording. She had no visual image, nor sense of the surroundings, the feelings, the odours of the situation. Although she has the sounds in her head, the text has only its inscriptions to be read. There is always a transformation, some would say, a reduction, a loss and thus an impact on validity, truth. Recording and the processes of transcription and of representation, from another point of view, are processes of work, of building, or of creating. Again, it is not that one view is right and the other wrong, it is rather the question of how the researcher and the reader engages with the interviewing process from its inception to the traces that remain. Too often there is a naïve acceptance of the 'data' as something like a found object on the beach, a piece of driftwood, or an apple that falls, or points of light viewed through a telescope.

Data has to be *understood* as data. Lacan (1977a: 194) gave the example of wandering in the desert and happening upon a stone inscribed with hieroglyphics that have never been seen before. Even though not a single meaning can be deciphered, there is the sense of a language. Indeed, it is precisely that it cannot be straightforwardly decoded that it seems like a language. As a contrast, Lacan (1977a: 84) referred to the example of the so-called language of bees where through a kind of dance a bee indicates to others in the hive the source and distance of nectar. However, '(w)e can say that it is distinguished from language precisely by the fixed correlation of its signs to the reality that they signify.' In a language the value of a given sign is produced through the relations it has to the others in the given form that the concrete text or talk takes, as well as the way in which sounds may be accented or the way in which a word or phrase is employed varying the conventional forms of grammar or exploiting the sounds of words to produce puns, irony, satire and so on. The bees exhibit no such flexibility in the codes they employ.

The discoverer of the unknown hieroglyphics in supposing it to be a language 'like mine' has the sense of an encounter with an Other, a radical alterity that survives as a chain of signifiers (Lacan 1977a: 194). As data it may be *explained* in terms of being structured in some way. Each way of forming patterns may be offered as a way of describing its underlying structure, a structure that may be *interpreted* as a language. Yes, it may have the meaning of being a language to the discoverers, it may enhance their careers and have a number of other significations. However, there is no necessary access to the meaningful content of the given text. For that to be the case, there would need to be some further happy accident where a given number of key hieroglyphs could be related to things and processes. Until that moment, the signifiers remain empty. Some, it may be argued, due to their relative position and regularity of occurrence seem to have the role of describing subject positions or object positions or other functions. However, until it is shown how the signifiers related to the realities of the people whose language it was no message or meaning can be construed from the text.

The situation, of course, is very different from the opening interview extract. Although it is in a language still very much in use, there are some blanks, due to difficulties in transcribing, and some problems due to references to particular events, policies, roles that may not be familiar to a reader. Nevertheless, there are ways to fill the blanks and resolve the troubling references. Yet, is it possible to read this text 'innocently'? The bees in their sign system were able to faithfully inform fellow bees of where to find nectar. This might count as an innocent process of both coding and de-coding. However, human needs and actions are both mediated and transformed by language. When a baby cries, how is this to be interpreted? Context may provide a clue: is it cold? Or, has the baby not been fed for some time? Or, is it discomfort due to needing a nappy change? Each experience of the baby will be interpreted in some way and eventually the child will come to use the words that the parents are using for various experienced states. But as Fink (1995: 6) points out:

> If a parent responds to its baby's crying with food, the discomfort, coldness, or pain will retroactively be determined as having 'meant' hunger, as hunger pangs. One cannot say that the true meaning behind the baby's crying was that it was cold, because meaning is an ulterior product: constantly responding to a baby's cries with food may transform all of its discomforts, coldness, and pain into hunger. . . .
>
> The Other as language is assimilated by most children (autistic children are the most notable exception to the rule) as they attempt to bridge the gap between inarticulate need that can only cry out and be interpreted for better or for worse, and the articulation of desire in socially understandable, if not acceptable terms. The Other in this sense can be seen as an insidious, uninvited intruder that unceremoniously and unpropitiously transforms our wishes; it is, however, at the same time that which enables us to clue each other in to our desires and 'communicate'.

Language is not innocent. There is a weaving of the concrete particular, the individual life into the general categories of language. What is the truth, the validity of the interpretation of the child's cry, that simple, uncorrupted state? There are those, like Rousseau who yearn for an age of innocence, before language, a Garden of Eden, pre-knowledge, where all was honey and people were bees. If language has its material aspect in the signifier, then signifiers literally make an impression on the nerves, the flesh, as sound waves, light waves, rhythmic pulses. This impression in the flesh itself then literally carves up the 'innocent' flesh, rendering each part a location associated with a signifier, creating of the flesh 'a subtle body':

> Words are trapped in all the corporeal images that captivate the subject; they may make the 'hysteric pregnant', be identified with the object of *penis-neid*, represent the flood of urine of urethreal ambition, or the retained faeces of avaricious *jouissance*.
>
> (Lacan 1977a: 87)

For each part of the subtle body formed through language, a given culture, a given family will prescribe what can be seen, what should be hidden, what is clean, what is dirty, what is beautiful, what is ugly. Confronted by the body of the other, to look or not to look, to show or not to show? And what to wear? How shall I dress – to call out serious, solemn responses, or seem casual, relaxed or be flirty, seductive? Each presentation, each form of dress is an address for the looks, the judgements, the touch of others. The body, its look, its dress, its postures, its movements are readable. How will it be interpreted? How should it be interpreted? And what are the implications for the identity, the sense of self?

Already there is a sense that there is no straightforward reading. Each part of the named body carries with it the weight of sensory impressions and associated meanings accumulated over a lifetime. What is intended as attractive may be read by another as filthy. However, to address another as being 'filthy' may not be possible in certain contexts – polite society, or a group where judgements as to what is attractive or daring but not filthy differ. The judgement may have to be hidden and even substituted by some polite or even complimentary comment. This generates a game of who is aware of what is in play during a given interchange (cf. Glaser and Strauss 1964). I am aware that you are aware that ... yet neither of us are making this public and even if I do, I know you will deny my accusation. In such a game the truth or validity of the statements made are blurred, meanings hide one behind another. Thus, although Saussure provided an image of language as being articulated linearly through time, one word at a time, each word selected from a stack of possible substitutes (see Diagram 2), each word may have gathered about it a connative cluster as in Diagram 3 which gives it a multiplicity of meanings (structured as a chain of equivalence). And 'one has only to listen to poetry, which Saussure was no doubt in the habit of doing, for a polyphony to be heard, for it to become clear that all discourse is aligned along the several staves of a score' (Lacan 1977a: 154). Whether or not I want or like, some of these meanings along the staves of the score through which the harmony or the discord of my life is expressed, become manifest as signs or symptoms or as slips of the tongue, as a voice from somewhere else ready to be read by an alert interpreter:

> While political discourse as a general rule tries to present itself as a transparent medium through which reality is portrayed in an unmediated fashion, no discourse succeeds entirely in concealing its socially constructed and therefore, ultimately contingent nature. A careful reading of a particular political discourse will reveal the mechanisms through which that naturalisation occurred and the discourse was dissimulated.
>
> (Norval 1996: 3)

How then is the extract that opens this chapter to be approached?

There is something called the 'third strategic priority' which with a bit of prior knowledge is known to refer to a UK policy where Higher Education institutions seek income from business as well as teaching and researching. This then would qualify for additional government funding. It is a key policy mechanism which in effect divides research intensive universities whose income is principally from research bodies from those universities that cannot attract such high levels of research income and thus require a 'third leg', that is business, to contribute alongside teaching incomes. For many commentators this means that universities can then be ranked prestige-wise in terms of what kinds of activity they pursue. This background information can be found in policy documentation, research publications and media accounts. Such information contributes to revealing the unannounced 'staves' along which meanings can be located. The pro-vice chancellor describes the response of his institution as one of trying to identify what they were already doing that would meet the requirement of obtaining 'third leg' funding. The attempt then is to try to marshal particular activities (contents) already engaged in under the general signifier 'third leg'. By looking at areas of strength and weakness, the identity of the university is being modified, shaped towards being recognized as not a research intensive university under the new policy. Rather, what research it does will be redefined as 'third leg', or applied. The university, then has responded to a powerful policy mechanism that is having profound impacts upon its various departments. It reads like a positive united response. There is little sense of division under the unifying signifier 'we', but just a hint: 'We had to be quite strong . . .'. Does this imply there was some resistance? What counts as a 'fairly objective view'? Does this imply a degree of bias? And the departments for which the strategy is to be a 'low priority' does that imply they were the weak departments, the departments that would get less funding? Such questions may emerge to the mind of the listener who has the chance of posing them at some suitable point during the interview. For the reader, there is no chance unless they were actually posed and unless a second interview is possible. Interpretation, then, begins with the interview itself, before, during and after.

Reading Between the Lines

The temptation is to fill in the gaps. Listening to the other speak, in a language that is familiar, of circumstances that are common, there is no need to question. Or is there? Rather than encountering alone in the desert Lacan's object inscribed with the hieroglyphics of an unknown language we are all too familiar with the other who speaks. Yet, there are times when someone says I know that you're the sort of person who ... And is wrong. You say something, or you do something that is interpreted very differently from what you intended, yet to say otherwise would cause offence. How much during an interview should one assume to know?

During an evaluation of the development of 'competence' for trainee nurses and midwives we took the decision from the beginning to treat the word 'competence' as an 'empty space'. How would people fill it with contents? For example:

> It's a hard question. One aspect of it is actually having a good grasp of the kind of nuts and bolts of the job, like when it comes to psychiatric nursing ... you should as a competent nurse know the relevance of the sections of the Mental Health Act thoroughly so you're not fumbling around when the situation comes up ... and similarly when it comes to carrying out procedures like intramuscular injections, dressings and so on ... I think when you're at least familiar you're far more competent in things like that and I feel more confident and then I think that sort of flows over you into sort of the other areas. (pause) I find it difficult to put into words, but part of it is a sort of sensitivity to other people because it's very much about personal relationships and building relationships and a rapport with people who you know are in various kinds of mental distress ... So to me that's quite an important part of being competent. I mean there's so much involved in that, it's not always what you do it's what you don't do ... knowing when to actually say something to somebody, when to get into deep conversation, when to play it cool and when to stop a conversation. (student)
>
> (ACE project 1991–1993)

This is a student talking about issues of being and becoming competent to practice as a nurse. It involves 'knowledge', skilful practice, and a sensitivity to others. However, none of these are easy for her to define. Competence is a hard question because there is an existential quality to its accomplishment that defies categorization. Yet there seems as if there ought to be a way of answering fully and adequately. Competence was often defined in terms of a cluster of skills required if one was to be fit to be left alone to accomplish a job. Others saw it more in terms of the ability to identify and solve problems with the skills component being subordinate. Many talked about confidence as an essential criterion. The research literature also provided a multiplicity of approaches to defining and assessing what was to count as competence (see Bedford et al. 1994). University courses drew upon models developed from the literature in order to provide frameworks to assess students as they developed from novice to competent practitioner. At every stage of development there were distinguishing criteria such as those made popular by Benner (1984), drawing upon the work of Dreyfus (1980), who saw five stages: novice, advanced beginner, competent, proficient, expert. Each such category, however, was difficult to define fully for practical decision making about the level of a given trainee. The particulars of a given situation never quite fitted. Mostly, there was a kind of negotiation between the student and the assessor and often the trainee would define for the assessor what the criteria meant! The situation was no different in two later projects that covered similar territory (TYDE project 1992–1995; PANDA Project 1997–1999). These covered virtually all the universities in England. There were similarities with Schostak and Schostak (2001) which involved five medical consultants from different specialties talking about the nature of expert thinking. It was something difficult to talk about. Yet, all could provide endless stories about particular decision making events which illustrated their 'expertise' and the lack of a similar ability in trainees.

Without being fully defined, terms like novice, competent, expert when used in dialogue or negotiation, work in relation to each other to make practical distinctions by saying what you did was better than a novice but not yet quite competent, perhaps more like expert beginner. This then calls out for an explanation of what would be needed to make it competent in the eyes of the assessor. Thus during interviews, the focus was on trying to get detailed descriptions of actions, events, situations, circumstances. It is not enough to hear: 'it's not always what you do it's what you don't do ... knowing when to actually say something to somebody, when to get into deep conversation, when to play it cool and when to stop a conversation.' Give me an example of 'playing it cool' or when it was appropriate not to do anything.

Slowly the contents of a term like 'competence' get to be filled out with stories from a range of trainees and practitioners. Rather than a single definition that would satisfy all, words such as competence often key into different discourses about the nature of a given profession. Each discourse defines a way of thinking, speaking and acting as well as the kinds of available subject positions and identities. In our research, for example, we found those who embraced new definitions of nursing and caring as well as those who yearned for, and indeed mourned the loss of, old views of nursing. In the old days a trainee would have to learn a key range of practical skills during 'on the ward training'. With the move towards university based training, much more theoretical based understanding was required with an emphasis upon problem solving and flexibility. It was perceived by one school of thought that the newly qualified nurses seemed to be less practically competent than those trained in the older methods. However, others stated that those qualified through the new methods were more flexible, learned faster and were more independent, overtaking the more traditionally trained nurses within a few months.

Such distinctions between the 'old' ways and the 'new' ways of training may be seen in other contexts and other professions. Should children be schooled in the basics or should they learn through play? Should trainee doctors work without sleep for excessively long shifts because that is the only way they will see enough and do enough; or should the hours be shorter and a more problem solving approach be developed? A term like 'competence' may well become politically critical in the arguments that develop between alternative views. How it is interpreted may well favour one view rather than the other. Thus, the key term – or signifier – becomes a battlefield. It is a battlefield because there is no essential definition that can be pointed to, that would end all further discussion. There is then no way of representing something called 'competence' that would be true for all possible situations and contexts. However, 'competence' remains a desirable aim. Since there are different interest groups struggling to control the definition of what counts as the profession of say, nursing, then the definition of competence may become the focus of that struggle. In that sense, there is no interpretation that could be politically 'innocent' and thus mimetically, bee-like, valid or true.

Reading between the lines means that there is no single axis upon which to read a particular account. Even distinguishing the polyphony of accounts each with their own line of reasoning does not exhaust the meaning because 'I find it difficult to put into words, but part of it is a sort of sensitivity to other people.' As the student struggles to find words, there is beyond words the impact of being with others, the sensitivity towards others, an openness that is felt. Each signifier partly points then is cancelled in the deployment of 'sort of' as a way of indicating that this is not it, but may be getting closer. But no signifier brings with it a signified that fully captures what is meant. Whatever is the case, then, this sense of an inexpressible something deconstructs any view that says a particular category can fully capture what is meant in particular. The category, at best, implies only an absent fullness or totality as Laclau calls it (1996: 42), that is, although such contents (or signifieds) are impossible, the category implies that it is possible to have such universally valid contents. It is in this sense what Laclau calls an empty signifier, a signifier without a signified. As an empty signifier if one particular interest group can marshal its contents under the flag of the desired signifier then those contents take on the aura of universality or necessity that the signifier lends to it. Thus one view predominates, controlling the field, denying alternative viewpoints because the one view has become the total view, the natural view, with all other views being nonsense, impossible, mad. There is the political manufacture of truth or validity as particulars are marshalled and modified to fit. The political process through which this takes place and its further implications for the inter-view and for representation will be developed in Chapter 6. The implications for coming to a view about what is the 'case' are developed in the next section.

Representing the Complexity of Views

Is a view like an empty signifier? Or is there yet some way of gaining an interpretation of what a speaker or an author *really* meant without it falling into a political contest to control some field of meaning, truth and validity? If the latter is the case, then there must be something positive that can be addressed, something that fixes meaning in a way that is independent of what others might wish it to be or become. One way of thinking about this is to take the case of the translation of a text written in one language to that of another:

> One problem that anyone working in the field of translation studies has to confront is the relationship between the text termed the 'original', or the source, and the translation of that original. There was a time when the original was perceived as being de facto superior to the translation, which was relegated to the position of being merely a copy, albeit in another language. But research into the history of translation has shown that the concept of the high-status original is a relatively recent phenomenon. Medieval writers and/or translators were not troubled by this phantasm. It arose as a result of the invention of printing and the spread of literacy, linked to the emergence of the idea of an author as 'owner' of his or her text. For if a printer or author owned a text, what rights did the translator have? This discrepancy has been encoded into our thinking about the relationship between translation and so-called originals. It is also significant that the invention of the idea coincides with the period of early colonial expansion, when Europe began to reach outside of its own boundaries for territory to appropriate. Today, increasingly, assumptions about the powerful original are being ques-

tioned, and a major source of that challenge comes from the domains of the fearsome cannibals, from outside the safety of the hedges and neat brick walls of Europe.

(Bassnett and Trivedi 1999: 2)

Something of the problem faced by translators can be seen in the interview process. There is an 'original' interview which is directed towards the 'original' or eye-witness accounts of an interviewee. Is the original the bearer, the 'home' of truth and the criterion by which to test the validity of interpretations? Thus, when an interviewee speaks – who owns what is said? Who owns the 'Truth'? Who holds the power to ascribe meanings? Is the recording a mere copy of the original, the actual acts of speaking and the actual play of intentions that were shaping the meaningful utterances? Hence is the recording really owned by the speaker, the interviewee? If this is so, then procedures need to be established to ensure that any transcribed representation of the interviewee's view is both accredited by the interviewee as the data owning author and also agreed by the interviewee as owner to be placed into the public domain. Stenhouse's (1984) Library Access in Sixth Form Schools Project (LASS) effectively followed this procedure. Each interview was transcribed then returned to the interviewee for checking. The interviewee could remove and change the text in order to accord with what was really meant. Then the transcript was placed into a box file with other such 'corrected' transcripts to provide the case record of a given school. What, however, is the relationship between 'correction' and 'censorship' in this case? If as in a psychoanalytic view the speaker or writer is divided in terms of a conscious statement and an unconscious message, then perhaps what is being excised includes the unconscious 'slip' that a Freudian or Lacanian analysis might interpret as the unwelcome irruption of some repressed contents. Can there be an innocent 'correction'?

The Hermeneutic Turn

If there is something being 'corrected' or 'censored', it would imply that there was something positive that could either be expressed or withheld, corrected or censored. That is, there is an interpretation of what is *really* meant whether or not the speaker wanted that meaning to be known. The problem now looks rather like that of hermeneutics as described by Ricoeur (2004: 3–4), an approach having its origins in:

> *exegesis*, that is, within the framework of a discipline which proposes to understand a text – understand it beginning with its intention, on the basis of what it attempts to say. If exegesis raised a hermeneutic pro-

blem, that is, a problem of interpretation, it is because every reading of a text always takes place within a community, a tradition, or a living current of thought, all of which display presuppositions and exigencies – regardless of how closely a reading may be tied to the *quid*, to 'that in view of which' the text was written.

The 'that in view of which' something is said or written refers either to something outside the text, a positive something (or referent), or to some other text which may in turn refer on to other texts without ever coming to rest in some positive, final reference, an infinite intertextuality without any central point to fix meanings. Ricoeur reminds us that hermeneutics involves the modes of comprehension such as myth, allegory, metaphor, analogy, a poetics of the real. These are ways in which reality is approached, grasped, understood, that is 'by meaningful expressions, not a selection of so-called impressions coming from the things themselves' (2004: 4). This is one way of understanding Derrida's statement that there is nothing outside the text (1974), that in trying to understand, we employ further meaningful expressions. Hence we are relayed from text to text.

Hermeneutics at the opening of the twentieth century seemed to offer to Dilthey (1914–) an approach appropriate for the social sciences. It focused upon the production of meaning by social agents not upon the observation of behaviour as in the natural sciences:

> The human sciences are distinguished from the natural sciences in that the latter take as their object features which appear to consciousness as coming from outside, as phenomena, and as given in particulars; for the former, in contrast, the object appears as coming from within, as reality, and as a vivid original whole. It follows therefore that for the natural sciences an ordering of nature is achieved only through a succession of conclusions by means of linking of hypotheses. For the human sciences, on the contrary, it follows that the connectedness of psychic life is given as an original and general foundation. Nature we explain, the life of the soul we understand.
>
> (source Howard 1982: 15–16; Dilthey 1914–, V: 143–4)

Thus in coming to understand, hermeneutics had to take into account not only 'the laws of internal connection, of context, of geographic, ethnic, and social environments, etc' (Ricoeur 2004: 5) but also the psychological and social processes involved, in particular, 'the con-nectedness of psychic life'. This connectedness is a unity effected within experience not outside of it, '(i)t involves particular memories of items and events in one's own history' (Howard 1982: 17). There is no external vantage point which can give a total – or transcendental – view of human life. In order to interpret a particular or phenomenon of social life it has to be placed within its context, its epoch, its way of life. However, to understand a way of life one has to see how it is enacted, articulated in the instances and phenomena that comprise that way of life. There is then a kind of circle where the part is understood in the context of the whole and the whole is comprehended in relation to the part. However, if this is the case then a distinction may be drawn between what an individual thinks is being said, or intends to say and what it 'means' in the context of the whole of which it is a part. Interpretation, then, may have as its aim to represent both.

From Phenomenology to Post-structuralism

In order to know what a person is meaning, it seems straightforward enough just to ask them. If someone suddenly bangs their fist on a table – what was the purpose? Asking might reveal: to kill a fly, or to express anger, or to attract attention, or to emphasize a discussion point. The symbolic is only revealed by asking. Besides the hermeneutic approach of Dilthey, this symbolic dimension became the focus for studies of social interaction through the pragmatism (later referred to as symbolic interactionism) of Mead (1934) and the social phenomenology of Schutz (1976). If all one had to do was ask, a kind of naturalistic frame of mind creeps back into methodology, one which both wants to study things in their 'natural setting' and which assumes that by 'just looking' and 'just asking' one gets at the truth, or at least, at the ways in which truth is socially constructed. Phenomenologically speaking, one suspends such natural interests, or beliefs in the reality, truth, ontological validity and so on of the world in an act resembling that of Descartes methodological doubt or Hegel's project of the presuppositionless philosophy. This according to Husserl's phenomenology reduces the world to phenomena that appear to consciousness. In the process one cannot suspend that there is a thinking ego carrying out the act of suspending the natural attitude toward the world. Schutz wanted to exploit the results of this process at a philosophical level and apply them to the world of the natural attitude. Everyday life he said, was characterized by a pragmatic attitude of taken for grantedness. The sociological task therefore was to describe the social structures and processes that are taken for granted. This could be done by focusing on interaction in social settings and recording the ways in which people accounted for their actions and their experiences. From such accounts invariant structures, or ideal types, could be drawn out from the features that were shown to be common to a range of different actions. So, for example, by studying what teachers say about their classes, the 'good' can be distinguished from the 'bad'. In Chapter 2 an illustration can be seen in Jane's interview extract and Diagram 3. Suppose all the teachers of that school and other schools sampled from across the country picked out some or all of the same features. Then the two ideal type classes would be constructed of the features that were common to all. A similar process can be carried out to construct ideal type teachers, pupils, parents, workers and so on. These ideal types Schutz likened to puppets endowed with consciousness. Of course, people are not puppets. Are they?

Garfinkel (1967) demonstrated what he considered to be the taken for granted structures underlying social action in his various experiments. By causing trouble in a given social situation the tacit or hidden rules of how one ought to behave would be brought to light. By arbitrarily moving chess pieces across a board, for example, one's opponent would soon remind you of the rules. Similarly, try adopting a self conscious scientific style in response to an ordinary greeting like 'Hi, how are you?' instead of responding 'Fine thank you' you might query the meaning of the question: 'do you mean how am I in my work life, or my health, or my love life, or . . .'. When such experiments were tried by students of Garfinkel the response was often angry, even violent. It was read as an insult, or as making fun of someone. The rules of everyday life are powerful, taken for granted, and call out emotional responses if challenged. There is a routineness, a kind of puppetness, to many of everyday practices that are seen only when disturbed. Yet, in the disturbance, the uniqueness of life is perhaps glimpsed. Both the typification and the singularity are dimensions of identity. The danger inherent in the reduction to types and taken for granted practices is the loss of the uniqueness, the singularity of the individual, the existential quality of life.

It would seem then, a cross fertilization of the ideas of hermeneutics, phenomenology symbolic interactionism and existentialism could be powerful in describing, representing, interpreting, understanding and explaining social life (cf. Ricoeur 2004; Gadammer 1989). By focusing on the lived experiences of individuals and setting them within the complex contexts of their times perhaps the multiplicity of views and their interactions that comprise those times can be analysed to aid understanding and to explain why things happen the way they do. In the process, the very focus on meaning, text and language draws in further reflections and debates on the issues of representation, interpretation and understanding stemming from literary theory and cultural studies drawing on the debates following from the French readings of Hegel, Nietzsche, Husserl, Heidegger and Freud. Where phenomenology focused upon privileging what appears to consciousness, psychoanalysis focused upon the unconscious and how the apparent unity of consciousness was fragmentary and its privileged position illusory. Where Hegelianism, structuralism and hermeneutics focused upon the whole and the relation of the part as subsumed under the whole, to the post-structuralists this unity itself became both undesirable as an aim and untenable philosophically, epistemologically. Reason, whether as the I-think, of the Cartesian, Kantian or Husserlian cogito, or as the Hegelian Absolute Reason, came under attack.

What was at stake was a view of reality, its fundamental nature as defined under 'Reason' or the metaphysics that Derrida critiqued. Was such a view possible? And if it were, was it desirable? These questions are at the heart of the quest to know whether sense can be made of the complexity, the division, the fragmentation apparent in the world about. The focus on the rational methodologies inaugurated by the I-think of Descartes claimed to provide a method whereby reason could come to know and to explain. The Hegelian project sought reconciliation of individuals with society under Absolute Reason. In either case, the aim was to bring about freedom for people through enlightenment. By finding their values and their projects exclusively within their own minds (rather than through tradition, authority or religion) they distinguished themselves from all previous ages, they were the Moderns. Such views privileged the thoughts, the endeavours and the achievements of particular actors (as great philosophers, scientists, artists) on the one hand and the rule of reason to encompass all, explain all, and be the criterion for action, on the other. Similarly, it downgraded the masses, the ordinary, the particular (in favour of the universal), the emotional and values (in favour of 'facts'). There was much then, in the personal and social life that was overlooked, ignored or even scorned. In constructing alternative approaches, the elements that had been discarded, de-valued or ignored were drawn back into view. In doing so, the authority of Reason and its methods was challenged. Such challenges have their costs, provoking counter attacks.

When Barthes (1963) did his study of Racine, it outraged the scholar Picard. Davis (2004) describes Picard's approach as the painstaking uncovering of 'facts' which produced an important 700 page but 'monumentally dull' publication in 1956 (2004: 11). Whereas Barthes produced 'a sort of structural anthropology of the Racinian world' (2004: 13). The conflict led to considerable media coverage which made the careers of both! Over 30 years later a similar conflict occurred when Sokal (1996a,b) submitted an article to the journal *Social Text* and then later admitted in another journal *Lingua Franca*, that it was a hoax. Sokal, a physicist, wrote his paper after the style of postmodernists but laced it with a use of science he considered to have no intellectual merit. That it got published by a leading journal seemed to prove his point. A media furore arose. He later published with Bricmont (1997), a book discrediting postmodernists called *Impostures Intellectuelle* which detailed, in their view, how leading writers misused science. Those attacked included Derrida, Lacan, Kristeva, Deleuze, Baudrillard and others. As Davis points out:

The common stakes of the two imposture controversies are relatively clear. In the name of responsible values of objectivity and truth, an array of French thinkers are denounced for their obscure jargon, relativism, scepticism, intellectual shoddiness and implicitly the corruption of youth. Yet Sokal and Bricmont, like Picard, employ a rhetorical virulence bordering on overkill, which suggests that something is going on here which exceeds simple academic infighting. Barthes is not just sadly misguided, he is aberrant, absurd, frightening; thinkers associated with postmodernism are not merely wrong, they are vacuous or banal, deliberately obscure, charlatans, irrationalist or nihilistic. This rhetorical extravagance certainly does nothing to raise the level of the debate. Moreover, the emphatic distancing of Self from Other (I am rigorous, you are shoddy; I am rational, you are irrational; I am responsible, you are dangerous; I am genuine, you are an impostor) looks more like an implicit acknowledgement of proximity than a marking out of real differences. Without resemblance between the genuine and the false, imposture would not be possible, but the resemblance also disturbs the secure position from which the distinction can be confidently maintained.

(Davis 2004: 31–2)

The argument about the original as 'True', combined with Reason as *the* framework for the production of knowledge is threatened not just academically but politically, emotionally. Yet, as Davis points out the post-structuralist maintains its resemblance to the modernism that it positions itself as being 'post'. It is the resemblance of the lure that mimics food, friend, shelter. Finally, how does one settle the truth of the matter? Davis refers to the websites that have sprung up around the debate (e.g. http://www.physics.nyu.edu/faculty/sokal/index.html) which clash with claim and counter claim, each hyperlink leading to a host of other links. So, 'it is impossible to read through all the articles and sites that can be readily accessed, and there is no authoritative means of deciding in advance between what is or isn't worth the effort' (2004: 30). Each attack requires a counter attack to explain what was *really* meant, with Sokal and Bricmont needing to 'dispel a number of misunderstandings' (1998: ix).

In Davis's account several features stand out. First, a struggle for a location, a place in the public arena between protagonists who stand for ways of thinking that are mutually subversive. Second, there is the impossibility to read everything and take each text into account. Third, a sense of undecidability in terms of what is or is not worth the effort to read. These are all characteristics of the postmodern scene. Sokal and Bricmont have ironically not only been caught within but have contributed to the entangling webs they sought to eradicate with every correction to their views that are made. Representing this complexity is at one level fairly easy: just report that a variety of views exists. But this is not the same as covering and deciding between these views in order to assert a 'truth'. There is no totalizing view, no single archimedian point from which a view can see everything and draw it all under its explanatory gaze and produce a single decisive view. Thus, this is what is at stake in the views of writers like Derrida who claim to show that the principles of certainty and the structures upon which rational or scientific or philosophical explanations are built can be deconstructed:

> The Undecidable remains caught, lodged, at least as a ghost – but an essential ghost – in every decision, in every event of decision. Its ghostliness deconstructs from within any assurance of presence, any certitude or any supposed criteriology that would assure us of the justice of a decision, in truth of the very event of a decision.
>
> (Derrida 1990: 965)

Undecidability is at the heart of being – is that the 'Truth'? Any sense of a decisive total view already carries within it the shadow of its opposite at least as a possibility and the very possibility sows its doubt. If all is undecidable and all is re-interpretable in the light of an infinity of future views, then all is open to contestation. If there is no Archimedian point, no absolute foundation and no Absolute method for attaining Truth, then matters are decidable only by alternatives such as force, whim, desire or the politics through which these are organized by the powerful. Yet what is not undermined is the process of criticism itself – its logic is maintained and employed right to the point where the quest of modernism ends and finds rest in its supposed certainties and 'facts'. This relentless critical process is an echo of Hegel's pressuppositionless philosophy (Houlgate 2005: 26–47). As in the Sokal case, there is no final resting point to the debate (apart from boredom), a decision about the meaning of a text is altered by every other text that is produced to date, and infinitely on into the future, in relation to it. Since there is no final, complete decision there is always another occasion when that decision has to be either made again or modified or rejected. The continual iteration of the decision implies uncertainty. Each iteration is made in a different context and hence is necessarily different from its previous announcement, that is, it *differs from itself*. Since, no decision is ever final there is an inevitable *deferral* at the heart of the decision, that is, its finality is continually deferred until the next pronouncement. In the Sokal case the choice was between positions that could only be defined in terms of their *difference from each other*, that is, they took their meaning and their identity in the debate as the 'other' of each other. Moreover, each 'side' attracts, like it or not, and 'knots' together other kinds of interests – for example, on the side of Sokal this might include traditional, conservative interests very different from his own socialist interests. Hence, as Grosz writes a particular decision cannot be fully present to itself because it is always open to whatever is encountered next. Its meaning then is always *deferred* to the future, a future that extends infinitely. The kinds of difference that I have just described that befall a given decision together comprise what Derrida calls *différance* and what Gasché (1986: 142–54; 185–224) in his discussions of Derrida's work calls an 'infrastructure' and later, a 'minimal thing' (1999). Such a complex structure (or more appropriately, structurality) through which different kinds of differencing are knotted together (deferral over time, difference within itself, difference from itself, difference between others and difference from totality and from particulars) is entirely negative. It recalls Saussure's insistence on the arbitrariness of signifiers and of signifieds which exist only because they are in a system where each is defined as being different from all others. The significance of this system is that it provides a powerful model for the analysis of societies as structures connecting subject positions with the rules, codes and plays of signifiers and signifieds to construct meaning and identities. In this system all views are subsumed under a totalizing structure, each view and each individual just an element in the system, defined only by their position as being different from all the others. This negative structure is transformed in the approach of Derrida and other post-structuralists in that their form of criticism and analysis does not assume a system. Laclau (1996: 37) more formally defines the difference from Saussure this way:

> We know, from Saussure, that language (and by extension, all signifying systems) is a system of differences, that linguistic identities, – values – are purely relational and that, as a result, the totality of language is involved in each single act of signification. Now, in that sense, it is clear that the totality is essentially required – if the differences did not constitute a system, no signification at all would be possible. The problem, however, is that the very possibility of signification is the system, and the very possibility of the system is the possibility of its limits. But if what we are talking about are the limits of a *signifying system*, it is clear that those limits cannot be themselves signified, but have to *show* themselves as the *interruption* or *breakdown* of the process of signification. Thus we are left with the paradoxical situation that what constitutes the condition of possibility of a signifying system – its limits – is also what constitutes its condition of impossibility – a blockage of the continuous expansion of the process of signification.

Saussure's conception of language as a system of differences implies that it is a totality able to cover all possible differences, exactly. If it were not possible to ensure that the system could allocate signifiers that were mutually defined as being different from each other then it would be like trying to follow map directions where co-ordinates could not be guaranteed because a given longitudinal line could not be properly distinguished from any other longitudinal line. Thus no unique intersection (with a given latitudinal line) on a map could be constructed. However, Laclau points to a problem inherent in the nature of such a system. The system itself cannot include itself. This is a classical problem in philosophical logic. If it could signify itself, it could only do so on the basis that it was signifying a difference that was different to all the other differences. That is to say, this new difference just adds to the totality of differences within the system of differences. So the problem starts all over again, how to signify the new totality of the system of differences? The horizon of differences simply expands each time to include the new difference and no final signifier of the total can be made. The hope of completing the system is just that, a hope that cannot be fulfilled. There is thus a breakdown of signification, that is, a final, stable assignment of meaning, a final view of all. Similarly, the case cannot be a finished, total bounded system, even one as complex as a language in Saussure's sense. Yet, there is the sense of such a completion, it hovers ghostlike, promising its existence but never fulfilling that promise. In Laclau's sense, it is an empty signifier, that is, a signifier of universality – say, Patriotism – that has no signified (that is, no content that cannot be contested by other different contents). The case, then, is like an empty signifier.

Rather than reconciling complexity and difference in the production of a total system, a total view, the approach adopted by Derrida, Gasché, Laclau and others attempts to guarantee the continuation of complexity and difference. What is at stake in accepting such reconciliation is the loss of openness, complexity, novelty and change that is implicit in any total system where all is covered, the book of Reason can be completed and the end of history announced. In post-structuralist views, the essential emptiness of the signifier that can unify All means there is always another view to add to the multiplicity of existing views. It means total mastery of the field of interpretation is not possible. Thus, conflict and struggle about 'ends', 'meanings', values', 'purposes' and the nature of 'reality' is inevitable. Where the Enlightenment and Modernism seemed to promise that Reason would provide a straight road to freedom, knowledge, social improvement and reconciliation postmodernism seems only to deconstruct every straight road into its detours, its false avenues, its illusions. How does this impact on a project that desires to be emancipatory? If there are no certainties, no rational social totality is emancipation only the gloomy realization that we can be free from illusions but not from conflict and alienation? If there are no certainties, why *believe* anything? Why not believe *anything*?

Reading a text, listening to an interview, reading its transcript, the same issues arise. In making an interpretation some sort of whole is prefigured, but in doing so, this excludes alternative views and thus alternative understandings and interpretations. In this sense, an innocent reading is not possible. In admitting that such exclusions are inevitable implies a desire to be read as innocent. However, in admitting this, at least *the* view that there are alternative views in conflict and in struggle or even in indifference to each other are possible, therefore innocence is implicit. However, *the* view excludes . . .

Moves in a Maze

Each chapter has ended in a move forward. But is 'forwards' a real move? Is it more like being trapped in a maze constructed of 'howevers', or perhaps like Escher's ants ever moving forward but caught in the spatial logic of a moebius strip thus always going in circles without ever realizing (Schostak 1999b)? How can the case now be interpreted?

Perhaps reading the case as an empty signifier, the absent fullness of community, or a unifying category, that haunts the sociological imagination is a way forward? As a signifier it cannot make sense without other signifiers (and thus other 'cases') and without actors riven by signifiers who construct signs in relation to signifiers. A project case study then may be constructed around the signifiers that attract conflicts and struggles, the processes through which signification is produced, the embodiedness of the signs, the practices through which signifiers are incarnated or materialized. What are the subject positions that emerge around these signifiers, how do they stand towards each other, or resist each other? What enables one (or more) position(s) to attain dominance over others? The inter-view strategy then involves obtaining the accounts of the subject positions that are defined by each protagonist. Interpretations are made according to the ways in which each protagonist describes the other in relation to their selves. The certainties that are expressed are then open to an examination as to whether these certainties are founded upon illusions, myths, contradictions. But, no final reading is possible since there is always an interpellation, a 'calling out', a 'calling into being' of another reading. Each further reading contributes to the play of difference, a change in what can or cannot be done, said and hoped.

The interpellation of different readings adds to the possibility of what people may become, how they may see themselves, how they may see others, how groups may unite under different views, or merge, or dissolve or generate new contents to fill the signifier of being a People. It stimulates the possibility of new ethnographies, writings about people, of people for people. The cultural possibilities of 'peopling', of becoming a people, of becoming other, is encouraged with every reading, every interpretation. The cultural horizon – as final limit – recedes ever from view. However, what is to stop such processes leading to social discord, wars, genocides? Nothing. Cultural enrichment is as much a possibility as apartheid or a war of all against all in the Hobbesian sense.

Action and evaluation allied to some political view as to 'good' social order seems to arise 'naturally' at this point. If it is maintained that postmodernism leads to the conclusion that there are no grounds for making decisions that can be held with rational certainty, then the temptation under conditions of rapid change that unsettles the taken for granted, is to seek some location for belief and authority based on other grounds through which such order can be reimposed. Strong Government, the Church, Big Corporations, the People, may be a source for such belief and/or authority. There may then be a demand, and thus 'invitations to bid' for funds for action research and evaluation to find ways of establishing, strengthening or shaping behaviour towards order defined by policy makers that represent each such interest group. Does each project focusing on increasing numeracy or literacy scores in schools or increased innovation in businesses, or a reduction in waiting times in hospitals add to the power of policy makers to control or free children, workers and professionals to act according to their best interests? An answer can only be given if there is some indication of the range of interests in play, what is at stake for each actor in a given situation, and criteria for choice. The purpose of the following three chapters are to explore both the theory and the practice of how this may be done.

5

Positioning Subjects, Framing Selves, Making Worlds

There is nothing quite like being stuck face-to-face on a train with strangers. I was listening to a recording of Descartes meditations in French – a vain attempt to improve my French as well as my philosophical acquaintance with Descartes. Recently I had attended a seminar at Manchester Metropolitan University, called the *Bladerunner* group, which had focused on the reading of Deleuze and Guattari's *Thousand and One Plateaus* (1987). The following was addressed by e-mail to my fellow readers at the seminar:

> 'All we are saying is that animals are packs, and that packs form, develop, and are transformed by contagion' – Deleuze and Guattari p.242

> On the train ... there I was, ears plugged with some French actor 'sonorisant' René Descartes *Discours de la Méthode* ... when reluctantly, conscious attention fled towards a young woman diagonal to me (I could give a Deleuzian page reference here but will resist) who took her place with two other strangers, a business suited woman in her 40s and a young man in his early 20s. Well suited woman asked the passing ticket inspector whether there would be a stop where she could get out and have time to have a smoke. 'Yes luv, Sheffield.' Young woman was quasi Goth in her dress, obligatory bare skin about the waist, constant big toothy grin, she slouched her five foot nothing across the entire carriage – space was no problem to her though it might be to others – and angled her bare breasts towards the young man. She took out her Walkman and before plugging her ears asked the woman next to her to wake her should she fall asleep before Nottingham 'Just give me a kick, luv'. The woman confessed she wouldn't know Nottingham if it struck her in the face. The young man shrugged helplessly. Desperate the Goth looked

around – I dodged her glances, deep in communion with Descartes – and accosted two others who said they were leaving well before Nottingham. 'God, you lot are the most useless bunch I've ever travelled with! I'll just have to stay awake.'

Staying awake meant talking. Incessantly. First it was about the strategic positioning involved in choosing a seat on the train: 'I like to sit on the outside. Most people won't try to sit on the inside so you get a double seat . . .' All the while she was rolling a cigarette, glancing about furtively. Once rolled she stood and looked about for the toilet where she smoked it. Returning, relaxed, all smiles, breathing fresh smoke she awaited the snacks trolley which duly arrived. She bought a bottle of whiskey and a coffee and commenced talking about the price of liquor, particularly vodka. This turned quickly into anecdotes of drinking until paralytic – a conversation the entire carriage could not avoid hearing, particularly the bit about waking up totally naked after a heavy binge where she was told, but could not remember taking her clothes off in front of the delighted masses. Oh, how embarrassed she was, she said. Loudly. Several times. The whiskey bottle nearly empty.

By this time the carriage had a faint pink glow from the rows of red faces, attempting not to listen, attempting not to laugh. Descartes had all but lost my full attention. What did it was hearing, 'I don't mind admitting, I was a drug addict. It took me a long time to get off it.' There followed a long discourse on the problems of methadone. Eyes darted about, no one was listening, the carriage glowed redder. I decided to write these notes.

At last, the train crawled towards Nottingham. But dammit it stalled outside. She looked around, getting confirmation from all that this was indeed Nottingham. She collected her things, sat back down, stared at the young man opposite and said, very loudly, 'you look as if you need a strong drink.' He was nonplussed, 'why?'

'You just do. You know, you're REALLY CUTE.'

The entire carriage was hooked, mouths open, barely suppressed guffaws. The carriage glowed brighter as the young man blushed.

'Yeah, you're really cute, if we had time we could go somewhere. Why don't we meet up?'

'My girlfriend might have something to say about that.'

'She needn't know.'

The train mercifully moved. She, almost panicking, stood, grabbed her baggage and made her way towards the exit. The train stopped as she halted in front of a man in his late thirties. She said something. He blushed. Laughter filled the carriage as the entertainment unfolded. The young man stood and fled in the opposite direction. She noticed and followed. The entire carriage turned, watched, laughed. And they disappeared onto the platform. The train moved off.

But it didn't end there. Something had changed, people talked to each other. Smokers got emboldened. Furtive moves to the toilet became common as business suited woman encouraged others. Returning giggling, red faced. At each stop at a station, first one, calling to others around the carriage, until a little gang ran to stand just outside, sucking in relief . . . becoming pack. Business suit woman had found a man she fancied during the smoking episodes and went to sit with him . . . they went to the toilet several times together.

I returned to Descartes.

Written for fun, it describes a complex of encounters that open up relationships and modify identities and behaviours. In a Saussurian inspired structural analysis, the train carriage can be visualized as a matrix of places, a totality with positions. It is a system where each empty seat relates to each other empty place under the unifying structures of 'carriage', 'train', 'train company', 'train timetable' and so on – each position defined as different from all other positions. People come and go, momentarily occupying a seat – rather like signifiers sliding over signifieds. Or is it more like one signifier dominating the other, transforming the other into its signified? Some seats are reserved by a ticket inserted into a slot, people search for *their* seat. A signifier (ticket held by passenger) transforming another signifier (seat ticketed) into a contents for a subject (passenger): this seat is reserved, it is *mine* and I *ought* to sit in it – I am its subject. Sometimes the staff do not have time to place the tickets onto the seats and in a crowded train, exasperated ticket holders search for their seat only to find it occupied. A contest may then take place as to who has the *right* to the seat. The whole system has been thrown into disarray. There are many ways in which systems are vulnerable to disarray.

This then, is the context into which the prime actor enters, the young woman I described as the Goth – hair dyed black with strands of violet, dress black, evoking some vampirish look. Her image, like that of 'business suited woman' – call her 'the Suit' – signifies connections to values, ways of behaving that are typically placed into opposition. The carriage is a rule governed system of locations. When the Suit asks the ticket inspector when she will be able to smoke she recognizes that rules apply. When the Goth asks those about her to wake her at the right time she ignores the embarrassed glances, the averting of eyes, the reluctant replies that signify having crossed a boundary. However, when someone speaks it is a rule that one should in some way reply, or indicate 'listening'. In this way she generates relationships that lead to accounts of experiences witnessed and provokes the presentation of identities-in-action. Each relationship, as a being-towards, offers ambivalently both gift and trap. There is an opening up as in gift: a desire to make contact and to be open to contact is expressed through each look and utterance directed towards others, inviting a response. There is a snapping shut as in a trap reducing the other to victim to be exploited: the attempts to reduce others to their use-value as instruments to awaken her; the flirtation with the young man opposite her to arouse her and amuse her; the provocation of those around to keep her awake, amused, in control, to turn them into a 'pack'. But of course, this interpretation is open to challenge. Why should the representation be accepted as accurate? It too visibly includes the agenda of the writer, even to the extent of there being a citation from Deleuze and Guattari that orchestrates thinking and interpretation towards the image of the formation of 'packs'. Isn't it the case then, that the real focus of the text is not the young woman and her impact on the others about her but the writer and his audience of the seminar group? However, that is not sufficient either. The writing was the *effect* of a coincidence of effects, events, interests: the reading of *A Thousand Plateaus*, the seminar discussion, my interests in philosophy, methodology and writing, the collection of strangers who boarded a train and arrived in the same carriage with each other, each with their particular biographies, interests, values, hopes, fears. None of these had the slightest causal or otherwise historical relationship with each other before the event of being on the train and being a witness to what took place. So, what is going on here?

Experience, if it is to be social and hence personally assimilable, has to be open to articulation in some way. What I mean by this is: through language conceptual unities or syntheses can be produced from otherwise disparate elements. The articulation of differences into synthetic unities – albeit however fleetingly, provisionally or indeed historically persistent – is essentially how social life is patterned, made predictable, made usable. It is also why social life is essentially precarious, under the right conditions open to subversion or deconstruction as the syntheses fall away to be replaced by others. Now, the reason for the Delueze and Guattari quotation becomes apparent. The group of passengers otherwise broadly disinterested in each other had undergone a number of transformations as a result of the effect of the young woman. They recognized each other as audience to her antics, eyes glancing towards each other, smiling, raising eyebrows. Taken for granted ways of behaving were challenged by her antics leading to blushing, embarrassment. Her need to talk and her frankness, led to her neighbour also revealing aspects of her life. Her need to smoke and her flouting of anti-smoking rules led to other smokers engaging in similar behaviour, together as a group, a pack. The pack, the audience, the shared, silent gestures of embarrassment among the neighbours who otherwise had no relationship to each other are examples of social syntheses, temporary unities which knot people together. And of course, the written account is a synthesis of these and other syntheses – my interests, the seminar group and now this book – articulating, perhaps, with a project of reflection upon the constitution of social life.

Wherever we go we are in some position, rather like that of the train carriage. In a supermarket, the shelves are categorized and under each category other categories are ranged to be filled by particular contents. We choose a checkout queue – the shortest – slot into position and await to register payment. Each registration of payment is further coded into items bought, cash paid. Cash then flows to another category of income to be set off against other payments called costs to produce profits that eventually end up in a shareholder's personal account. It is a more complex system of locations than that of the train carriage, each defined as different from all the others through which contents can be marshalled toward other locations. And, analogously with the train carriage, there are those who have 'reserved' certain locations as theirs – their bank account, their inheritance. Of course, their rights of possession can be challenged, either within the rules that are recognized (at least by some) as governing access, or by changing the rules, or by sheer force.

The positioning of subjects therefore cannot happen without a recognition of some location to occupy in relation to some other location. In a train carriage there are a fixed quantity of such locations, some of which are seats, others are corridors. Here the seats are more desirable, generally, than standing in corridors. Similarly, living in a rich household is generally seen as more desirable than a poor household. Occupying a particular position in a system – being a subject of the rich environment as distinct from that of the poor – organizes how subjects are related to each other. What allows people to change the rules, change places and what stops them from changing places?

Identity and the Power to Frame Views

To what extent is any individual, as a living being, a subject in a free (not necessarily mutually free) relation to others? If possible, that presumably means free to occupy any position. However, if a given position can only be occupied by a single subject at any one time then there is the possibility of contest unless the other is not free and so can be removed. If the other is not free then the free subject is always a potential thief of the other's position, indeed, their creative possibilities. Therefore in general:

> ... domination is achieved by removing the rules constraining one's own freedom of choice, while at the same time imposing as many restrictive rules as possible on the conduct of all the others. The wider

my range of manoeuvre, the greater my power. The less freedom of choice I have, the weaker are my chances in the power struggle.

(Bauman 2001: 34)

The ability to remove others at will defines a kind of identity in relation to the other who does not have this power. It ascribes a positive content to the subject of a given position in the social matrix. In Hegelian terms this might be the identity of the Master or that of the Slave. In everyday terms, the paradigmatic menus of substitutable terms (see Diagram 2) include: the owner or the employee, the teacher or the pupil, the parent or the child, the government or the citizen, the bully or the victim. Each identity filling the slot of the powerful and the less powerful is generated through its rule governed associations with other subjects of other kinds of positions. More generally and theoretically, subjects are indexically related, that is to say, each subject from their positioning in an inter-subjective matrix can infer or produce hypotheses about the probable relations between individuals, objects and events. In employing the term index I am modelling this conception of an intersubjective nexus on Gell's approach to developing what he considers to be an anthropological approach to art. So what is an index?

> An 'index' in Piercean semiotics is a 'natural sign', that is, an entity from which the observer can make a causal inference of some kind, or an inference about the intentions or capabilities of another person.
>
> (Gell 1998: 13)

This kind of inference is in logic called 'abduction'. He explains the relationship between 'index' and 'abductive inference' as follows:

> When we see a picture of a smiling person, we attribute an attitude of friendliness to 'the person in the picture' and (if there is one) the sitter or 'subject' of the picture. We respond to the picture in this way because the appearance of smiling triggers a (hedged) inference that (unless they are pretending) this person is friendly, just as a real person's smile would trigger the same inference. We have, in short, access to 'another mind' in this way, a real mind or a depicted mind, but in either case the mind of a well-disposed person. Without pausing to unravel the very difficult question as to the nature of the relationship between real and depicted persons, the point I want to emphasize here is that the means we generally have to form a notion of the disposition and intentions of 'social others' is via a large number of abductions from indexes which are neither 'semiotic conventions' or 'laws of nature' but something in between.
>
> (Gell 1998: 15)

Similarly, the inter-view is a methodology of 'inbetweenness'. It cannot be captured within semiotic conventions otherwise it would be reduced to them and could never establish the basis of those conventions. Nor can it be framed within a 'law of nature' since then it could not explain semiotic conventions as a system different from and not reducible to laws of nature. If there were no differences, then semiotic conventions would be laws of nature. Each abductive inference is an act of framing, that is, an act that creates the conditions for differences (inside the frame, outside the frame) to emerge. More subtly, it could be argued that the interview is more like Derrida's use of the term parergon, the threshold to a frame, since a frame is too substantial. In everyday life we do not see, nor can we touch the 'underlying structure' or 'infrastructure', the structurality that structures our ways of seeing to perceive differences. The identity of the other that results from such an act of framing is real in the sense that it is a depiction that has effects. In this way, intersubjective space is populated by subjects depicted as having certain identities. How one depiction rather than another is brought about under given circumstances involves a complex play of power to construct and manipulate subject centred views, where such a view is a complex knotting together of opinions, judgements of value, and sensory perception into 'knowledge', 'ways of knowing' and forms of expression that create a dominant sense of perspective unifying a sensory field, as pictorially, a field of vision in a renaissance style landscape painting to create a sense of depth, unity, realism. Thus:

> By focusing on a field of vision and of visual culture operating within it, we create the space for the articulation of (but not necessarily the response to) such questions as: What are the visual codes by which some are allowed to look, others to hazard a peek, and still others are forbidden to look altogether? In what political discourses can we understand looking and returning the gaze as an act of political resistance? Can we actually participate in the pleasure and identify with the images produced by culturally specific groups to which we do not belong? These are the questions which we must address to the vast body of images that surrounds us daily. Furthermore we need to understand how we actively interact with images from all arenas to remake the world in the shape of our fantasies and desires or to narrate the stories which we carry within us.
>
> (Rogoff 1998: 16)

If in this passage vision and visual are replaced with the appropriate words for hearing, smelling, tasting, touching, or indeed reaching out, grasping, moving towards, occupying and so on, something of the sense of the complex field that inter-view methodology 'maps' and 'unthreads' as a realm of possibility appears. Now, instead of thinking of the field of vision as a space organized by a single point of view, but as a space where no point of view predominates, the unity of the field dissolves. Furthermore, if the field is not closed but as in Laclau's argument described in Chapter 4 (Laclau 1996: 37) it is an infinitely receding horizon, power, then, operates differently. There is no longer a master view that can dominate and unify the field rather there is a multiplicity of positions from which possible views can be constructed. Either the plurality of views are in conflict, or they have nothing to do with each other, or they can co-exist in some complementary fashion. If they have nothing to do with each other, then each is like a unified island, each island different from each of the others but living in peaceful isolation. However, at the moment when a move is made by one to possess the location of the other, there is the potential for a conflict.

Consider the city as a place of complex exchanges between locations. In historic cities for example Tokyo, Rome, Calcutta, there is a city boundary that changes over time but its design has never been planned from beginning to end. Its structure has emerged over time through a complex set of interactions. Such a city can be rethought or re-read as a locus of signs, a play of signifiers and agents producing, meanings, nonsenses, order, chaos, growth, decay – a maze of streets, alleys, corridors. What is important – or seems to be so – for people in the company of each other is the production of networkable spaces where locations can be addressed, by the energy of people to interact through 'looks', 'sounds', 'gestures', 'postures', 'mimicry' – all these call attention, orient it and seek to maintain and manage it. From such interactions patterns emerge, get reinforced, modified or erased.

Johnson (2001) has discussed such emergent patterns in terms of the mathematics of complexity theory which is used to explain the sophistication of phenomena ranging from ant hills to the development of cities and increasingly applied in computer software development. No planning agent is required. Why did one area of a city become known as a theatre district, or another for street markets or yet another for the trading of antiques or jewellery or yet another known for its Bohemian life style? As one or more traders set up shop and if customers take note then other traders may well be attracted to the same area. There are advantages in coming together in one location – a reputation develops as the place to go to buy gold. The more that customers are attracted to an area, the more traders want to set up there; the more traders, the more customers. Thus the conditions for power emerge as people consolidate, compete and seek to control locations and how those locations are to be viewed and how people are to act in those places.

The control of space to produce locations, places, passage ways, boundaries, margins and so on and thus to position subjects can be seen in the subtle play of a network of glances, as one individual notices another, and one or more others notices the noticing, and the original individual notices the noticing of the other or others . . . that is sufficient for a network to emerge through which meanings can be constructed and played out. I call this kind of network of glances a 'dense' intersubjective space. Suppose there are other people in the region of those who are engaged in this 'dense' network of glances. They may either notice or not notice. Not noticing, they are excluded, 'on the outside' in a way that may or may not prejudice them. Now the game-like feel or tone of this network of glances begins to emerge. What if some inside the dense network notice that others who are outside either have not noticed or are beginning to attend to the patterns of glances? They can for example include them or exclude them; or, act in such a way that those original members 'inside' the dense network who have not noticed the obser-vations of the outsiders are prevented from noticing, or are brought into awareness. Multiple levels are clearly in play. The actors can either multiply the levels by creating boundaries to awareness, or boundaries to engagement and inclusion.

From this relatively simple example of a game of glances meanings about inclusion and exclusion are already beginning to emerge – without a word being spoken. There is in effect a language of glances, a coded set of practices that is co-extensive with the emergence of the network, a network founded upon awareness of the other and the acts of the other with respect to a given subject. Subjects are either willing recruits or trapped into identities recognizable as 'one of us' or 'one of them'. In either case – at whatever scale from a play of glances in a train carriage, to the emergence of districts in cities, or the global operations of multi-nationals and financial networks – individuals are not in an absolutely free relation to others, their identities are produced through the multiple plays of multiple networks of subject positions that emerge complexly in ways that no single individual can master. What are the implications of such an approach for the development of research projects?

Framing Projects

Returning to the account of events on the train, supposing the project became 'public behaviour on trains' or 'the culture of the carriage' or 'chance meetings, conversations and embarrassment'; or any number of other possible working titles, a strategy might be worked out to identify the range of interactions, the roles people adopt, the ways in which they incorporate 'train stories' into their repertoires of anecdotes, the events that take place and the impact on people's sense of identity, behaviour and attitudes towards others. Many possibilities begin to multiply as one brainstorms ideas for the research project to be. After noting a few more such possibilities, there may then be the temptation, or indeed, the perceived need to systematize these in relation to a research design that would be acceptable to some potential funder or, in the case of students, course supervisor/examiner. At this point the fun dilutes as the project becomes increasingly dominated by discourses of academic mastery. There is no one voice, however, some voices are more dominant. For some it is the voice of Science, the science of the laboratory, of measurement, of sampling and statistical or mathematical manipulation. For others, it is the voice that privileges human experience, consciousness and meaning situated in the contexts of everyday life. The researcher may further be positioned by other voices: the voices of Control, Progress, Emancipation.

Science entails the view of a world dividable into clear and distinct entities open to being witnessed and indeed manipulated by an observer able to apply reason to detect patterns, necessary relationships and causal relationships to generate explanatory theory. Such a science masters the world through reflective reason. One of its approaches is the randomized control trial (RCT). Here a sample drawn randomly from a total population, say, of train journeys around a given region, country or indeed trade blocks such as Europe or the Pacific Rim or Latin America, or across continental land masses. Of course, a funder or supervisor will be quick to curb the global ambitions of such a study. Perhaps, a sample from the total train journeys between two or more cities? Maybe a city and a seaside resort or a rural town in order to generate a sense of comparison and contrast? Having established some strategy for randomization – like, using random numbers tables to pick train journeys, carriages, seats, passengers – the next issue will be how to control for the variation within each carriage and across trains so that results can be obtained that are not caused by spurious factors. Some trains or carriages would have to be designated the controls. All the conditions within these designated control carriages or trains would have to be identical to those pertaining in all the trains and carriages where some experimental change is going to be introduced. Making the trains and carriages identical is, theoretically at least, a mere technical problem. Trains and carriages can be manufactured to the same design. Unfortunately human beings cannot be so manufactured, at least not yet, and not without ethical controversy. However, it can be argued, people do not have to be absolutely identical for the RCT framework to work, just sufficiently so. Any unclear results can be attributed to 'noise' which does not upset the basic coherence of the design. Hence, what is required is that in each carriage the composition of the people is sufficiently alike for research to take place. Into each carriage, therefore, one could pop an individual sufficiently like the young woman of my story and see whether the same behaviour occurs in all cases, a significant number of cases, or an insignificant number of cases, or indeed, not at all.

My RCT example is a spoof. But suppose it was worked up to become a realistic project plan. No matter how sophisticated the design, it would stand or fall on at least three points: that the material conditions were the same (i.e. the trains), that the people involved were sufficiently the same (otherwise the variables would be out of control) and finally that one could engineer compliance from the train operators and the passengers. The first is theoretically possible but practically unlikely. On such a large scale ensuring the 'sameness' of trains, their fittings, their level of cleanliness, their temperature, their punctuality and so on is a massive task. Then what would be the definition of 'sufficiently the same' to define the participants? It can be argued that people look very much the same and generally act in very predictable ways. The clothes they wear are rarely dramatically different – even those between the Goth and the Suit. The values expressed by one white, 40 year old, university edu-cated, male, middle class, conservative voter may not be startlingly different from those of another who fits these same broad categories. Hence they are sufficiently similar. Already, there is a lot of skidding over possible problems and a necessary suspension of disbelief to make this work. I have indicated six key variables focused on ethnicity, age, edu-cation, gender, social class and political preferences. Taking the category 'white' – is this a truly homogeneous category into which can be lumped those of Polish, Italian, German, British, Irish, Scandinavian and so on background? Of course, these could be handled, but how many more internal qualifications of the category 'white' would need to be made? What about size, weight, attractiveness? It could be argued these were irrelevant. But how would we know before hand? What experiments would have to be conducted to find out? Similarly each of the other four categories can be indefinitely subdivided. But then what about categories other than the six? What about: personality, intelligence, religious beliefs, articulateness, health, the biographical history that has formed their outlooks on life and the worries, concerns, interests that each individual has in their work, community and home lives? Already this process of splicing categories to admit further differences is getting out of hand. Indeed, it is beginning to look like the complexity of language itself. To reduce this complexity into frameworks that can be measured and manipulated as a basis for developing 'knowledge' involves, in my view, an heroic suspension of disbelief. Finally, there is the issue of bringing about the compliance of both people and train operators to conduct the RCT. Again this is theoretically possible but why would one do it?

Apart from the enjoyment one might gain from the sheer absurdity of the exercise what might be learnt? One comparison might be Stanley Milgram's (1974) experiment on the extent to which people would obey authority figures. A surprising number increased the level of electric shock to fatal levels as the prescribed response for 'learners' who failed to get a nonsense word correct simply because an authoritative looking individual in a white coat was present. With the intervention of the young woman, we might, for example, find out the extent to which people with a range of backgrounds would be prepared to break social taboos and engage in illegal behaviour in public contexts. However, does the paraphernalia of the RCT framework add or detract from this aim? In my view it detracts and distorts because its reductive method assumes too much, glosses over complexities and excludes the inconvenient. By its very methodology its reductive techniques exclude or distort the very conditions and processes through which individuals engage with each other in everyday life in order to meet RCT criteria.

The RCT framework has focused on individuals as interchangeable members of isolatable categories rather than as individuals who are beings uniquely, complexly and historically related towards others and the world about. Individuals who are interchangeable within a given category lose their quality of 'difference', 'otherness', 'irreplaceableness'. That is, they lose essential qualities of what makes them human. Furthermore, the very role of the researcher as 'master manipulator', seeking control through the research design and its procedures over all conditions – or at least 'sufficient' to justify the application of statistical method – is adding a key social variable that is nowhere examined within the design: the will to mastery over all conditions in order to control effects. Traditionally, Western metaphysics and the reflective subject of Descartes and Kant privilege the subject over the other/object. This is characteristic of what has been called the Enlightenment Project and of Modernism underlying the development of both capitalist market economics and socialist forms of economic planning as well as the great scientific and engineering achievements of the last 200 or so years. Nevertheless the accuracy with which scientists can control the flights of space probes to the outermost planets of the solar system is nowhere near matched by the ability of economists, let alone politicians and sociologists, to control everyday social processes. For example, Pawson and Tilley (1997) drawing on the work of Bhaskar and others admonish those evaluators of social and political programmes who have modelled their studies on RCTs. Their complaint is that RCTs employed as the methododological framework for evaluations of social processes, even the best of these, tell us very little. They give the example of evaluating prison reform where an exhaustive review of the literature by Martinson (1974) yielded the conclusion:

> I am bound to say that these data, involving over two hundred studies and hundreds of thousands of individuals as they do, are the best available and give us very little reason to hope that we have in fact found a sure way of reducing recidivism through rehabilitation.
> (Martinson, 1975: 49; source Pawson and Tilley 1997: 9)

This was the answer under the title of 'what works?' It is not so much that little seems to work, but that the methodology chosen is not fit for the purpose of providing an answer as to why.

Yet wherever we look there is control, there is predictability and there is order. The trains run to a schedule, not perfectly, people by and large get on and off trains in an orderly manner, and the whole system is managed by thousands of employees each responsible for different functions who keep the system working in ways which are typically only noticed when things go wrong. These considerations give another approach to conducting the research: as a complex of relationships, positions and strategies of co-ordination. In dividing, subdividing and displacing such categories as 'white male' the notion of identity as a self contained circle has already been punctured. An individual is no longer reducible to a single broad category but participates in many possible relationships with others where each relationship modifies the identity of that individual. Faithfully going to an Anglican church and participating in its various social and religious functions modifies the ways in which individuals present themselves and think about themselves just as going to learn martial arts or taking a course in philosophy or night clubbing, or campaigning for human rights. No individual can be thought simply as an interchangeable member of a category but is rather more like the knotting of many threads connecting that individual to many others, each in some way modifying the identities of the others as they engage together in harmony, in tolerance of differences, in creative discord or in conflict and so on. At any moment the knots can come undone. It is at this point that another view on the nature of the research project takes shape:

> For Foucault, knowledge (particularly that of the human and social sciences) and power-relations constitute one another by rendering the social world into a form that is both knowable and governable, each being dependent on the other. If something is established as an area of investigation, this is only because relations of power have constituted it as a 'possible object'.
>
> (Fox 2003: 80)

Similarly, if some methodologies are privileged over others – constituted as the 'gold standard' of research – then it is because they have been constituted as possible ways of viewing the world by relations of power. If answers are not found by such methodologies, then it is perhaps because answers are not supposed to be found. Finding answers may undermine the relations of power. Finding answers, however, from another point of view also defines an emancipatory project. Such a project is disturbing in many ways because its impact includes the very relations in which individuals, *as* individuals, are enmeshed:

> A *self* does not amount to much, but no self is an island; each exists in a

fabric of relations that is now more complex and mobile than ever before. Young or old, man or woman, rich or poor, a person is always located at 'nodal points' of specific communication circuits, however tiny these may be. Or better, one is always located at a post through which various kinds of messages pass.

(Lyotard 1984: 15)

What is at stake here is the formation of the 'judged self', the self that arises as some identity for another, as a locus of these multiplicities of messages, the drip-drip of attention, the look, the tut-tut, the nod and wink. All of this is composed as anecdote, narrative, biography (see Chapter 8) and made available to the researcher as recorded through the microphone or on the note pad. The casting of judgement, as a spell is cast, frames individuals through a grammar-like structure of positioning. How does one get into a position to create moves?

Creating Moves

Parodically, each carriage of the train example, or indeed each train can be seen as 'a bounded system', a single instance. It is organized like a matrix, each seat, each carriage, each train numbered. Each character in the story took a place and became locatable by their position in the matrix:

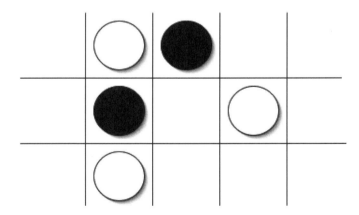

Diagram 4: A matrix of subject positions

Like the diagram, each individual can be defined by their subject position in a matrix constructed to position boss or worker, male or female, black or white and so on. As in a game, any move is defined by the subject position occupied and the rules by which an individual piece can act. If the game is describable in, say, Marxist terms then those who are workers will share common interests and see bosses in oppositional terms as wanting to exploit employees. If workers do not however rise up and unite against the exploitation of their labour then it could be argued that they do not understand the real conditions underlying their circumstances – a false consciousness of reality. Similarly, a woman should recognize in another woman their subordinate position in the context of a male ordered system and thus have a basis for uniting in common interests to challenge and change the system. Similar cases can be made in terms of race, religion and so on. However, such cases only hold if the system is dominated by a master discourse through which the matrix of subject positions comes into being. If there are multiple possible discourses, then each individual is a locus of not one but many possible matrices of subject positions:

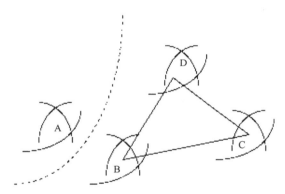

Diagram 5: Inside and outside the pack

Each individual is criss-crossed with connections to others whether on the basis of gender, ethnicity, level of economic income, age, employment status, occupation, fashion, cult – and so on. There is no one that necessarily dominates over the other. Different circumstances may make moves according to one or more positional connections more appropriate, more desirable, more successful than others. In the story about the Goth and the Suit what seemed to dominate and create connections was the need to smoke which gave a rebellious, daring feel to the temporary alliance – the pack, as I called it, B, C and D, in the diagram – that then followed. Thus a boundary, however subtle, is constructed between those inside and those outside the pack that could be called upon to rush for a smoke when the train paused for long enough at a station.

If this is to be treated as the germ of a case study, how should it be defined and elaborated? Perhaps, one move, rather than conceive it as an instance, or a bounded system, is to conceive of the 'case' as a mental construct generated for some pragmatic reason (because it seems like a good 'unit' to focus on, like a school, a pub, a supermarket). However, as a mental construct it mentally limits ways of thinking by creating a non-necessary category into which to fit a rather messy, knotty, slippery, complexly connected reality. In Schostak 2002 I argued for a different approach to the case study founded upon the tracing of relationships. So, starting from my observation of the train episode, an arbitrary starting point, a mapping of relationships can begin that reveals the implication, imbrication, or woven and knotted strands of relationship as between people and things of the world as well as the boundaries that they erect between each other and things. Each individual becomes a possible focus for interviews, for observation, for the collection of artefacts they use or produce. Each individual provides a point of view and a locus for action that takes the other and otherness into account. Each view as a direct-edness towards an other carries also its sense of limit or boundary between subject and other. That is to say, with every view directed by a subject towards another there is an inter-view, a space between views. It is this betweenness that ensures no single view can fully saturate the views of others. There is in every view always a difference, a 'between-ness' that cannot be crossed as subject looks towards, or reaches towards the other. The interview, in this sense, is constructive and de-constructive of cases not as singular instances, nor as bounded systems but as infinitely extensible, richly connectable plays or weavings of ever expanding differences.

A case study is then constructable by elaborating and generating accounts of the density of relationships that actors have with each other, the boundaries that emerge under given circumstances, the transforma-tions and dissolutions of relationships, and the events that take place from as many view points as possible. Indeed, it could be argued the event illustrated in the story is the kind of fluidly evolving and dissolving event so characteristic of postmodern societies that it therefore constitutes the only kind of ethnography possible of those who are members of such a society. However, just as there is no necessary reason as to why one subject position should dominate due to the 'objective conditions' of social life, so there is no reason to suppose why one should not. The potential for a dominating subject position to unify a field and so create the conditions for a People is always available – as in Norval's (1996) description of Apart-heid. How ways of life that govern people's sense of self, their identities and their views concerning others emerge, become sustainable, transform or dissolve is vital to any emancipatory project. It provides the insights necessary for action and the promotion of visions and practices for change, whether through Action Research or evaluation. Understanding the poli-tics of change requires a mapping of the politics implicit in the emergence of subject positions, their fragmentation and their transformation.

Mapping The Politics: A rhetoric of circumstances, motives and action

You never quite know what to expect:

> From the taxi window the terraced houses of the area look neat, poor, but generally well kept. Down one street I notice a mosque just before we turn and enter the drive way of the primary school. I pay, hop out and look around. I spot what seems to be the remains of an archway acting as a centre piece for a little garden area. I slightly detour to walk past it before entering the school. Off to the right is a room being used by a local women's group and as I follow the sign to the head teacher's office I'm passed by a local man who seems to have been doing some work in the garden areas. Before reaching the headteacher's office I'm greeted by a receptionist who says the headteacher is off somewhere around the school. She'll get him for me.
>
> After he arrives, we settle down for the interview in his office. He keeps the door open, sips from his coffee mug, takes out a cigarette, lights it and allows the smoke to trail out the window behind him.
>
> I ask him if he knows about the project I'm involved in. No not much. So I tell him. Of course, I won't use his name or that of the school nor of the location. All will be anonymized. He is agreeable to be interviewed. I switch on my digital recorder and wait momentarily for it to be ready.
>
> '... it takes a little while. There we go. It's fairly sensitive, so, you don't have to shout,' I chuckle.
>
> 'Well this is a beacon school um School achievement, we've won the school achievement each year since it's been going for good SAT results in comparison with similar schools. Um, 410 children on the roll and 850 waiting to come in.'
>
> '850 waiting to come in? ... Slightly overbooked then ...' laughing.
>
> 'mmm, yes yes uuum there are something like 99% ethnic

> minority pupils and about 98% have English as an additional language. Um, 97% are Moslem. The heritage groups ... there about 16 at least, 16 identifiable languages spoken here but I I guess there's maybe a few more um The communities stretch from ... children who were born here and their families maybe were born here. Mainly that's the Pakistani heritage group. But then we've got families from the student population who tend to do Ph Ds at the (university) who only stay for three years and go back and are mainly the Libyan community and some other Arab speaking communities and Malaysian and Indonesian. Um, which gives us something like a 35% transient population. So, 7 children get from nursery to your 6th. And a third of each class changes, roughly, each year. Um we have ... Then at the other end of the spectrum we have refugee asylum seekers, not so many but mainly from Somalia, Bosnia, Kosovo uhh Afghanistan and one or two from Pakistan, for various reasons. Does that give you the background?'

That's how it began, no hesitation, no waiting for initial warm up questions. What do you do? Do you disrupt the flow, interject your own questions, or just chuckle. In many ways this is just what I want. Not so much the 'background' but whatever it is that the interviewee deems to be important to talk about. However, I also have a purpose. I need to find out some examples of ways in which the creative arts, and arts practitioners can be employed as an approach to learning about cultural diversity. That's what the funders are paying me to do. But I hold back my questions. There is time for that. I want to know more about how this man's world looks to him. He is telling me what he seems to think I want to know – the background – but this interpretation of 'background' and what I want to know are the seeds of what it is he wants me to know in the context of how he sees his world.

I look around his office, stacked with papers, his desk littered with in-trays and out-trays and between the trays. His door is open, but entering there are few places to position oneself: the door way, the side of his desk, the chair in front of his desk. That chair is lower than his. He can look down. I have to look up. He angles himself towards the window to smoke his cigarette and drink his coffee. I was never asked whether I minded the smoke, nor was I asked if I wanted a coffee. Nevertheless, he created one safe boundary for his action: the smoke went outside, not inside. On sheer positioning, I was in the subordinate place. However defined, he was in control. I continued his theme of background, asking, what's the area like:

> 'It's pretty much all white, economically, socially, spiritually deprived. Someone called Professor (XXX) did a health and did did uh a survey some years ago on health and social deprivation levels uh and they looked at the cities in uh major cities in western Europe and we fell off

his chart (. . .) it's got the highest crime rate in the city uh, prostitution, drugs, shootings, car thefts, burglaries – it is all here in excess. But . . . the community that the school serves is maybe economically deprived, even if you're a student your grant's very small for a young family – but socially, spiritually and all the other ways, no. (. . .) The surroundings around the school is pretty bad in every single way. But our students tend to come from the other side of the (. . .) road. It's only more recently, in recent years that they've started moving this side because this side was such a terrible side that nobody even wanted a new house. I mean this is bad enough here but that does not impact on the school, at all.'

'Right, wh' what's the unemployment like?'

'Well, I mean you take away the student population, they're quite high, they must be way, way higher than national. Uh, most of our families are maybe small, uh taxi drivers, small shop keepers, work in shops that sort of thing. And I guess a significant number unemployed. I I I met one guy a few years ago he was sat on the garden wall crying' the word crying is accompanied by a kind of laugh, 'I said "what's the matter?" He said, "Well I've got so many qualifications, I've been to so many training courses and I can't get a job." '

At last. This is more like it – a story. The background I can get anywhere – newspapers, local government and national government statistics, an internet search and so on. What are the stories that fill this man's head? I could, of course, just ask. But I don't. Stories work differently from that. They spring to mind to make certain points to compel a view, unasked. But stories are not to be hurried. The tone of the interview however has changed – not much – but has started to become more conversational. I asked if the school could make links into the community. His answer was 'we can do anything'. He listed his links which included being a lay preacher in the Mosque, connections to different schools and communities in the countries to which the schools heritage communities had links. He talked of his interviews by the media. He talked of his links with influential politicians. He talked of his fund raising and of ensuring that children, when they returned to their country, had been following the same curriculum as their home countries. There then followed a list of the achievements of the school's pupils. As the talk drew closer to the theme of everyday school work, ten minutes since the beginning of the interview, I saw my chance to pose a question on the relation between the creative arts, the connections to the cultures of the communities of the school and the needs of the curriculum.

'when I first came here it was very much a thematic approach. So you might choose water as your topic, bring in your Mosques, bring in literacy, bring in stories, bring in art, bring in dance, drama and so on and so on. (. . .) But then of course with the advent of uh the literacy and numeracy strategies and the foundation subjects *as* subjects you then moved to a very curriculum driven situation. For example if you're going to have an OFSTED inspection then they'll say well can we have copies of your timetables and they'll expect to see all the subjects on it. They would not expect to see theme, theme, theme. And they would not be looking at that kind of fluidity. Now of course with the document on Excellence and Enjoyment yes they would. Well, I don't know because' he laughs, 'sometimes there's a difference between policy, between DFES and OFSTED they are two separate departments (. . .)'

The politics of the curriculum has begun to emerge after the initial background listings of deprivation, connections with the community and pupil academic achievement. From his presentation of background and now of more detailed accounts, a political mapping and strategy is beginning to take shape. It is very much about making connections across a range of dimensions in order to create an environment. For example:

'But the arts can come into anything. And we use it in lots of ways, particularly the outdoor environment. I mean, when they built this school they ran out of money and they left us with two pieces of land with broken bottles and tyres. One we just grassed over and said, OK we can use it as a sports pitch of some sort. And the other we developed into a community garden with a pond and willows and all sorts of stuff. And we can use that as a resource for artwork.'

When I arrived at the school, the arch I had seen was the entrance to this garden, made by the children. The garden had been constructed with the help of parents, many, refugees who had provided their skills. He talked later of the garden as an unending project with new things to grow and experiment with. He mentioned how the school received very little vandalism in comparison to other buildings in the local community. The little it got was mainly through the summer holidays and local people would come in to remove it. I recalled him saying 'we can do anything' in answer to an earlier question.

Finally, I wanted an image of integration. How could it be done? I never asked this question. I never needed to:

'We teach steel bands, to quite a high level, I mean they've played at the (name of theatre) but there's no West Indian children here. Um to see a Malaysian, an Indonesian child, Pakistani children, a Bosnian child all playing steel band is quite an interesting sight in itself. Let alone the quality of the music.'

He remarks that 'it's about opportunities. Opportunities for life. Life long learning.' But, of course, I persist. How does it all get worked into the curriculum? Now 20 minutes into the interview, example after example follows showing how one idea led to another idea pulling together activities in art, music, food, poetry and so on, drawing in local artists, crafts people and parents:

'We had a lady from Pakistan who couldn't speak any English and she brought a child to the school . . . and wanted to learn English so we put her in a class and treated her as a year six and said what did you do in Pakistan if we're going to teach you English. And she says uh Oh I do slippers, then I do handbags – Great – and I do art – Fine, how's about we do some of that with the children as well in return? So we did some fantastic calligraphy out of leather, on velv on velvetine. We did some beautiful Islamic pattern work using leather. Some really nice artwork painting-wise. All Islamic oriented, even right down to the children producing their own. And then we got them laser cut into the floor.

His excitement and jokiness grew with every anecdote as he proclaimed we have so many advantages, advantages from all over the world to draw upon in terms of skills, art, culture. So what could other schools learn from this?

'they can learn what they want to learn. They may not wish to learn. . . . I mean, during Ramadan we fast. The majority of the school fasts. And a couple of nights during Ramadan we break our fast (. . .) So what happened, we extended our day from half past three to the time of breaking the fast. The boys and gir', the boys and *men* prayed in the hall, the women and girls prayed in the community room. And after the prayer, wh' while that was going on the non-Muslims staff actually set out the dining area and all the classrooms for the food that had been cooked during the day by our staff. And then we can break the fast. We pray we go to the hall and break our fast. It's all been laid out by the non Muslim. Staff. And the Muslims think this is wonderful. Why should the non Muslim staff do it it's not Christmas it's Ede (. . .). So we say, we're one community.'

He also invited pupils and parents from another all white school where he had worked to watch or partake. 'They had never seen 700 people all fed in one school before.' He contrasted this experience with the experiences told to him by many other headteachers who consider that behaviour becomes problematic during the fast because in his view the spiritual meaning of the fast had never been explained.

At the back of this is a sense of lack of recognition. He talked of how the National Curriculum essentially leaves out the varieties of British cultures to be found let alone those of the various ethnic heritage communities he had named earlier.

'There's no example for Moslem children of good role models in the sense (. . .) Well if you look at the Mosques they're all prefabs. What really hit me was when I took the kids to (Names a Cathedral). I said, "what do you think folks?" they said "Wow . . ." and the history, and the size. I said "I've gotta take you to somewhere Islamic." So we went to Istanbul and stayed with a friend of mine and we looked around (name of Mosque) and they said "Wow." ' He laughs. 'And you know "I

> wish all these Americans would stop flashing their cameras." I said "Why?" "Well, it's in our Mosque." But I said, "it's not in your Mosque. It's in Turkey." "Ah, but" they said, "it's the same thing, it's our Mosque. We're Moslem." '

After 40 minutes, the interview ended with a tour around the school. He pointed out many of the examples of work that he had talked about. We ended in the Garden. In its midst was a living willow arch shaped into the Islamic symbol for Peace.

The Rhetoric of Struggle for Position and Recognition

Recall the imaginary meetings I described in Chapter 1. When faced with approaching a stranger in an isolated place there is perhaps a sense of wariness. As Hegel tells the story, the encounter is essentially between two warriors. Each wants recognition as a value in itself. It is not enough to assign value, a sense of worth, to one's self, each 'wants this *particular* value, his own, to be recognized by *all* men, *universally*' (Kojève 1969: 58). The interview described above ends with a personal anecdote about the need for recognition and the symbols of recognition that are a focus for cultural identity, whether these are role models or monuments to cultural achievement and spiritual life. It is how the life of the particular human being relates to the universal in a given culture. Running throughout the interview this positioning of the individual in relation to the universal has been elaborated. It's a kind of weaving, like the many artwork textiles I saw around the school, or the rope work, or the living Arch of Peace in the garden.

Weaving is a metaphor of unity, drawing diverse strands into a unified whole, knotting them into place, it is the articulation that Laclau (1996) refers to as differences are formed into a synthetic whole or unity for particular political purposes. At this point I use the metaphor of weaving and articulation to refer to this process of knotting strands together. Plato employs weaving as a metaphor of statesmanship where opposites that are at war are plaited together, a process called *symploke*. Unfortunately, in order to get the perfect weave inferior products have to be eliminated, such as:

> those children who 'cannot be taught to be courageous and moderate and to acquire the other virtuous tendencies, but are impelled to godlessness and to vaunting pride and injustice by the drive of an evil nature. These the king expels from the community. He puts them to death or banishes them or else he chastises them by the severest public disgrace' (. . .). The totality woven by the *symploke* – a totality of concurring and complementary opposites – is thus a function of the expulsion of absolute heterogeneity.

> (Gasché 1986: 97)

Hence the weaving that is taking place does not bring together all the diverse elements. A school and its headteacher can only do so much, of course. The headteacher referred to the crime rate of the area, that is not what he can deal with. However, the diversity of what he calls cultural heritage groups is to him a rich resource to weave into the children's education. Thus when he talks of connections into the community, it involves only the desirable connections. The undesirable have no impact on the school. In fact it seems some are leaving the area.

There is then a broad positioning taking place across a mental matrix that is roughly divided into the local community, the organizations that compose the education system both locally and nationally, and a range of other useful and influential organizations (e.g. religious organizations, media, business, charities). The matrix can be made more sophisticated and detailed by including the range of positively defined diverse heritage groups, and the language, skills and occupations of the local people. Diversity runs the risk of falling into conflict as different groups feel that their individuality – their differences – are not recognized and supported. This poses a considerable political problem, one which the headteacher is aware that many other schools and indeed institutions nationally do not deal well with – as he discussed in relation to his example of Ramadan. Although diverse, each group faces and thus may well fear any descent into conflict and chaos. Hence, there is something that could potentially unite them. Furthermore, although diverse, those who see themselves as members of a particular heritage or faith group or as having particular needs due to their refugee status, their poverty, their lack of employment face in common at least two kinds of additional implicit threat: first, the threat of the criminal activities that make their homes unsafe; and second, the threat of a lack of appropriate education for their children should the school fail. This latter threat would condemn their children to very uncertain futures as unskilled and unemployable in an area of high unemployment and perhaps leave them vulnerable to criminal street cultures. Hence, even if diverse, they at least face common fears and issues. What kind of political organization can both recognize difference and create a sense of order, safety and hope?

The strategy of the headteacher is clear. It is concerned about achievement, about opening opportunities for children, to providing role models, symbols of achievement and generally instilling the belief that 'we can do anything'. To meet these goals he brings diverse groups together into educational projects and fundraising events. As in his West Indian steel band without a single West Indian but composed of children from a multiplicity of heritage communities he offers symbols of unity, working together, feasting together. It is a powerful political message. But implicit in that message is a message about leadership and the position of those being led, or brought into harmony.

In his stories he is very much the central player, the weaver of the fabric. In classical philosophy, the self as subject is privileged over the other, that is to say, in Hegelian terms the subject desires to dominate the other, whether this other is another human subject or the raw materials of the world. Thus the self's desire is to master the other which in turn means that the Master wants universal recognition by each and every particular individual. Each story told by the headteacher is a story of leadership, of galvanizing others, of organizing others, of providing opportunities to others, of generating the conditions for sharing, of teaching others. With few exceptions in the interview, the flow of influence and of power is one way. Where he uses the 'we' it is a community 'we' defined or directed by him. In his domain he commands the field. Running like a sub plot during the interview are the plays concerning recognition between myself as interviewer and he as interviewee. From the first encounter the positions are defined as I enter his office. Such positioning plays are about micromanipulation: the organization of the room, its furniture determines what positions can be occupied; the way one enters, the first words to be said, the organization of the agenda; when and whether a drink is offered, when and whether permission is asked in relation to socially problematic actions such as smoking – he did indeed ask, half way through the interview, but by then our positioning play had evolved into a more conversational mode. These micromanipulations can be seen in each encounter. As we walked around the school, it was revealed in his entrance and self positioning in a teacher's classroom as he or she worked with the children. It was revealed in his asides to pupils, to passing parents and other members of staff. In each case, he could interrupt and command attention. Not noisily, but with a calm assurance.

There was no challenge to his authority. Continuing reading the interview alongside the Hegelian drama helps to draw out further political themes and issues that are at stake. For Hegel, universal Mastery, is only fully accomplished when the one, as particular, *recognizes* the universal superiority of the other. Clearly, the headteacher did not have this kind of universal mastery, only a mastery within the limits of the school, creating a kind of peaceful haven in the midst of a neighbourhood where violence and other crimes were common. In the fight between the Hegelian warriors, it is a fight to the death – and those kinds of territory battles did indeed take place as the headteacher indicated in his background description to the neighbourhood. The school could not suspend the politics, the struggles, the conflicts of the world outside. Other teachers in other schools in the area talked about the emotional scars that the violence left on the children. Children experience other political models in other spheres of their lives. What is the impact on a young child of seeing a member of one's family killed or raped by gunmen as battles rage around their homes? The refugee children in the local schools had such stories to tell (cf. Schostak et al. 2004). There are many images of mastery, brutal as well as compassionate. It is implicit in Hegel's drama when as a result of the battle, if one should die, then the winner fails to achieve the desired universal recognition since the other is dead. Similarly, if both should be fatally wounded then there is again failure. The state of mastery is only achieved should one of the warriors give in to their animal fear of death, and recognize the victory of the other. In this circumstance, the loser has no choice but to become a slave to the desires of the winner. The winner, however, in being recognized as 'master' only by a slave still does not gain what is most desired: recognition by an equal. To be recognized by a slave cannot possibly be satisfying. As a further irony, the slave in having to meet the desires of the master must work to transform the material resources of the world, eventually learning to make tools in order to be more efficient, perhaps inventing better weapons for the master's use. In short, the slave is educated through work. Thus:

> If then, at the start, in the given world the Slave had a fearful *'nature'* and *had* to submit to the Master, to the strong man, it does not mean that this will *always* be the case. Thanks to his work, *he* can become other; and, thanks to this work the *World* can become other.
> (Kojève 1969: 52)

Gradually, therefore, in the Hegelian story, a different vision of political organization emerges through work and the cultural knowledge that derives from this. An idea of being able to transform the conditions of the world begins to grow, which includes the possibility of freedom from the Master. However, having an abstract idea of freedom is not the same as having the courage to realize it (Kojève 1969: 53). Returning to the interview transcript, what kind of freedom is being offered by the headteacher? It involves a freedom to take the opportunities being offered by the school, the freedom to develop abilities, it is the freedom offered by the slogan: 'we can do anything'. Each example involves how through work, through the employment of skills, through the exploitation of resources, given circumstances can be transformed. Nevertheless, such work still implies submission to a given social order and the continued need to work and to produce the symbols of achievement (high qualifications, children who go on to universities and particularly prestigious ones) and to be like those few who symbolize high achievement. High achievement implies its opposite, that there will always be those who the high achievers are measured against – the failures, the losers, the average, the wannabes, the mass. So, if this is freedom, what kind is it? And if this is desirable, how is it justified?

Kojève describes then the 'alternative ideologies' that the slave employs to justify the continued slavery. Each ideology though proves to be ultimately unsatisfactory. The ideology of the *Stoic* was to think one is free without acting to make it the case. While a possible solution, it is fundamentally insufficient because, as Hegel maintains, if nothing else, inaction is boring. The next ideology of the *sceptic-nihilist* also finally fails because in denying the value of everything there is nothing to live for, leading most logically to suicide. The final ideological move is that of the *Christian* (or more generally, the Religious) where there is no 'need to fight to be recognized by the Master, since one is recognized by a God' (1969: 55). Under God the slave and master are equal. God is the Absolute Master. The faith of the headteacher is clear and it gives him great strength and conviction in his personal dealings with others. It is reflected in the beautiful image of the symbol of peace in the garden created by the community of children, parents and staff. It is symbolized in his children's response to seeing the magnificent Mosque in Turkey. At that moment they found themselves. They saw themselves as part of the people, as Moslem.

Hegel, of course provides an alternative reading. Taking Christianity as his focus, he considered this meant for the believer there was no need to do anything about the issue of freedom since it will be realized in the next world, the Beyond. This however, he notes, does not really solve the problem of freedom in the present world. For Hegel the religious solution is accepted by the slave basically because the individual cannot face up to the reality of death, of finitude. The only solution to be free from the Absolute Master and free from the Beyond, according to Hegel is to overcome this consequence of religious belief by realizing freedom in the present world. This can only be done if the slave overcomes the fear of the master.

Each such ideology represents a particular move in a mental game that effectively does little and at worst nothing to alter the fundamental relations of power in the world. There is no head on confrontation with how power operates, nor is there any vision of an alternative way of organizing social relationships in the contemporary world. What then, is the next move?

Confronting the State We're In

From a religious point of view, since God is the Absolute Master in Hegel's terminology, there are no real masters and thus no real slaves. The next step in Hegel's saga is the emergence of the *Bourgeois*, the private owner of property. Without slaves, work must be carried out in order to live. For that, property is required. To ensure the fruits of work, law and order is required. However, real Hegelian freedom can only be realized in the formation of a State or Society

> in which the strictly particular, personal individual value of each is recognized as such, in its very particularity, by *all*, by Universality incarnated in the State as such; and in which the universal value of the State is recognized and realized by the Particular as such, by *all* the Particulars. Now such a State, such a synthesis of Particularity and Universality, is possible only after the 'overcoming' of the opposition between the Master and the Slave, since the synthesis of the Particular and the Universal is also a synthesis of Mastery and Slavery
>
> (Kojève 1969: 58)

What is achieved is a state of Absolute Reason where all the prior conflicts between individuals are reconciled. The State is the incarnation of Absolute Reason, that is, the concrete realization of the universal recognition of the worth of each individual. If the initial struggle between the warriors was the initiation of human history through war and work, then the State is the end of history (that is, the end of struggle, war and work, where work is defined as the work of the slave to meet the needs of a master).

Although a fiction, the Hegelian story has a number of elements that are persistent themes in the development of poststructuralist and postmodern readings of contemporary social, political and cultural issues and that are essential to inter-view methodology as inaugurating an emancipatory project: face-to-face encounter, the desire for recognition, struggle, domination and subjugation or control, education and cultural development through work, the ideological rationalization of failure, the synthesis of differences. They pervade the headteacher's interview. But now, rather than return to that account, consider Frank's description of his approach to managing the world about him, as a businessman running a pub:

> because you know running a pub um I was educating customers in how to behave, customers who didn't er behave very well in one pub up the road, always be in fights always shouting obscenities, would be quiet as a lamb in my pub (...) because I just made it clear to them that these were my rules. This is how they behaved if they wanted to come into my pub. They could come and enjoy it, it was a lovely pub but everyone was going to be happy here but if you wanted to upset that then you have to leave and there was never ever any question about that and, and that's what made the pub successful, the fact that there were clearly defined boundaries and that every one understood that it was a nice pub because it has strict rules.

The fit between the Hegelian drama and Frank's account cannot be read as a simple, literal, one to one correspondence. Rather, it suggests a range of possible strategic actions that individuals may adopt in an encounter. Frank establishes in his account the rules of engagement between himself as pub manager and his clients. He had a very strict view of how people should behave and sought to impose that view through a process of what he called 'education'. He could not be described as a Master in relation to his clients as Slaves, just as the headteacher could not be so described in relation to his staff and pupils and their parents. However, Frank does describe his approach in terms of mastering the unruliness of others, transforming them to become 'quiet as a lamb' – not slaves but tamed, rendered docile. They had to recognize *his* rules as pertaining universally throughout *his* pub. He was the ruler of *his* domain – his property – and in that sense each particular potentially unruly person had to *submit* or be forced to leave. All of these are Hegelian themes. That is to say, the discourse Frank is employing is formed in an oppositional relation to the unruly others. His and their identities are thus formed in relation to each other. Indeed, his pub echoes the State as a place where each could recognize the universal value of 'nice pub' because of its 'strict rules' that acted as the common, rational underpinning of this highly controlled quasi-state. So, he thought he could draw upon this model and apply it in all aspects of his life and in particular to his new career as a school-teacher:

> I have an image of whatever … I have an image of my life, I have an image of my environment that I try to create about me um and I have an image of what makes a good pub, I have an image of what makes you know a nice garden, a nice home or and and I have an image of … what makes a good class. Um there are things that will happen along the way which are you know happen … just to make that work but they in themselves aren't objectives, it it's the overall picture that's the objective um (…) My objective wasn't to make them behave my objective was to have a nice, … nice friendly pub. My objective won't be to mould kids, you know to fit a a precise model it'll be, whatever groups of kids I've got, make them enthusiastic in their own way um but I'm not into the moulding and … dictating fashion.

The view through which he defined his pub as 'nice' then extends to every sphere of his life. He denies he wants to mould, or dictate to the children of his classes, yet desires to make them 'enthusiastic in their own way'. Thus, rather than he as Master dictating, it is the concept of 'class' like that of 'pub' that generates the conditions under which the desired image is realized: there could be difference, but only if it fitted into the image. It depends very much on the other recognizing that this is a desirable condition. However, sadly, this was not to be. After two months of becoming a qualified teacher, Frank resigned because: 'To find that I'd asked for quiet or I'd started to explain something and there was just a total lack of manners and courtesy. It just shook me. It is something that has just not been part of life to this point.' He described to me the sleepless nights he'd experienced before making his decision. It wasn't that he was incapable of teaching or indeed getting the class to work, it was because of the lack of recognition of *his* view of what a class should be. In short, they could not be transformed into enthusiastic lambs. How could Frank reconcile his failure?

What was lacking in Frank's view of the world was any sense of dialogue with others who are perceived to have different yet valid views. That is, Frank had no sense of the inter-view between himself and the children of his class. His only recourse was to resign rather than face further failure. At the time of my last interview with him he had not made any final decision but was thinking in terms of becoming a private tutor. He had not given up on his dream, but was looking for a suitable place where the dream and the reality, or at least its appearance, could fit.

Both Frank and the headteacher saw education as offering life chances. Yet, they had very different political strategies for dealing with the realities of a world consisting of a diversity of views. The headteacher saw rich opportunities. Frank saw rudeness, disrespect. How are the political conditions for mutual recognition and thus mutual respect to be generated? And are there alternative views to be encompassed in the process? What about the problems facing the wider community? Where does the politics start and where does it end? Is it enough to build a quiet garden of peace?

Mapping Political Complexity for Action

It is easy to look around and say, how tragic that with all the world's resources so many live in poverty and die miserably. Research does not need to tell us this. What we need research to do is tell us why and how to make the difference between people living in misery and people living well. A tool that gets at the reasons, the desires, the fears, the understandings and the misunderstandings that steer, release, stockpile and block the flows of wealth is critical. No clear, unambiguous tool exists. The history of philosophy and the social sciences is full of methods for exploring the ambiguities, the complexities, the confusions of the world about that are themselves implicated in all the difficulties of representing and understanding the lives and actions of people.

Politics is often called the art of the possible. This, of course, is only a gloss for the reality of politics. Where politics, theoretically, is about managing the possibilities for people to realize their potentials, practice involves facilitating and blocking, according to the norms of a given group or society. Thus the political actor engages a personal set of agendas in relation to the agendas of others in a material and symbolic context that limits and empowers according to the position of the actor in relation to others in those systems or structures. There is a crisis of the possible today. This is not to say that people in other times and places have not experienced the same, but that today, all is possible in a way that has not been possible before. Yet, billions are prevented from having access to resources while others who have a considerable range of resources are psychologically and socially inhibited from using them creatively, justly. And finally, a few, a very small percentage in each country have access to immense quantities of resources which the laws and powers of those countries are deployed to ensure they keep.

An interview provides a means of mapping the position of actors in the worlds that they co-create but also which constitute them as subjects in relation to others and to the symbolic and material world about. Interviewees are presumed to know and to provide access to their world(s). However, since they are not sole authors of their world(s) they are in a sense divided from it. That experience of division is not just a split between a sense of self and a sense of the other. It is a split within the sense of self. The self, as partly constituted by the processes and structures of the world about, thus has within itself this alien other. This split was represented in Diagram 5 of Chapter 5. It can now be more fully politically interpreted in relation to an earlier model of political organization I called 'stealth architecture' (Schostak 2002). It is the sense of splitting, that is, of being both constituted by and multiply connected to the world about, that enables political action to be composed. Recall the example of the Goth and the Suit in the train episode of Chapter 5. The Suit has connections to her world of work where the convention of formal dress is required. Her work-based view of the world is in part composed from the discourses about the opinions, values, philosophies and knowledge common to her occupation. Suppose she is a business manager. Her approach to management could take one of many forms. It might be authoritarian or democratic, for example. Her practices will be very different according to whether her chosen management philosophy is authoritarian rather than democratic. She may wish to institute performance indicators that she believes are appropriate and to ensure these are met she may choose to monitor performance by regular audit procedures. She will want resources that will enable her to keep control over her staff. This might include appropriate software that monitors the time staff are working at their computers, that enables the creation of flow charts of activities to be undertaken, that identifies who does or does not meet targets. She will want to be able to have the resources to be able to reward and punish. Thus her views in combination with her practices and the resources she has available will – in her view and her experience – lead to particular outcomes. If she fails to get the outcomes she desires she might attribute this to say, lack of resources rather than to her authoritarian views. She will be able to connect to others who share her views and perhaps scorn those who do not. In another dimension of her life, as a woman attracted to men, she will have another set of views as to 'what men want' and how men and women ought to behave towards each other. She will have her own ideas as to what she wants. Over the years she will have developed ways of acting, perhaps a repertoire of practices which she has employed in a variety of contexts. Each context will require different kinds of dress, accessories and resources. By aligning her ideas, practices and resources as to what is appropriate for a given context she will tend to get the outcomes she expects. If she does not, then she may consider this due to being not on form or to the peculiarities of the circumstances. Some parts of her life, of course, she might want to keep very separate from others. The views and practices she engages in with some people she may want others never to know about.

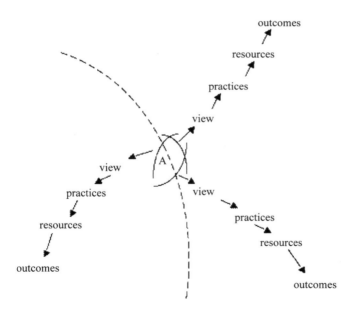

Diagram 6: The multi-dimensional 'sides' of the split subject

The diagram expresses the multidimensional 'sides' to the life of an individual. In church she expresses views and acts in ways that may or may not have an overlap with those views and practices of another sphere of her life in business. However, they may be complementary, filling out her personality for others as a respected member of a community. However, there may be sides of her life, as in 'A' that she wishes to keep separate, even hidden from her community identity. Depending on what this involves, of course, it might make her vulnerable. When people meet, in what ever circumstances, each of these 'sides' are potentially available to be accessed to make a 'connection'. Particular circumstances may encourage one side rather than another to be expressed. Other more ambiguous contexts – meeting on a train, on a dance floor, on holiday – may provide opportunities for other sides to be expressed. The needs, interests and desires that are satisfied by one side may not be the same as for other sides; or at least, will not satisfy them in the same way. The multiple sides then develop in relation to the ways in which needs, interests and desires are met, at least partially, under different circumstances and contexts. What holds it all together – as *my* identity – is her political imaginary. In this imaginary, to get what you want involves connections with others. What do they want? And is it similar to what I want? How do I get them to give me what I want, or make it possible for me to get what I want? To do this, self has to position the other in some way.

Politically sophisticated positioning requires the ability to imagine and model the mental states required for a particular subject position and then to project these states onto the minds of the other in that position:

> The Dutch primatologist Frans de Waal tells a story of calculating sexual intrigue in his engaging, novel-like study, Chimpanzee Politics. A young, low-ranking male (named, appropriately enough, Dandy) decides to make a play for one of the females in the group. Being a chimpanzee, he opts for the usual chimpanzee method of expressing sexual attraction, which is to sit with your legs apart within eyeshot of your *objet de desire* and reveal your erection. (Try that approach in human society, of course, and you'll usually end up with a restraining order.) During this particular frisky display, Luit, one of the high-ranking males, happens upon the 'courtship' scene. Dandy deftly uses his hands to conceal his erection so that Luit can't see it, but the female chimp can. It's the chimp equivalent of the adulterer saying, 'This is just our little secret, right?'
>
> (Johnson 2001: 197)

Although crude, the elements of this sequence dramatize the political management of desire. Of course, it might be just the little secret between the 'adulterers', but what if another, not the high ranking male, saw or guessed that something was going on? Then the situation would be reminiscent of Edgar Allen Poe's short story 'The Purloined Letter'. Lacan analysed this story to explain how unconscious contents could impact on social realities. A letter was handed to the queen, we are never told its contents. As she was reading it, the king entered. She placed the letter down on a table as if it were of no relevance. A minister of the court saw this and guessed that the contents of the letter were such that the queen did not want the king to know about them. The minister then passed by the table and picked up the letter. This, of course, gave him power over the queen. Hence the queen needed to get the letter back. The dynamics of this situation are a function of the political imaginary through which desire is managed. Knowing, or suspecting, people's interests and desires is part of the process of creating strategies to manage these in one's own interests. When those interests or desires are hidden, *that* gives a power of threat over the individual – comply, or all will be revealed. If however, they are open then those interests and desires can be managed in a different way. Like the headteacher creating his garden of peace, the diverse interests of many can be united by finding a common focus for opposition, in this case, opposition to all who would bring violence. Thus, as in the diagram below, all that may be in common among the diverse individuals – or groups – A, B and C, is their opposition to, or fear of D:

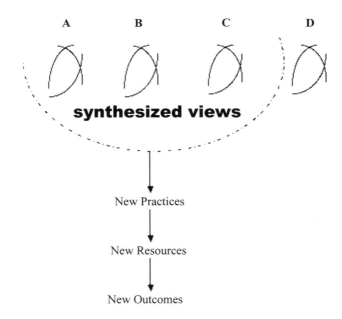

Diagram 7: The synthesized views of split subjects

On their own A, B and C are engaged in struggles to make a life for themselves and their families. Whether they have a particular religious belief, are working class, unemployed, male or female they seek some respect, recognition of their human worth as they express their personal and cultural identities in their different ways. Suppose what they lack is the political order to enable them to get what they want. Various possibilities might fill this lack. One could be the use of force, the violence of the gang leader. Perhaps that is what D is offering. However, that would involve submitting to D's desires and whims. Opposing this might be the approach offered by the headteacher. This would involve the different groups joining forces to establish an ordered community: the parents from the different heritage communities, the religious organizations, the local business people and others. Each retains their cultural identities and practices. However, in order to work together some new practices need to emerge in order to generate a kind of synthesized identity which comprises all the differences. Each difference rather than being seen oppositionally is evaluated as an 'advantage', a resource for the community. There are new practices to enable people from different groups to negotiate about decisions, to ensure some sense of fairness where all views are included. Working together may enable access to resources, such as through fund raising, or through sharing skills and knowledge. With the new resources new outcomes can then be achieved. Such a community is produced through what Laclau and Mouffe (1985) call an hegemonic strategy: a knotting together of diverse interests into a synthesis that enables diverse groups to act as a community. However, the community developed by the headteacher had its limits. It could not be a panacea for the severe problems of the neighbourhood. Between the community and the neighbourhood there is a fragile boundary. It is at this edge between order and disorder, the rule of law and the rule of arbitrary violence, that people become vulnerable. The hegemony can splinter at any time into its different groups and power be diffused and re-fused into different hegemonic patterns. The inter-view strategy then focuses on the emerging or dissolving sense of position, fragmentation, synthesis, boundary, marginalization experienced by people in order to describe their views of what practices and resources are under threat or can be employed to create the events and outcomes they desire, avoid those they fear or endure those they can do nothing about.

Edge-Moves

Political positioning requires a sense of order. The modern mind, for Bauman (2001: 66) is characterized as 'legislative reason, and modern practice is the practice of legislation'. It is about the compromises made between security on the one hand and freedom on the other, and then learning how to accept this order as a 'freedom', or, at least, the price to pay for a civilized society. Alternatively, it may be expressed as how to manage anxiety by replacing the pleasure principle with the reality principle: ' "Reality principle", in simple terms, means cutting the "I want" to the size of "I can"' (Bauman 2001: 66). For Bauman the modernist project in its early aspiration to apply this rational vision of a reality principle to the whole of society has failed and has been abandoned. And, the strategy of ensuring that needs, wants and desires were to be subordinated to the reality principle, that is, the objective ability to actually satisfy them, now only applies to:

> ... the 'underclass', the 'new poor', the 'welfare recipients' – to people who by common consent are incapable of managing the endemic conflict between their wants and their abilities; only in respect of their case does the argument 'we cannot afford it' strike a receptive chord. As to the rest – the majority, the main body, the pattern-setting part of society – it is the wants that have been assigned an unqualified priority and given the role of the initiating and driving force as far as the potentialities of society are concerned. We measure 'economic growth' and overall 'health' of the economy by a rising demand for commodities, and economic success by a rising 'power to spend'.
>
> (Bauman 2001: 67–8)

In this view, the prevailing political imaginary sustains the conditions for the few to exercise power over the many and close their eyes to the damage people endure as a result of inequalities. How are people persuaded to accept this? How may they counter it? What should they believe in? Such questions are concerned as much with the conditions people live under as with the conditions that open possibilities for change.

Research can be employed for many purposes. However, emancipatory research has only one purpose: to create the conditions for people, as a group defined as much by their differences as by their commonalities, to map and understand the structures and processes governing their circumstances, wherever that may lead, in order to contribute to the kinds of strategy that build practical visions representing diversity and difference within human communities. Implicit in this quest is a sense of justice. How does one define a difference: as good, as bad, as irrelevant, as to be rejected? If they are to be equally valued, how does one ensure this? How does one choose between alternative political visions and practices? Just on a basis of power or a fear of consequences? Emancipatory research, whether case study, ethnography, action research or evaluation, or some other permutation, lives at the edge of all boundaries as they form, de-form, dissolve, transform, re-form into different patterns through which individuals shape their lives with or in opposition to each other. At the edge, what counts as truth? And who gets betrayed?

7

Truth, Witness and Betrayal: The ethical framing of interview based research

We make judgements all the time.

I recall during an interview with a recently retired man who was retraining, a point in the interview when he said: I hate Gypsies, they're the scum of the earth – but don't use that. The recorder kept going and I made a mental note on the ethics of the double bind. In a chapter on ethics that would be a good instance to use – a nice juicy quote as we say in the trade. This was a man in his fifties who would now work with people of all different cultures, including Gypsies. He was very certain in his mind about right and wrong. Yet, is this what I want to say? There's this other quote, very dramatic, that my colleague, Heather Piper wrote in a collaborative paper (Schostak et al. 2004) a group of us gave at a conference about a school assistant listening to a refugee child recount his experience of his brother being snatched by police. He was hiding behind a door, listening to his brother being dragged off. They never saw him again. There's something of what I want to say there in the horror of being a silent witness to the unspeakable (cf. Caruth 1995). But that's not it either. What I'm trying to get at is something much more everyday. Much smaller, much less noticeable. No, it's not the out-stretched hand of the homeless person sat on the pavement next to the cash machine, coat collar pulled close up around the lower face. No not that.

I recall reading in Berman (1982: 148–9) about Baron Haussman reshaping Paris with great boulevards. I admit, I love those boulevards, the space, the traffic, the shops, the crowds, the mixing of all social classes. He quoted an extract from a story by Baudelaire describing a family in such a street who for the first time can look through the window into a restaurant to watch the rich dine. He called it a family of eyes amazed at what they saw. Is it then the spectacle? You know, being able to switch on a television and see the Boxing Day devastation caused by the Tsunami of 2004 or reading the accounts of tragedy each day as the death toll mounts and the charitable giving grows. And then hear about the billions of profits made by corporations, or the multimillion bonuses given to directors. It's all there nakedly on the table as we get up to go to work or come home to relax. But that's not it either. It's something closer to home.

Being with others as a researcher who witnesses their lives, their words, involves a strange kind of intimacy – neither a friend nor a stranger. Both inside and outside. Lacan coined a word for this: *extimacy*. He applied it to the experience of the unconscious, the sense of the stranger within, the alienation of language, so intimate yet so foreign. How to sum up the life of another when one's own is such a mystery? I use the words they speak and play with their sense to reveal hitherto unsuspected meanings. Each meaning a new view opening up to hidden connections with the words of others. Is it then as Lacan, Derrida and others suggest that we do not speak but are spoken by language? Or is there in this extimate relation with language some tiny place where a bargain is struck to keep everything as it is?

There is a guilty secret in truth. Politics and ethics are two sides of the same double bind. To reduce discussion to the one or the other is to miss the point and hide the 'truth' of a situation, a life. What is this 'truth'? If politics is about the force necessary to impose a claim, ethics seeks to justify a claim. Ethics, however, cannot enforce its evaluation over those who disagree without the force of law, without, that is, generating a sense of wrong or injury in those who disagree (cf. Rancière 1995, 2004). If the ethical move is to be open to the differences of others – or, in Derrida's (1992) terms, the force that is inherent in *différance* – then the political cannot be avoided. And the political is born in division, heterogeneity, conflict as views and claims are contested under the force of Law, a law that is always founded upon a violence concealed by tradition, religion or reason to create a sense of a community bound by the Law. However, the Law itself is not reducible to the particular laws passed by a government. Those laws cannot be sustained unless there is sufficient popular support for them. Popular reason can be explored as a weaving of 'truths' of 'views' into a unifying vision of the 'people' that defines what is 'right, 'good', 'proper', that is the Law composed of universal categories (cf. Laclau 2005). What, in this context, then, does it mean to be open to the differences of others? What emancipatory strategies can challenge the Law?

One example that comes to mind is Stenhouse's Humanities Curriculum Project (HCP). This was a radical curriculum development project funded in the late 1960s in the UK (Stenhouse 1975). Briefly, it involved working with 15 year old pupils who were the first cohort to have to stay on for another year of compulsory schooling until they could leave at 16 years old. HCP was targeted to those who did not want to take examinations. Really, they wanted to leave and go to work. The approach adopted was to engage these young people in debate about real world issues that were typically controversial. Rules of debate were established. Teachers were to take the role of being neutral chairs of discussion. The young people would be provided with packs of evidence that they could draw upon in their debates. An old colleague and friend of mine, Bev Labbett, had been at the time a young HCP teacher. One of the great problems, he said to me, was how do you deal with the young Fascist at the back of the room? One of the principles underpinning HCP was that each person had the right to make their views heard. The teacher was to be neutral, that is, could not espouse a political position, had to ensure that all could make their views heard and that all had access to evidence. It might be hoped that rationality and evidence is all that is required to bring people to the right views of the world. It was, Bev lamented, not something to which he felt he had a solution. Yet he was a passionate promoter of the Stenhousian approach and a brilliant teacher (see Labbett 1988, 1996). It was, for him, a double bind.

Ethics demands some kind of commitment to universal categories concerning the true, the good, the right. The HCP imaginary is all have the universal right to express views in a framework of rational debate underpinned by access to evidence. Implicitly the belief, rightly or wrongly, is that debate under such conditions will lead to a more tolerant acceptance of the views of others as well as a modification, indeed, a transformation of those views in the light of reason. Yet, the confrontation with the Fascist views of the young man seemed to prove the opposite. Rorty, of course, would not be surprised:

> consider the principle 'Thou shalt not kill.' This is admirably universal, but is it more or less rational than the principle 'Do not kill unless one is a soldier defending his or her country, or is preventing a murder, or is a state executioner, or a merciful practitioner of euthanasia?' I have no idea whether it is more or less rational, and so do not find the term 'rational' useful in this area. If I am told that a controversial action which I have taken has to be defended by being subsumed under a universal rational principle, I may be able to dream up such a principle to fit the occasion, but sometimes I may only be able to say, 'Well, it seemed like the best thing to do at the time, all things considered.' It is not clear whether the latter defence is less rational than some universal-sounding principle which I have dreamt up ad hoc to justify my action. It is not clear that all the moral dilemmas to do with population control, the rationing of health care, and the like – should wait upon the formulation of principles for their solution.
>
> (Rorty 1999: 15)

To the question of what to do, Rorty is only able to answer that while he has no rational solution he prefers to adopt strategies minimizing cruelty. Rather than resting his preference on some transcendental first principle he suggests: 'it is best to think of moral progress as a matter of increasing sensitivity, increasing responsiveness to the needs of a larger and larger variety of people and things'. (Rorty 1999: 81). If one asks why, there is no other answer than to say it depends on upbringing and the social context within which one has lived. Philosophy provides no further foundation. Hence:

> there is no neutral, common ground to which an experienced Nazi philosopher and I can repair in order to argue out our differences. That Nazi and I will always strike one another as begging all the crucial questions, arguing in circles.
>
> (Rorty 1999: 15)

This debate underlines serious questions as to the role of philosophy in the harsh world of politics. Put it simply, can philosophy address the question of whether there is a direct relationship between the philosophy adopted and the kinds of education and politics that then ensue? If there is, then perhaps Rorty's Nazi philosopher may yet be convinced. If not, then how do we proceed? Are we then simply drawn back into the Hegelian continual struggle for mastery without anything founding the struggle other than the desire to win?

Unsurprisingly, Rorty considers there is no necessary relation between a philosopher's philosophy and the politics adopted. He cites Heidegger's involvement with Nazism. What then is philosophy good for? Perhaps not much more than for self fulfilment. Rorty called Derrida a private ironist (1999; Mouffe 1996). By this he means to make a distinction between the kind of philosophical thinking that leads to self fulfilment and the kinds of discourses that are necessary for active engagement on the public stage of politics. For this reason, Rorty has no time for a politics grounding itself in an ethics whereas Derrida sees in the ethics of Levinas a way to ground a sense of responsibility towards the other.

This move towards Levinas draws us back again to the face-to-face event which for me is the foundational instance of the inter-view, that essentially split, impossible space where consciousnesses regard each other at a moment before either battle or friendship, a moment where decisions have to be made but in conditions of undecidability:

> If I conduct myself particularly well with regard to someone, I know that it is to the detriment of an other; of one nation to the detriment of another nation, of one family to the detriment of another family, of my friends to the detriment of other friends or non-friends, etc. This is the infinitude that inscribes itself within responsibility; otherwise there would be no ethical problems or decisions. And this is why undecid-ability is not a moment to be traversed and overcome. Conflicts of duty –

and there is only duty in conflict – are interminable and even when I take my decision and do something, undecidability is not at an end. I know that I have not done enough and it is in this way that morality continues, that history and politics continues.

(Derrida: in Mouffe 1996: 86–7)

Does this tell us how to judge? No. Both the political and the ethical act are radically free. However, does this freedom mean it is arbitrary? No, because Derrida appeals to to a 'quasi-transcendental' to produce a 'quasi-stability' in the otherwise potentially random collapse:

> Do I speak just speak of this 'quasi' in an ironical, comic or parodic manner, or is it a question of something else? I believe both. There is irony and there is something else. As Simon Critchley said, quoting Rorty, I seem to make noises of both sorts. Now I claim this right to make noises of both sorts in an absolutely unconditional manner. I absolutely refuse a discourse that would assign me a single code, a single language game, a single context, a single situation; and I claim this right not simply out of caprice or because it is to my taste, but for ethical and political reasons. When I say that quasi-transcendentality is at once ironic and serious, I am being sincere. There is evidently irony in what I do – which I hope is politically justifiable – with regard to academic tradition, the seriousness of the philosophical tradition and the personages of the great philosophers. But, although irony appears to me to be necessary to what I do, at the same time – and this is a question of memory – I take extremely seriously the issue of philosophical responsibility. I maintain that I am a philosopher and that I want to remain a philosopher, and this philosophical responsibility is what commands me. Something that I learned from the great figures in the history of philosophy, from Husserl in particular, is the necessity of posing transcendental questions in order not to be held in the fragility of an incompetent empiricist discourse, and thus it is in order to avoid empiricism, positivism and psychologism that it is endlessly necessary to renew transcendental questioning. But such questioning must be renewed in taking account of the possibility of fiction, of accidentality and contingency, thereby ensuring that this new form of transcendental questioning only mimics the phantom of classical seriousness without renouncing that which, within this phantom, constitutes an essential heritage.

(Derrida: in Mouffe 1996: 81–2)

In claiming the right to refuse, *absolutely*, discourses having a single code, language game, context and situation, Derrida is in a sense incarnating a universal position. He usurps the place of the Hegelian master who makes demands that have no further foundation than the desires, the whims, the caprice, the taste of the master. In this act of mimicking the master, the force of *différance* appears. There is a difference between the Hegelian master and the Derridean in that a claim to a universal 'right' is made in a *manner* that is absolute and unconditional and according to *reasons*. The Hegelian master has triumphed in a struggle and brought the other to submission. There is no such submission of the other in Derridian discourse, there *is* the claim and its *manner* of claiming.

What then remains to explore is the place of ethical and political reasons in making the claim. These reasons are not identical with reasons employed in the classical sense (Hegelian, Kantian and so on) but mimic them. Where Hegel brought all differences under Absolute Reason or Husserl sought to formulate the conditions under which certainty could be established Derrida displaces this discourse into one of quasi-transcendentals, that is, a way of thinking which poses ways of bringing together differences under categories *as if* they were universals, or under universal-like categories on the understanding that these categories cannot be finalized, closed. There is then a fundamental irony involved in the approach. It is a matter of taking things very seriously as in one interpretation of an ironic statement knowing that there is also an alternative interpretation that undermines taking the first interpretation in *all* seriousness. Since there can be no final closure to the claim to universality, and since the claim keeps on being made across an infinitely expanding range of contexts of application, there is an infinite deferral of the claim being accomplished in its fullest possible sense. This is the force of *différance* at work in the claim: the continual evocation of the difference (and thus mimicked similarity) between the Hegelian and the Derridean demand, and the universal and the quasi-universal; together with the infinite deferral of closure.

Applying this to the frustration felt by my friend the ex-HCP teacher confronted by the fascist statements of the youth at the back of the class requires a further detour, a brief one, through the political philosophy of Laclau. Fascist sentiment typically makes appeals to the People and to Patriotism as unifying signifiers that can be exploited in order to exclude those who are not considered 'pure' (cf. Norval 1996). What it means to be patriotic will depend on the historical circumstances of the time when the call to be patriotic is made. The content that fills the signifier may be capitalist, fascist, socialist, democratic, revolutionary depending on which faction wins. Laclau (in Butler et al. 2000: 82–3) tells the story of a preacher, Antonio Conselheiro, in Brazil who was unsuccessful for most of his life in gathering followers. One day he entered a village where people were rioting against tax collectors and said 'the Republic is the Antichrist'. These words became the universalizing signifier gathering the people together, under its banner and starting 'a mass rebellion which took several years for the government to defeat'. In effect, the particular becomes universalized under the signifier. The effect is to generate a quasi-transcendental which stabilizes meanings for a period of time, that is, until another contest takes place. For Zizek (in Butler et al.

2000: 100–1) Laclau's position is that 'each Universal is the battleground on which the multitude of particular contents fight for hegemony,' thus 'all positive content of the Universal is the contingent result of hegemonic struggle – in itself, the Universal is absolutely empty.'

In the moment of decision, both the ethical and the political stance is born. Each are shaped by the force of *différance* which creates the conditions for the knotting together (as well as the deconstructive un-doing) of the different interests of individuals and groups. Making an appeal to a universal as a 'right' sets in motion a struggle with those who demand other rights, or who define those rights differently. In the example of the young man making Fascist comments at the back of the class, the mistake is to define him under the category 'Fascist', as if all his interests, all his needs, all his hopes, all of what he is, is reduced to that one category. The mistake is an ethical one. Excluding him in practice is a political one. What then is the ethical strategy?

The Ethics of Emancipation

There is something of an urgency to the idea of emancipation that Derrida makes clear:

> Emancipation is once again a vast question today and I must say that I have no tolerance for those who – deconstructionist or not – are ironical with regard to the grand discourse of emancipation. This attitude has always distressed and irritated me. I do not want to renounce this discourse.
>
> (in Mouffe 1996: 82)

If emancipation is again a vast question, it is because judgements about the conditions under which people live are being made that need to be questioned in order that they may act in freedom. How does one witness a state of freedom or of unfreedom? Such a question brings the issues of validity, objectivity and generalization back into the debate but with a very different spin. What counts as a valid, objective and generalizable state of freedom? Ernie described the kinds of decisions that he made in his everyday life. To what extent are they made in a state of freedom?

> The 'old firm' is the gang of which about sixty or more male adolescents would claim some association. Its location is the city centre and it is called the city gang. These associations made up largely of working class male adolescents have existed for some generations in the area. They are usually connected to particular regions or housing estates and their names derive from them. For example, the young male adolescents living on the Redbourn housing estate would be called the Redbourn Boys; similarly those living around the city centre are called the City

Boys. These associations are territorial and will occasionally be antag-
onistic to one another or alternatively join together to support the local
football club against visiting fans. New faces come in as others grow up
and leave. According to Ernie people who become associated with these
groupings are *'you know, people who want to be the hardest geezers in the city,
you know, a mean Harry, that sort of thing. Whereas'* Ernie now says *'they are
just a bunch of saps'*. To qualify as a City Boy you have to be an *'arcade
lad'* first particularly in the city centre arcade *'you sort of get to know them,
you know, and have a laugh and all that and then you sort of start fighting'*. He
adds *'the Old Bill are just waiting for the chance to get that lot now'*. He began
hanging around the arcade he says *'we had nowhere else to go and nothing
else to do'*.

(Schostak and Davis 1990)

For most people who pass by on the streets of the city nothing will be
known of the 'old firm', a gang that has existed in the city for several
generations. However, for those who know, different kinds of judgements are being made about where it is safe to be and who it is safe to be
seen with. Identities are formed in relation to the different addresses of
the city – arcades, streets, housing estates or regions. Each provides a
simple sorting mechanism which generates an identity solely on the basis
of being a different address than the others. Each address has its gang,
historically formed over generations – a mechanism for being recognized
as 'the hardest geezers in the city'. With nowhere else to go and nothing
else to do the young boys end up hanging around the arcade, the only
resource for amusement. Here they meet members of the gang which
enables them to have a laugh and inducts them into fighting and
encountering their old enemy, the Old Bill, the police. At no point was
Ernie actively pressured into the gang. Later he talked about being drawn
into borrowing money to play the arcade games. The amount to be paid
back doubled each week of the loan. Soon it reached sums too high to
pay. Those that couldn't pay would be severely beaten:

> However, Ernie refused to pay and he is now careful when he goes into
> the city centre. He is trying, he says, *'to keep away from a broken face'*. He
> does not regret no longer being a member of the City Boys. He calls his
> previous involvement *'a bad mistake that'*. If he met himself as he was at
> fourteen he would not be impressed, he says. *'I was a right little cunt'*. All
> he learnt, he says, was how to fight *'to fight dirty'*. But that is all over now
> as far as he is concerned. He will not even go in for fights today *'I keep
> myself to myself'*.

Ernie's refusal has consequences. It could be seen as a free act rejecting a
former way of life. It could be seen as the only thing he could do since he
could not pay back the money. However, on the basis of it, he has
modified his identity. Nevertheless, he is still trapped in a game of hide
and seek and confrontation, not with the Old Bill, but with the old firm,

the City Boys. This is a gang that will be around his neighbourhood all his life. He could leave, but traditionally, few leave their neighbourhoods in this city. The task is to live with it. One such story of living in the neighbourhood, Teresa, 14 years old at the time, told was:

> Once they had trouble with a gang from another large village. There were about eighteen boys and girls in this gang, aged about 16 years 'They were really hard'. Teresa, her friends and some boys from a neighbouring suburb were 'Trick or Treating'. This gang shouted at Teresa and her friends and 'just all sort of came after us'. But Teresa and the others managed to get away. Unfortunately they knew where she lived because one of the boys in the gang recognized her.
>
> The next night when she was doing her homework she looked out of the window 'and there they all were standing outside my house'. She shouted 'Dad, they're all out there!'. She was naturally a bit scared because of the previous night's events. Her father told her to ignore them and they left it at that. But then the gang threw an egg at the window and then they smashed a window in her father's van. Her father 'went mad. He ran out on the road – he's pretty hard, my dad, he goes mad and he really hits – He ran out after them but he couldn't catch them. So he went in his van. They thought he was gone when he ran back for his van ... he went bombing after them. He got out and said to one of them "Right you're the biggest I'll get you". The youngster he picked out was going "please, mate, please, mate, I didn't mean to do it". All the rest just stood there. Usually they pile on top of people. But they just stood there going "We'll have a whip round". And my Dad go "You lay a finger on my kid and I'll really hurt you". They were just bricking, some of them'. She's not sure but she thinks her dad 'head-butted one of them'. She thinks they all stood there because they had not expected such a dramatic intervention from her father 'your dads usually go after them but they don't usually get hold of them'.
>
> (Schostak and Davis 1990)

For many like Teresa and her family, dealing with such conflicts is just a matter of everyday life. In what sense, can the actions of any be considered a state of freedom to make a decision, or judge, or act? Following the incident, Teresa was left alone, they even smiled at her when she walked down the street. A realignment had occurred, a new pecking order. Her father was recognized as being 'hard'. The fundamental rules had not changed.

What does it take to make a real change? That is, a change that changes the rules, an emancipatory project. In the traditional view, emancipation involves a radical break from one reality to another (Laclau 1996). Take for example the following:

> *Thesis*, a thesis asserted by urban people starting in 1789, all through the nineteenth century, and in the great revolutionary uprisings at the end

of World War One: the streets belong to the people. *Antithesis,* and here is Le Corbusier's great contribution: no streets, no People. In the post-Haussman city street, the fundamental social and psychic contradictions of modern life converged and perpetually threatened to erupt. But if this street could only be wiped off the map – Le Corbusier said it very clearly in 1929: 'We must kill the street!' – then maybe these contradictions need never come to a head. Thus modernist architecture and planning created a modernised version of pastoral: a spatially and socially seg-mented world – people here, traffic there; work here, homes there; rich here, poor there; barriers of grass and concrete between, where haloes could begin to grow around people's heads once again.

(Berman 1982: 167–8)

The thesis and its antithesis can be applied in many spheres of social life. Thesis: same schools for all the people; antithesis: different schools for different kinds of people. Now substitute in turn the following words for schools: neighbourhoods, homes, hospitals, income, life chances, futures. If emancipation is simply about getting rid of those encounters where difference is displayed and contradictions brought into confrontation, then the politics is straightforward. The mechanisms that are required are all those that sort people according to particular criteria and then increase segregation between those people. There are of course a range of such mechanisms in place in most nations: for example, people can be sorted according to social class, gender, ethnicity, religion, language, academic achievement. An apparent rationality can then be employed to conceal inequality and injustice as in the extreme case of apartheid (Norval 1996). Or, inequality and injustice can be seen as challenges to overcome through charity or political initiatives focusing on the poor and dis-advantaged.

In 1983 I described the dream of a new town, built in the 1960s to rehouse slum dwellers from a neighbouring city. It was a radical break from the past. But by the time of my study, those dreams were crushed. Few of the children who went to the school of my study had parents who were working. The town soon developed a national reputation for crime and violence. One of the teachers described to me how it had felt like they were building the 'New Jerusalem' in the early days. It was perhaps about building the organic community where each individual would fit as a part of the whole. This is a traditional view of politics, one which Zizek, com-menting on Rancière (2004) calls a defence against the reality of politics. The reality of politics for Rancière (1995) is that of disagreement, the existence of a wrong, an injury. This, for Zizek, is the reality of politics, the Lacanian Real that bursts through the appearance of the whole, the organic, the symbolic order. For the people and their hopes of the New Jerusalem, the government subsidies to the local industries were with-drawn and the town nosedived into a slump. The area has never recovered.

From emancipation to betrayal in one generation. An alternative political philosophy reigned during the 1980s which focused on the progressive dismantling of the welfare state and returning to schooling based on selectivity (Schostak 1993). This political discourse was moralistic rather than ethical. It focused upon undoing the 'nanny state' and returning to Victorian values of self reliance and working hard for ones money. This, of course meant that the culture of dependency fostered by welfare had to be overturned. Society, famously said Margaret Thatcher the then Prime Minister of the UK, did not exist. There are only individuals who have to make the right decisions in their own interests. Alongside working hard, of course, there was merit. Some people are simply worth more than others because of their talent, their business acumen, a merit properly rewarded by earning more money per hour than the untalented. It was a neo-conservativism fuelled by monetarist economics – often called at the time Reganomics after the then US President – a return to a survival of the fittest through competition without safety nets. The poor were poor because they did not work hard enough and there was inequality only because there was genetically an unequal distribution of natural talent. In this way the existence of 'real' poverty could be denied and measures introduced, like cutting welfare, to encourage the poor to go out and find work; and inequality due to talent in combination with 'working hard for one's money' could be judged both natural and right. The proper role for government thus was only to secure the conditions under which work could be generated. To do this the economy had to be an attractive place for global enterprises:

> Politics has become today a tug-of-war between the speed with which capital can move and the 'slowing down' capacities of local powers, and it is the local institutions which feel as if they are waging an unwinnable battle. A government dedicated to the well being of its constituency has little choice but to implore and cajole, rather than force, capital to fly in and once inside to build sky-scraping offices instead of renting hotel rooms. And this can be done or attempted to be done by 'creating better conditions for free enterprise', that is, adjusting the political game to the 'free enterprise rules'; by using all the regulating power at the government's disposal to make it clear and credible that the regulating powers won't be used to restrain capital's liberties; by refraining from everything which might create an impression that the territory politically administered by the government is inhospitable to the preferences, usages and expectations of globally thinking and globally acting capital, or less hospitable to them than the lands administered by the next-door neighbours.
>
> (Bauman 2001: 26)

Hence, as governments changed, the policies changed little. A new game ruled, one not dominated by States but by the mechanisms of globalizing communications which facilitated the flow of capital and the globalization of work: a memo dictated in New York might be typed in Calcutta. Such work could be transferred to the cheapest labour market anywhere in the world. The role of the State had to modify in order to create hospitable environments to attract globally acting capital.

The regionally focused innovation research project described earlier in Chapter 3 is one such response to the need to create hospitable environments. Its focus was upon the development of knowledge based enterprises along 'corridors' between one city and another as well as developing business parks and science parks. The idea was that wealth would trickle out to other areas. Cities and their regions are being structured as a key mechanism to attract global capital. Within this structure, the worlds of Ernie and Teresa are irrelevant and there is no New Jerusalem for the New Town where unemployment is, at the time of writing, as high as ever. If they are not structured into the system, then there is no way of witnessing their lives that makes a difference to the processes of development. The ethical moment is just this: the point at which a decision is made to represent the otherness of others in the structures and processes of decision making. If the worlds of Ernie and Teresa as well as that of those in the New Town are the Other to the discourse of technology corridors, the knowledge society, the business park and the science park, then they will continue as quasi-separate worlds noticed only when there are disturbances. The question then reduces to representing the other as a danger to be controlled so that disturbances will not arise.

One answer is to generate such control in highly complex societies, that with the right design, with the right mechanisms through which different views are included, the control of behaviour will simply occur:

> Under the seeming disorder of the old city, wherever the old city is working successfully, is a marvellous order for maintaining the safety of the streets and the freedom of the city. It is a complex order. Its essence is intimacy of sidewalk use, bringing with it a constant succession of eyes. This order is all composed of movement and change, and although it is life, not art, we may fancifully call it the art form of the city and liken it to the dance – not to a simple-minded precision dance with everyone kicking up at the same time, twirling in unison and bowing off en masse, but to an intricate ballet in which the individual dancers and ensembles all have distinctive parts which miraculously reinforce each other and compose an orderly whole.
>
> (Jacobs cited by Johnson 2001: 51)

The dance of the complex but orderly whole is a seductive social imaginary. In effect order arises by the exclusion of undesirable behaviours through the mechanism of an all pervasive surveillance. It even has an

Hegelian ring, where all the differences (that are acceptable) are subsumed under the rationality of the whole. Here Johnson is using an extract from Jacobs to elaborate his vision of how order can arise without any visible sign of leadership or of planning. Each is a witness to the other, a mobilization of the eyes, a total surveillance of eyes – or as a variation in other circumstances, CCTV, neighbourhood watch groups in conjunction perhaps with zero tolerance policing. How this order develops is similar, Johnson argues, to the ways in which ants build anthills and 'calculate' the shortest distance to food. Each ant communicates chemically to another that food is to be found in the direction from which they have just come. The more ants that send this message the more likely it is that large quantities of food are to be found and hence a pattern of search is reinforced. Such simple behaviour can produce highly complex outcomes. Their society is ordered without any urban planning or government. Johnson draws upon recent developments in mathematics which models how such complex patterns and life-like behaviour emerge. The algorithms that have been invented are at the back of sophisticated games where each character is able to 'learn' over time. Players can feel considerable frustrations when they want to exert control over characters that have been constructed to 'learn' autonomously in environments that appear to be controlled by some malevolent god:

> 'The challenge is, the more autonomous the system, the more autonomous the virtual creatures, the more irrelevant the player is,' Zimmerman explains. 'The problem with a lot of the "god games" is that it's difficult to feel like you're having a meaningful impact on the system. It's like you're wearing these big, fuzzy gloves and you're trying to manipulate these tiny little objects.' Although it can be magical to watch a Will Wright simulation take on a life of its own, it can also be uniquely frustrating – when that one neighbourhood can't seem to shake off its crime problem, or your Sims refuse to fall in love. For better or worse, we control these games from the edges. The task of the game designer is to determine just how far off the edge the player should be.
>
> (Johnson 2001: 186)

In this technological imaginary, just how far off the edge are we as life-players in the contemporary world? Increasingly, information is now distributed informatically, that is to say, through mechanisms – albeit created by humans – that generate information, distribute it and propagate ways of decision making without further human agency. Governments are increasingly like the players who wear 'big, fuzzy gloves'. In any emancipatory project the ethical and political question is how to represent the uniqueness, the 'otherness' of individuals into the structures, organizations, processes, practices through which everyday life can be constituted as a family of eyes who care unconditionally for the other.

Changing the realities of people is not just a matter of urban redesign, nor of the political agenda of the day, nor of changing the rules of a very complex game to bring people and/or governments back from the edge of control. It is an ethical issue where humans, not simulations, live lives. In this view an ethics of emancipation is not about a radical overturn, but is about the inclusion of difference and thus of different views into a community of decision making. Mouffe (1993) writes of democracy as an unfinished revolution, that is, of driving democratic representation deeper into the structures of everyday life. Democracy cannot exist unless its ethic of emancipation is about the unfinished inclusion of difference into the field of the political. In the post-structuralist views of Laclau, Derrida, Butler, Zizek and others it is a process that cannot be finished because the democratic horizon cannot be closed, it recedes infinitely, embracing new differences. Hence democracy and its ethic of emancipation will always be unfinished business. Emancipation is a vast question because it carries within it an infinite ethical charge to include difference, that remains well after politicians and their public have lost interest.

Moving and Removing the Ethical Edges of the Inter-view

The researcher is a witness to the ways in which different individuals and groups give witness to their experiences and views. Approaching their different interests through interviewing is itself an ethical as well as a political act:

> The current context in which we all work is that schools want to be more vocationally involved. They haven't got the resources or skills, so colleges are being asked to enjoin with them and deliver on site where possible and we're beginning to look at that. And so schools benefit by offering a more relevant offer to 14+. Colleges benefit from a closer working relationship with schools and ultimately [providing] progressional opportunities for those young people. So, there's a business case sort of way down the road but that wasn't the reason we went into it.
>
> (from CIEL project interview 2004)

As a researcher, with a multiplicity of interests, I create frames for the interview, each edge connecting to others: political interests, philosophical interests, economic interests, cultural and educational interests. Face-to-face with the interviewee there is an ethical demand to be open to the other. But what does that openness mean? Does it mean revealing my views? Or does it mean that, like Bourdieu (1993) I listen, actively?

An edge emerges between myself and the interviewee. As a listener I don't have to tell my interests. However, I do have to enable a telling to take place.

The above interviewee is a senior person in UK Higher Education talking about a policy initiative focusing on young people aged 14 to 19 where there is a perceived lack of provision for certain groups. This age range crosses institutional boundaries between schools and colleges. The strategy is meant to cross the divide and provide an integrated package. It is particularly focused on areas of disadvantage in order to increase access to vocational courses or minority academic subjects. There is, it would seem, an ethic of inclusion which is underpinned by synthesizing the interests of different organizations which either would have nothing to do with each other, or be in competition. What at this point am I listening to?

By the time of this interview, I had not only interviewed many others in connection to this project, but also many others in the same area with respect to other projects involving young people like Ernie and Teresa, as well as policy makers, and business people who were interviewed in relation to urban and regional development. This enabled me to formulate questions I might not otherwise have been able to do. I am looking for connections: how is what he is saying relevant to what others have been saying in different arenas of action? Thus I am able to unpack the logic of the interview in terms of its connections with other areas of everyday life. So I ask a question about the impact of young people getting better qualifications who leave the area which then leads, potentially, to a further decline in the area as it loses its young people. Is there a strategy for bringing appropriate jobs into the area that would make use of the skills and qualifications of the young people and so make the place an attractive area for the young people and for business? He knows of no such co-ordination of strategy. Further unpacking the logic of what he is saying reveals a more complex picture involving elements of noble motives, playing the game of compliance, manipulating resources for alternative purposes, good business sense and policy imperative. There are already institutions 'sniffing around' he said, trying to see what's in it for them, jostling for position in a game that may well become highly competitive.

With each question, there is a truth, a reality that keeps shifting. There is a kind of trivial truth in the sense of the existence of a given policy document, the lack of resources of schools to provide students with particular minority or vocational courses and the local colleges working with schools to provide those resources. The existence of each 'fact' is a matter of true or false. There is then a truth in relation to the interests that each 'fact' evokes. How are these interests conceptualized and organized in relation to each other? That perhaps provides a sense of the political truth, that is, a truth regarding the nature of what is at stake for the different individuals and groups, and so on, affected. Outside of a controlled laboratory, a decision, no matter how well thought out, has consequences that cannot be predicted nor indeed conceptualized. And when discovered these may be thought unjust:

> But justice, however, unpresentable it may be, doesn't wait. It is that which must not wait ... to be direct, simple and brief, let us say this: a just decision is always required *immediately*, 'right away.' It cannot furnish itself with infinite information and the unlimited knowledge of conditions, rules or hypothetical imperatives that could justify it. And even if it did have all that at its disposal, even if it did give itself the time and the necessary facts about the matter, the moment of *decision, as such,* always remains a finite moment of urgency and precipitation, since it must not be the consequence or the effect of this theoretical and historical knowledge, of this reflection or this deliberation, since it always marks the interruption of the juridico- or ethico- or politico-cognitive deliberation that precedes it, that *must* precede it. The instant of decision is a madness, says Kierkegaard. This is particularly true of the instant of the just decision that must rend time and defy dialectics. It is a madness. Even if time and prudence, the patience of knowledge and the mastery of conditions were hypothetically unlimited, the decision would be structurally finite, however late it came, a decision of urgency and precipitation, acting in the night of non-knowledge and non-rule. Not of the absence of rules and knowledge but of a reinstitution of rules which by definition is not preceded by any knowledge or by any guarantee as such.
>
> (Derrida 1992: 26)

In Derrida's view, a decision is not the simple application of a rule. It is an act of madness in the sense that it is made under conditions of lack of knowledge, lack of rules, lack of understanding of the conditions. In the complex circumstances of everyday life there are times when decisions have to be made, even if the decision is not to make a decision. As in the case of responding to a policy initiative, moves are made to work out its possible interpretations and the implications of those interpretations for a given organization. Making a decision to privilege or not to privilege the interests of one organization or one group, or one individual over another takes it into both a political and ethical realm. It is no longer the simple application of a rule. For Derrida (1992: 24) 'A decision that did not go through the ordeal of the undecidable would not be a free decision, it would only be the programmable application or unfolding of a calculable process. It might be legal; it would not be just.' And it would not be true: 'La justice, y a qu'ça de vrai' (1992: 27), that is, only what's just is true. A true witness is thus a just witness.

Taking the broad themes and contexts together, a kind of politico ethico-mapping can be produced which sets the strategic thinking at national and regional levels in relation to those of major institutions charged with implementing, or at least taking into account, policy and the networks of influence of key local decision makers who in turn have an impact on the local communities and the lives of individuals. Traditionally one can map these contexts as concentric circles: the national embedding the regional which embeds the local which embeds the individual. However, recalling the discussions of Chapter 6, the map is more like a shifting network of connections each forming and reforming into patterns of alliance and opposition as circumstances change which, through mechanisms of inclusion or exclusion, dominance or subordination, either open up or close down access to resources and opportunities for given individuals, groups, communities, organizations and so on.

Engaging in an emancipatory project there is no possibility from the outset of knowing the case, if the case is the totality of relationships, actualizable and possible, that are in play at each given moment. If the case is conceived as the emergence of patterns, discoverable over time, then again it is impossible to know these in advance. The case, as Derrida (1992: 27) says of justice, has a future, it is always to come, *à venir*. Making a decision about the particular outlines of a case, thus cuts short the process of coming into being; necessarily so, because the time needed is infinite as the case is always in a process of coming into being. Any decision is thus made before all the facts are in, before all the rules can be known, before the end of time.

Yet a decision has to be made. Ethical protocols, designed by ethics committees, or professional bodies provide check lists of rules and procedures to be employed. But these, speak of law, perhaps politics, but not justice and thus, not ethics. I earlier defined the ethical moment in an emancipatory project as 'the point at which a decision is made to represent the otherness of others in the structures and processes of decision making'. This is not just a matter of including others in decision making, it is the *otherness* of others that is essential. To include otherness is to include that which is by definition unknown and inassimilable if the 'system' does not change. This opens up territories which have not been charted, yet call for decisions. It starts from the very first moment when the idea for a project dawns: as an invitation to bid, as a student assignment, or as a self initiated task. A future opens up: hazily at first, I have an idea and this idea connects with other ideas. Perhaps it is an idea about finding out how the economic, social and cultural life of regions can be modified, or improved, or transformed to meet the needs and interests of all people This hazy idea projects a future in which people will be interviewed, their transcripts interpreted and analysed in order to make representations, discussions, arguments and conclusions. This future point, no matter how hazy, points back to some beginning point, some origins to the current circumstances which are impacting on people's lives. The project idea, then, is acting as a framework to unify many particulars that might not otherwise have been thought about in this way. This has a controlling effect on what is seen, heard and interpreted. To be open to otherness, means to be open to the challenge of otherness, the alternative ways of envisaging futures through which to make sense of a past and a present. Under the impact of these alternatives, the project may change many times as its future conception of what is involved in emancipation alters to include an ever-expanding range of differences. Thus an emancipatory project is fundamentally historicized, not through a single final history of all, but through incorporating the possibilities of many histories. Each history creates the conditions for re-viewing thus moving and removing the boundaries between interest groups, revealing new edges that may come into contact and create new alliances, new futures (*l'avenir*) for new forms of justice through which emancipation may be realized:

> Perhaps it is for this reason that justice, insofar as it is not only a juridical or a political concept, opens up for *l'avenir* the transformation, the recasting or refounding of law and politics. 'Perhaps,' one must always say perhaps for justice. There is an *avenir* for justice and there is no justice except to the degree that some event is possible which, as event, exceeds calculation, rules, programs, anticipations and so forth.
>
> (Derrida 1992: 27)

Perhaps being the just witness to, and telling the stories of these shifting, dissolving and emergent events is the theme of the next chapter.

8

From Anecdote to Narrative Case Studies

There's always a first time:

> There was another thing that [Debbie] had to do in order to belong to the group at the home. 'They go "Are you a virgin?" Well like this. And I didn't know ... cause I'd been at school and at home. I didn't know nothing about this, I go "Yeah". This was not the best thing to have said "And so all the time I was there I had this ... I had people going 'You virgin! You virgin!. So that was one of the things I had to lose to get into that group. I had to lose my virginity. I always regret that. That's just to get in one group that was. And that was so horrible. You just get pushed into it. You don't like it. You don't like it. You just get pushed into it'. Pressure continued to be applied from both boys and girls until she finally gave way 'That's just one of the hard things. When you get forced into losing your virginity it is horrible'. But everyone in the home where she is now (which consists of semi independent shared houses supervised by a full time residential social worker) 'will respect a girl who has got their virginity because we have always wanted it back'.

> There was another step necessary for integration into the group. 'Everyone was doing nicking and to be in the troupe at all, you know, you had to go nicking, you had to smoke, you had to do all this stuff. To get into the group. To be one of the people at the edge'. It was necessary to 'do all this stuff and that stuff just to be in with them, if not they would just sit there and take the piss out of you. And you got a hell of a hard life in care if you don't join in with them'. Some people find it very hard to mix in with other people she says 'you have just got to know how to do it'.

> She used to skive from school in order to go 'nicking'. She remembers the first time she skived 'I was shitting myself'. But she soon acclimatised although the school did not: 'about two months later the school chucked me out'.

She was scared the first time she went 'nicking'. But this also, like missing school, became easier 'once you know you could nick something you just keep on doing it, keep on doing it, don't you'. She was young enough to find it exciting. They always went in a group. Some of the group were at another school and they only had mornings available for these sprees. At first she was only required by the others in the group to go in the shops and observe. The others meanwhile had told her what they were going to do. 'We all have to like pretend to be looking at stuff and everything and we had to cover where the mirror is or something. We have to cover her so they can't ... the mirror can't see anything. And they used to do the same for you. And we just used to work round like that'. She says the whole thing was very easy.

(Schostak and Davis 1990: profile 6)

A life is not composed as a narrative, a linear sequence of clearly separated events joined by adding 'and' between them: ... this happened *and* then this happened *and* then this happened *and* ... Nor is there some place to start. Nor even a place to end. However, the researcher as an accountant of experience, like the obituary writer begins at the beginning and ends at the end.

A narrative kills. Debbie, as 'profile number 6' from the report (Schostak and Davis 1990) is now fixed into a kind of textual preservative: 'Debbie is 16 years old. She went into care in 1986. Before that she says "I never been anywhere before, I ain't done nothing. I was out in the country and I wasn't allowed out or anything at home".' How might such a brief statement, suitable as the headstone to her profile written for a report, relate to her life 15 years later, or 30 years later? The profile is transfixed, borrowing its life from the interpretations made by others, haunting intertextually, later writings and readings. Barthes pronounced the Author dead (1977) releasing the text from the authority of a particular individual writer or speaker. And for Lacan (1977a, b) language kills by replacing the warmth of life by the abstract cold of the concept. Yet life goes on. A kind of excess frothing around the text that cannot and will not fully submit to the text. It is this tension, this eruption of life and the scarring effects of text on the flesh that shapes the narratives of lives.

In accounting for a life, as in a profile, the little snippets of narrative told in an interview are sewn together to generate a different kind of unity from any that may be perceived by the teller. It is the unity of data, not data-content as such, but the concept of 'data', this empty category into which must be marshalled the contents collected by the rigorous application of methods. Each method like the scrape of a scalpel or the crushing of a hammer sculpts or shatters the data into a shape that fits. It is the symbolic violence that Bourdieu (1993) seeks to keep to a minimum. It is the struggle that Nietzsche, Barthes, Laclau, among others see as the very stuff of social realities, the politics of interpretation, the clashing of representations, texts and lives. There is no primal, unmediated, raw, brute content-as-data that can act as the objective conditions, the foundational ground prior to representation for analysis and interpretation. If language is the mediating structure, then it provides the means for analytic and interpretational moves through which to explore the struggle itself. But it is not language as a unity, a total system of differences but language as the playground of those 'infra-structures' those 'minimal things' (Gasché 1986, 1999) such as differànce, trace, archetrace, mark, re-mark, parergon and so on that Derrida employed to prevent the closure of texts, meanings, interpretations. This return to the themes of Chapter 2 thus points to a way of re-thinking the work of the researcher as collector and honer of data. It is to focus on the practice of structuring – more exactly the structurality of the structuring – through which data gets to be shaped into quasi-unities for all practical, political and ethical purposes. To imagine this 'structurality' is like trying to see the negative image of the photograph when looking at the positive image. Without the negative, there cannot be a positive. Or, it is like the tain of the mirror, the silver lining that allows a reflection to be seen without ever actually seeing the tain itself (Gasché 1986). Analogously, differànce cannot be seen, but is the structurality of the structure of seeing, grasping, understanding a meaning that can never quite be completed.

What is then 'behind', like the tain, the snippet from Debbie's inter-view where she said: 'They go "Are you a virgin?" Well like this. And I didn't know ... cause I'd been at school and at home. I didn't know nothing about this, I go "Yeah".'? As she tells it, Debbie doesn't know the implications of the question. She has been dislocated from her old familiar world of home and school and so her words are being employed by another context of use that cuts across them, opening up alternative connections to other worlds of experience and judgement. Each word, as it were, sits at a crossroads, the intersection of different discourses that spin the word one way or another, opening onto one avenue, closing off access to another. As such the word 'virgin' is an intertext, a place of interconnection with a multiplicity of actual and possible other texts and discourses. The intertext enables a passage from one sign system to another (Kristeva 1984) and thus opens the space of the inter-view. As an intertext it is empty of any essential meaning and becomes the place where a polyphony of sounds, a plurivocity of voices struggle to impose a content and hence close or subject some views while privileging others. When she is relocated to yet another residential home where different discourses reign an earlier meaning of 'virgin' comes back to haunt her and the other girls as a regretted 'loss'.

The key word 'virgin' ties together a series of events into an account, a way of accounting for what happened. In doing so it acts as a point of transposition, where a subject position viewed under one discourse is dramatically transposed under the dominance of another. In order to establish her identity as one that fits the new circumstances she has to 'lose her virginity' by submitting to a new subject position sanctioned by the prevailing discourse. A discourse masters its subjects and ties them into structures of 'the same' and 'the different', or, 'like us' and 'not like us'. The intertext provides a structurality, not a structure as such, under which structure can take shape. However, there is a further requirement, an act of articulation, a speaking – or writing, or signing – subject who struggles to bring together the particulars, those contingent, accidental, surprising, devastating, frightening or pleasurable, desirable or satisfying and reassuring aspects of life into view as some kind of whole, unity, manageable synthesis, a quasi-explicable world. The result of these processes is an infrastructure capable of dealing with changing circumstances by providing the conditions under which alternative worlds and their discourses can be constructed and manipulated and shaped into accounts. This infrastructure may be called, for simplicity, an anecdote. There are a whole series of anecdotes that illustrate, that are the 'data' for believing that: 'To be one of the people at the edge.' It was necessary to 'do all this stuff and that stuff just to be in with them, if not they would just sit there and take the piss out of you. And you got a hell of a hard life in care if you don't join in with them.'

The anecdote organizes content temporally. In Lacanian terms an experience which may pass unnoticed as such takes on a shape, a meaning, retrospectively in terms of what it will have become at some future date (cf. Fink 1995: 10). Thus when Debbie was taken into care all the previous stabilities of her life were displaced, as symbolized in Diagram 8 below as three intersecting curves (representing also the split subject of Chapters 5 and 6). From this position where nothing seems to connect a notion occurs to her of a future community that she could join where again stable subject positions can be defined (symbolized by the triangle). Thus step one is to imagine or grasp the conception of a stable future community which then enables step two a comparison with an original state of wholeness (symbolized by the circle) which now lies forever in the past, defining her now remote origins. This then enables her to clarify what needs to be done in the present to resolve her present state of displacement (as the place of possible transposition), that is, lose her virginity, and steal goods from shops – this is an hegemonic strategy to synthesize connections with the others in the home. When she moves yet again to another residential home where she has more freedom a new sense of stability emerges which then enables her to look back again and regret her lost virginity. It is reassessed in terms of a lost value (innocence? Paradise lost?). The anecdote gives an explanatory structure for both change and sameness. To join with the gang she has to adopt a subject position that they recognize as 'one of us', as being the same as them. In order to do that she has to undertake work (losing virginity, nicking) to change. In changing, her previous life is on the one hand defined as knowing nothing and doing nothing and on the other as a place of lost values.

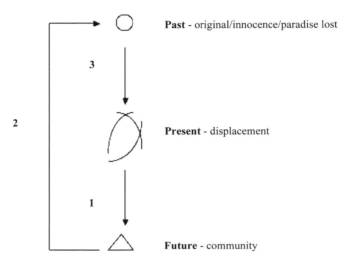

Diagram 8: The constitution of origins

Without the anecdote there can be no beginning nor an end, nor anything to explain or represent. In short it is a minimal thing, an infrastructure, through which a beginning and an end imprisons the sequences of 'ands' to produce a unifying narrative of something. One might call it the anding over of contents for their sentencing. It is either a sentencing to the 'same', a process of constructing stabilities, unities, syntheses; or a sentence of irresolvable conflicts, displacements, disintegration.

I have used the term anecdote because of its familiarity and its sense of triviality in an everyday sense. For these reasons the anecdote is often scorned and dismissed. The anecdote is not real data, the data of scientific procedure. Yet, each anecdote told formally structures its content into the hardness of a lived reality – this is the way it is, or this is what happened to me and this is why. Thus it can be argued that far from anecdotes being a weak form of 'evidence', they provide – in their formal (logical, structural, relational) and substantive (or content) dimensions – the route into the underlying structures and processes constructed by individuals who occupy particular positions or ranges of positions in intersubjectively maintained networks. Through the collection and analysis of anecdotes the dynamic, multi-dimensional and multi-layered narrative frameworks through which everyday and professional experience and action is organized can be studied. These in turn become the basis for the development of what may be termed 'narrative case records' (Schostak 1985). Such case records can provide a powerful means of establishing the evidence base necessary to inform the development of theory, critique and thus inform judgement, decision making and the implementation of courses of action – in particular, emancipatory projects – in everyday life, and with particular implications for action within multi-professional, multi-disciplinary and multi-organizational contexts.

Strategies to Compose Narrative Case Records

The inter-view, as a strategy, composes the case; that is, it composes the multiple views that have been recorded in a multiplicity of ways (sound, video, note taking, drawing and so on) together with any everyday artefacts that provide insights, representations, illustrations (documentation, clothing, ornaments, tools and so on). The case creates a structure, like the tain at the back of a sheet of glass, it provides the conditions for a reflecting surface, a mirage of integrity and cohesion. This is what may be called the mimetic function of the case. Mimesis is the imitation, the 'painting from life', the production of a realistic representation. In order to reach this state of realistic reproduction there are dangers to avoid:

> These [interviews] were all informal and semi-structured. Recorded on cassette with the agreement of the pupils, these interviews resembled somewhat one sided conversations prompted by the interviewer but following as far as possible leads offered by the pupils themselves. It was important that the interviews did not impose issues or concerns, ways of understanding, seeing or talking that were not the pupils' own. The fundamental strategy was to encourage the interviewee to set the agenda for the interview. It was important to know how alcohol featured in their lives, thus it had to emerge as a natural accompaniment to a description of their everyday lives.
>
> (Schostak and Davis 1990: 7.2.6)

Looking back, there is a naïveté or disingenuousness to this, a mimetic strain, a desire to attain a state in which appropriate data would arise 'naturally'. Yet, the duplicity is already there, the strategy underlying a struggle to impose an impositionless agenda: 'it *had* to emerge as a *natural* accompaniment'. That was to be its mark, its criterion of 'reality', 'objectivity', 'validity'.

It was important therefore to enable the pupils to answer from their own experience and not on the basis of received knowledge or what they considered the interviewer wanted to hear (this is not to say that the forms of received knowledge demonstrated by the pupils were not important cultural artifacts in themselves and a part of the pupils' world). In areas addressing controversial, difficult or sensitive subjects much bound up with the structural relationships of power and responsibility, of dependence and order, between adults, children and young people, it is vitally important that the adult interviewer enables the pupils' to feel the 'ownership' of their experience. On such a basis they are more likely to feel confident of giving responses relatively free of exaggeration, evasion or any of the other forms of truth dissipation. Tactically the interviewer volunteered information about himself at appropriate points in the interviews, articulating thoughts, reflections, attitudes and experiences. The purpose of such openness was precisely to equalise relationships in the interview, so avoiding any comparison with an 'interrogation' and to promote trust and relaxation.

(Schostak and Davis 1990: 7.2.7)

There is a game of positioning going on: positioning pupils into a feeling of ownership; positioning the interviewer as one who can be trusted; tactically positioning the interviewer as open; distancing the interview from that of 'interrogation'. The mimetic strategy in composing the project case is to lay the rhetorical conditions for the production and acceptance of the legitimacy of the naturalness of the data. To systematize this, there is further strategic positioning:

Qualitative research, because it focuses closely upon what people say and do can not involve itself in mass survey techniques. It is more important to achieve quality rather than quantity in these interviews. The emphasis is upon the internal validity of the interviews and the triangulation of perspectives that they offer. Internal validity, as used here, refers to the regularity and consistency of patterns arising within an interview and a series of interviews with the same person or group. Triangulation refers to the correlation of perspectives that can be achieved concerning a range of objects. Triangulation identifies the extent to which individuals and groups perceive the same objects or attribute the same meanings to objects. Objects which have been triangulated are said to be objectively valid for a given individual, group or groups. Such strategies are vital in determining the range and scope of youth sub-cultures and the influence these have upon the reasoning and decision making of young people.

(Schostak and Davis 1990: 7.2.14)

The first move is to position qualitative research from its other, quantitative research such as in mass surveys. This is not to say that qualitative strategies cannot be employed to generate coverage of a nationally significant range of people and contexts. Its techniques are different. I was to explore this in later projects as more fully discussed in Schostak (2002). Based on experience with several national projects, it is possible to combine both coverage and in-depth strategies in order to produce the mimetic effect of a survey. Essentially, the techniques are the same for both the in-depth and the coverage phases of a project. Two key techniques are mentioned in the passage: internal validity and triangulation. The third is what may be called a critical realist analysis of structure and process. These create mimetically the narrative of case construction for research purposes.

Internal validity and triangulation depend upon a presupposition of realism, that is, it is presupposed that given the right conditions – for example trust, openness, truth telling – a representation of the real, the authentic, the actual state of affairs, can be produced. Internal validity, as being constructed here, refers to the process of examining an interview transcript for regular patterns that construct a subject position that can be considered to express authentically (that is, as the author of an expression, an act, an interpretation), an enduring view for that subject position. Thus a representation of that view can be constructed for research purposes which can then be said to be 'valid' for that individual, or that group. Triangulation extends this process to make comparisons and contrasts with other individuals, groups and the objects that furnish their worlds. Intuitively, triangulation is rather like getting one's bearings by reading a map, a particular place can be accurately located by defining two or more views directed towards it: the longitude and the latitude that provide the grid reference for the place on the map. Similarly, if one person, says 'there's a dog down by the river', and a second person says 'there's a dog down by the river', and a third person says 'there's a dog down by the river', there is the chance that 'there's a dog down by the river'. However, two questions: is it the *same* river, and is it the *same* dog? Further questions, of course can be raised: what is meant by river? What is meant by dog? River might the name of a night club and dog the name of a gang. Each question further reduces potential ambiguities and misunderstandings until at some point agreement can be reached that each individual is intending the *same* object(s)/meaning(s). If not, out of frustration, one or more of the individuals may say 'well, come down to the river and look for yourself.' Going down to the river and looking for one's self provides another approach to getting the appropriate data: seeing, touching the water, stroking the dog all provide sensory information that this is indeed water and the dog is alive and not a plastic model. The idea of dog and water is filled out by the meaningful answers provided by the interviewees and correlated with further acts of conscious sensory input: a process of getting as many angles on the same thing as possible and in the process identify that the object in question matches the essential structure of the idea or concept in question, that is, of 'dog'. It is a brown dog, not black, with a long tail, not short, with a shaggy coat not sleek and so on. Some features may vary but all the essential features (that is, those features common to all dogs) are of a dog and not a cat. The process of generating such essential structures is in Husserlian phenomenology called *eidetic variation*. In brief, taking the example of a triangle one can vary each of its features, angles and length of sides. What remains common to all possible variations is that a triangle is bounded by three straight lines. If one of the imagined variations should make it such that a gap appears between two of the sides because the angle is too wide to make the sides join then the object can no longer be called a triangle as in object '2' of Diagram 9 below:

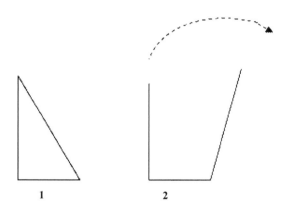

Diagram 9: Triangular realities

This simple process is very powerful in terms of focusing attention upon the acts employed by others to construct meanings and associate them with the objects of their world. Different groups may focus on different 'boundaries' to separate or include members of a particular class of objects: in one social world any combination of three lines joined together may be called a triangle, such as '1' and '2'; in another world (that of geometry), only '1' is acceptable because there is a further necessary feature which '2' breaks, that the three lines should compose three angles. There are different 'realities' at stake here, the researcher represents each according to the ways in which each view eidetically constructs the objects that feature in its 'reality' without making a judgement about it from some superior 'scientific' understanding of the world. This then means that no 'reality' is privileged over any other 'reality' during this process of creating the case record.

In order to gauge whether the representation of a given 'reality' accurately portrays that reality the researcher in a sense mimics (the mimetic strategy) the acts of consciousness of the actors in order to learn a way of experiencing, that is, sensually, intellectually, emotionally constructing this world. Thus the record can be created to provide all the necessary clues and instructions to carry out those acts of mimicry: acts of looking, tasting, touching, smelling, judging, reaching towards, recoiling from ... and so on. Consequently, the interviewee is positioned as the teacher, the expert in their own ways of seeing. Give me a picture explicitly or implicitly, demands the interviewer, of your world, what you do in it, who peoples it with you and the objects that comprise it. How do you value each of these and relate one to another? Tell me how to live in your world.

Acts of listening are made known in the questions asked, a close listening for detail, for an accuracy of understanding. The meaning of the other can be reflected in the form of the questions posed that ask about the details, that try to picture what is being said, that re-present what is being said through similar accounts. Thus a mutual triangulation of acts of consciousness directed towards 'this', 'not that', can be produced. Language, of course, is critical in this process by providing the means by which to differentiate and thus to identify. However, as has been discussed since Chapter 2, language is not a simple linear system where one sign refers uniquely to one signified, or one sign refers exactly to just one referent or thing in the world. Language, as a system of elements each defined solely by their difference from each other, is empty of positive contents. Thus it can be employed in the construction of multiple and conflicting meanings for any given object, multiple ways of seeing and hence multiple worlds of experience. Through the mutual acts of listening, meanings can be framed to include some but not all contents as 'valid', as 'true'. However, this does not mean that what has been excluded is irrelevant or false. The record that is composed through the acts of listening thus includes the acts of judgement, the acts of discrimination, the acts of repression concerning particular objects and meanings. In Lacanian terms, signifiers are strung out as if on the staves of a score and certain signifiers pass beneath the bar that separates the signifier from a signified. These signifiers that fall below the bar become the hidden signifieds of a 'surface' signifier. This is to say, that direct access to a given meaning is prevented in some way. Thus, as the mimetic strategy functions according to direct access, another kind of strategy is now required for the further development of the case record, this strategy includes hermeneutic, poetic, psychoanalytic, semiotic, ironic, rhetorical approaches that are capable of accessing multiply constructed dimensions of meaning. As a way of distinguishing from the mimetic strategy I will refer to this other strategy as the poetics of the real. A poetics of the real as I employ this term does not oppose a mimetic strategy, nor does it complement it. Rather, it suspends any assumption concerning what is or is not real. In that sense it suspends – and thus does not depend on – but does not do away with, any mimetic assumption that a real is being represented. In this sense, a poetics of the real enables the composing of the case as a site of multiple views for the construction, elaboration and exploration of experiences regardless of whether or not they can be counted as 'real'. Take an extract from John's account:

> He describes the development of drinking amongst his peers: 'At first everyone thinks it's some sort of contraband; they think "Ooh, it's a Bottle of Cider, here" and you sort of sneak around saying I've got all this stuff. It's banned, it's banned, it's taboo, etc, and then we went on a school trip and everyone is sort of smuggling in bottles of cider and all this thing. That's how it started and then once you get a taste to it, you progress onto, well, "Do I look old enough to get into a pub etc?" or you go down to the local little shops and buy something. Progressing from there, as soon as you're having a good time, you know, and you're getting drunk, and doing silly things and laughing; it's good times, so you think "if I have a drink, I'll have a good time".'
>
> (Schostak and Davis 1990: profile 5)

There is in this extract a theory, as it were, of how people learn to drink alcohol and equate drinking to having a good time. Certain aspects of it could be tested in relation to the views of John's peers amongst his friends, people in the neighbourhood, his school, other schools and so on. The mimetic strategy is interested in generating a description of this world as a valid representation of a given range of people's experiences. In John's use of it, it grounds his reality: this *is* what people do and why they do it. It has, however, a range of significances. It keys into a world of taboos, of bans, of contraband, of sneaking around as a way of creating alternative places for enjoyment. It cultivates tastes and it generates hurdles to overcome – do I look old enough? Each hurdle and stage generates a sense of progression. A poetics of the real takes notice of the resonances of words transforming the acts of getting hold of a bottle of cider and drinking it into a drama of transgression and through transgression gaining evidence of looking older and experiences of having a good time. The poetics of the account refers a reader or listener beyond the concrete events to the chains of significance that words like taboo attach to this representation of a young man drinking a bottle of cider. What texts refer to taboos? How do these texts organize people, things and 'realities' in relation to the 'taboo'? Thus those texts that refer to transgressive acts or events through which subject positions and interests can be constructed and organized are drawn into the case record. Indeed, for Bataille (1987: 65), 'Organised transgression together with the taboo make social life what it is.'

The account of the drinking as a mimetic structure and the significance of the taboo as an organizing framework are different dimensions of the same account. They work in different ways. Mimesis is a representation, using textual strategies, of reality. The poetics of the real is a way of drawing significance, of creating a sense of a unity that points to a truth. The distinction can be approached, analogously, with Riffaterre's (1978: 2–3) distinction between mimesis and the poem:

> Now the basic characteristic of mimesis is that it produces a continuously changing semantic sequence, for representation is founded upon the referentiality of language, that is, upon a direct relationship of words to things. It is immaterial whether or not this relationship is a delusion of those who speak the language or of readers. What matters is that the text multiplies details and continually shifts its focus to achieve an acceptable likeness to reality, since reality is normally complex. Mimesis is thus variation and multiplicity.
>
> Whereas the characteristic feature of the poem is its unity: a unity both formal and semantic. Any component of the poem that points to that 'something else' it means will therefore be a constant, and as such it will be sharply distinguishable from the mimesis. This formal and semantic unity, which includes all the indices of indirection, I shall call the significance. I shall reserve the term meaning for the information conveyed by the text at the mimetic level. From the standpoint of meaning the text is a string of successive information units. From the standpoint of significance the text is one semantic unit.

Of course, the extract from John's profile is not a poem. Nevertheless, there is a significance, in Riffaterre's terms, that 'points to that "something else" it means': the world of taboos that exists as a historical collection of texts produced and thus intertextually available as the (written or oral) heritage of communities. The specific significance(s) between the account of taboo behaviour by John and other taboo texts is thus a potential focus for data collection and analysis. Taboo, like Freedom or Patriotism or Truth refers to a powerful universal the contents of which are always under dispute, often radically and violently. In that sense, they are empty signifiers and are thus powerful attractors for hegemonic strategies (Laclau 1996), the strategies by which a unifying narrative can be told that holds together otherwise disparate individuals and groups to bring about control over ways of seeing the world, ways of organizing social practices, the ways of dividing the good from the bad and the ways of allocating resources to needs and interests in the maintenance of that hegemonically produced world view. In order to explore further the hegemonic structures, an additional approach to the composition of the case record emerges: the hegemonic strategy.

Chapter 6 (see Diagram 6) provided a means of analysing the multiple sides of subjective life that enables connections to be made where the

Goth was able to connect with the Suit to form a pack of smokers. The argument is that no individual occupies a single subject position but is intersected by many: for example, the subject positions composed by gender, occupation, religion, ethnicity, age, language and so on. This provides the basis for hegemonic strategies. So how is hegemony to be defined?

> Normally we think (or *I* think) of hegemony as the name for the (often unjust) domination of an already existing ruling power, whether within a given nation state or as exercised outside the state, for example in imperialism or colonialism. 'Hegemony' is another name for sovereignty. Laclau uses the term quite differently, to name the way a contingent group within a given society (the working class, say, or certain individuals within it in the case of the Russian revolution or a certain group within the Communist Party in Italy after World War II) 'takes upon itself the task' of political emancipation from unjust ruling powers.
>
> (Miller 2004: 218)

Hegemony, then, as used here is the taking on a task of emancipation from some unjust ruling order. What is just or unjust, of course, depends upon who makes the definition. The task consists in a group or certain individuals articulating a social imaginary, a myth, that resolves the sense of dislocation or crisis that people feel. Disparate groups or individuals may come to feel that they are at least fighting the same enemy. Thus the different groups and individuals are articulated under the myth in terms of what Laclau and Mouffe (1985) call a chain of equivalence. Thus:

> Consider, for example, the two sides in the affirmative action debate in California during the mid-1990s. The pro-affirmative action side includes civil rights organizations, people of colour community organizations, feminist groups, progressive trade unions and the AFL-CIO, student groups and small leftist organizations. On the anti-side, we have the Republican Party, neo-conservatives who oppose what they call 'special rights' and 'preferential treatment,' anti-feminists, racists who oppose the advance of people of colour in any shape or form and xenophobes who see affirmative action as an incentive for non-white immigrants to settle in California. Insofar as these groups form two opposed blocs, the following analysis can be suggested. On each side of the debate, the different subject positions are articulated together to form a chain of equivalence (Laclau and Mouffe 1985: 127–9). To the extent to which we are dealing with articulation – and not just superficial coalition – the value of each subject position in the chain is shaped by its relations with the others. Perhaps trade union militancy or radical feminism, for example, would become more multicultural as these subject positions were brought into closer negotiations with progressive anti-racist subject positions during the pro-affirmative action campaign. Ultimately, hegemonic articulation would occur on both a conscious and

unconscious level, as anti-racism began to operate as a compelling overarching framework for identification for anti-racists, trade-union militants and radical feminists alike. Wherever different subject positions are symbolically located together in opposition to another camp, such that their meanings are subsequently transformed by their overlapping identifications with partially shared sets of beliefs, then we are dealing with an articulated chain of equivalence. We should note, however, that a chain of equivalence never dissolves into a singular homogeneous mass; the differences between the subject positions in question are always to some extent preserved.

(Smith 1998: 88–9)

This, of course, is a speculative analysis. Recalling Diagram 2 of Chapter 2 where words are substitutable for each other under a given 'stack', the chains of equivalence can be mapped as follows:

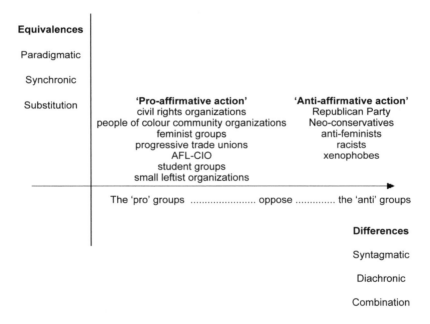

Diagram 10: Chains of equivalence

Each individual group is different from all the others. However, those stacked under the 'Pro-affirmative action' heading share an opposition to those stacked under the 'Anti-affirmative action' stack. Each group is thus positioned through their oppositional standpoints to particular other groups. In that sense each group under a given stack is equivalent, forms a chain of equivalence, in terms of being oppositional to those of the other stack who are seen as being equivalent to each other in being opposed to affirmative action. Politically, members of each stack have reasons to start to co-ordinate their actions. However, although on the same side, they are in fact different organizations that want to maintain their different agendas. In order to gain power, each group in the same stack will need to incorporate some of the key interests of the others in the chain of equivalence.

Suppose it was indeed the case that the pro-affirmative action side began to unify under one leading group as the symbolic focus of resistance and action. That one group might be the trade unionists or the anti-racists. In either case in order to keep the other groups on side the symbolic group, say the trade unionists, would have to modify its identity to include some of the interests of the others. In order to grow beyond the specific circumstances of the debate the modification of identity would have to include a symbolic dimension that could gather under its banner additional groups expressing needs and interests transcending the particular issues of that debate but who also saw themselves in opposition to the ruling elites. Gradually an hegemony of interests is synthesized under a particular symbolic frame or overarching myth creating a new imaginary under which needs, interests, desires are to be satisfied. The myth articulates a vision or complementary set of visions for community and for social order together with the practices and the allocations of resources that are necessary to underpin that order and thus compose the desired community.

Now let us take this out of the realm of party politics and single issue politics and back into the realm of everyday life where individuals negotiate the complex plays of subject positioning and alliance formation whether in gangs, families, streets, neighbourhoods, workplaces and places of prayer, leisure and entertainment. It is here that freedom or emancipation from the unjust has an altogether more existential, personal, fragile, complex, ephemeral feel that begin in the face-to-face encounters with others in particular circumstances like those of Debbie described in the extract at the beginning of this chapter. Her world is far from that of the debates of affirmative action. Yet, it is as much with her and her circumstances that an emancipatory strategy must begin as with the elites who command the powerful organizations that contest each other for power on whatever sides of the debates. How is Debbie connected to the powerful structures and processes that envelop her life? How can she take on the task of an emancipatory project? Such a project would have to take on board the total and very specific circumstances within which she lives. Adopting a Sartrean mode of analysis:

> Since each individual project has the quality of totalisation, it contains
> an interpretation and valorisation of the world which is connected to

living in the world in a determinate place at a given time. The project of going to work each day, for instance, involves an individual recognition that the existing order of production, and the socio-political systems which support it cannot at that moment be overturned. It is thus in the realm of subjective experience that revolution is negated or actively encouraged according to whether we choose to be resigned or revolutionary.

(Fox 2003: 68, 69)

The impression given by the extract may be that the choice between resignation and revolution is free. However, it is an impression qualified by the recognition that an existing order cannot at a given moment be overturned. The struggle is not one that is between equals. Debbie could have continued to refuse to submit to the demands of the boy dominated group but at the cost of having no community and no support for the development of her sense of identity, of being with others and being in the world. But the boys are not the dominant masters of the world and there are always different interests at stake:

She was never caught stealing as such but factors inherent in the situation itself caught up with the group. One day she was in (a department store). A friend of hers wanted a pair of shoes she'd seen in there. So Debbie went in and asked to try them on. When the opportunity arose she found she could only steal one of the shoes because her jacket was not big enough to take both. Just as she got out of the shop she slipped on ice dropping the stolen shoe onto the ground. She jumped to her feet and ran off meeting Gary, another member of the group, saying 'three times' that she couldn't go back into (the department store). She was really embarrassed she said. Grant (another member) returned to (the department store) and stole the remaining shoe. After this they went into (another department store) where Grant stole a pair of jeans while Debbie covered for him. Someone else from the home was also in (the other department store). This was Ian who was not at all happy about what the others were doing. He already had a criminal record and the consequences for him would be very serious if he became in anyway implicated in these activities. As a result he 'shopped' them to the police. Debbie explains why he did it 'He thought it ain't fair. Those can do it but I can't because I'm going to get nicked and put away. So he sort of grassed them up so we wouldn't do it'.

(Schostak and Davis 1990: profile 6)

This is not, then, an account of hegemonic plays but rather the play of interests and positions within already formed hegemonic structures that cannot at that time be overturned. The positional play as well as the possibility for change and development cannot be adequately understood without a record of the counterposing groups and organizations that together form the context within which subject positions are constructed, and identities and alliances are negotiated. Different subject positions are created according to whether a given individual sides with the group, the department store, the police. While stealing, the store staff are placed into subject positions oppositional to the group. Hence strategies are adopted to hide their activities from them. It is a game of transgression of a different kind to that of John's anecdote about breaking taboos. Nevertheless, as in the previous example the very possibility of transgression is fundamental to and constructive of social order. Ian is recognized as a group member but Ian has other interests in play – he is fearful of the consequences of being caught. Individuals are always intersected by multiple subject positions: for him, the critical choice is between being a group member and being someone with a police record. It is resolved as a question of 'fairness'. Thus within a context where the existing order cannot be changed for the time being, choices have to be made about how subject positions are to be negotiated, boundaries managed, practices adopted and resources obtained in order to meet particular interests in the construction of views. Records of these plays of interest, position and transgression contribute the final strategy to the composing of the narrative case record.

Narrative Moves

The key elements of the case record include:

1. The mimetic strategy;
2. A poetics of the real;
3. The hegemonic strategy;
4. Plays of position, interest and transgression.

What then, should the narrative case record look like? There are no recipes however there are strategies for elaboration of the record. The structurality of the anecdote provides a useful entry point to the mapping of the range of views identified through the process of generating the inter-view. Each anecdote synthesizes people, places, events, meanings, judgements and so on around a view or play of views. Each of these provide information concerning who to interview, what to see, what to listen to and how to value and connect the elements addressed by the anecdote into a view. Each recorded interview, each conversation, each observation guided by interviewees generates the ways of directing conscious acts towards 'subjects', 'people', 'things', 'objects', 'events', 'meanings', 'realities'. Each alternative view generated by adopting a range of alternative positions towards the elements of a given view provides a mapping of views and how those views relate to each other. Each view in that sense is constructed differentially from all the other views. The inter-view generates the possibility of dialogue between the views and hence a modification of views as different interests are or are not taken into account. Applying each of the elements described above:

1. Through the mimetic strategy, a narrative can be produced that seeks to represent the views of individuals who are being researched drawing upon their own words, their rationales, their values and judgements. Methods to accomplish include for example:
   a. Identifying, getting access to and generating the accounts of the key individuals who are members of a target community, organization and so on:
      i. Through conversation (deliberately initiated, overheard);
      ii. By interview;
      iii. Through collection of texts (letters, memos, diaries, e-mails and so on).
   b. Miming acts of consciousness towards some intended object:
      i. Identifying the instructions, as explicitly as possible, concerning for example:
         1. what and how to look at, touch, smell, touch, taste something;
         2. how to approach or withdraw from something or someone;
         3. how to reach out to, take, let go of, move, address others and things.
      ii. identifying how to:
         1. categorize;
         2. judge and evaluate;
         3. manage boundaries;
         4. express feelings, needs, interests, desires, pleasures and so on.
      iii. learning how to re-present accounts by:
         1. paraphrasing stories told to see if the gist of them is accepted as 'correct';
         2. re-telling stories heard and telling accounts of one's own.
      iv. learning how to pass for 'natural' by:
         1. dress – including hairstyle, make-up and so on;
         2. posture – ways of standing, walking, 'hanging around' and so on;
         3. activities – ways of doing things, events engaged in;
         4. knowledge – about people, things, places and so on;
         5. values concerning what and who are good, bad, normal and so on;
         6. language – specialized vocabulary, accent.

Not all the methods of the mimetic strategy may be possible within a given research project due to time, resources and other circumstances. However, the validity of the project is enhanced through as comprehensive a mimetic approach as possible. Each method contributes to the effectiveness of the triangulation of accounts and interpretations regarding people, meanings, things and events. Narrativizing the mimetic may be accomplished through employing a clear realist style of presentation that keeps interpretation to a minimum (see next chapter).

2. The poetics of the real addresses the symbolic, mythical and latent features of the accounts. To do this insights may be drawn from hermeneutic, psychoanalytic, semiotic, rhetorical and indeed poetic approaches. Methods include:

   a. Close textual analysis by exploring the patterns of tropes or figures of speech: puns, slips of the tongue, metaphor, metonym, catachresis and so on. Each of these can point to meanings that are hidden, repressed or latent or can point to key universalizing categories (freedom, justice, people and so on). The meanings and implications for personal, social and cultural life can be explored intertextually across the accounts recorded over time with the same person, between people and with other historic or contemporary texts that a given culture, community and organization has produced.

   b. Use of key symbols to identify the imaginary or the mythological frames through which features of everyday life are unified, made whole and meaningful; or, through which a sense of absence, loss and regret is made manifest. The source for such symbols and myths are the accounts, the texts, the images employed by those who adopt particular subject positions in relation to a present or desired but absent community.

   The shift in attention is from the validity of the mimetic level to the 'truths' and ethics of responsibility, duty, right and wrong expressed through the poetics. Narrativizing the poetics includes exploring relations to the myths, the legends, the construction of the imaginary of the people, as will be developed in the next chapter in relation to 'writing up'.

3. The hegemonic strategy describes how power is organized and the strategies employed, if any, to manage conflict and accomplish change. Specifically, of course, it is of interest to those forms of research that focus upon deliberative action as in Action Research and Evaluation. More broadly, it underlies emancipatory projects and in particular, the project of radical pluralist democracy as imagined by Laclau and Mouffe. Here the narrative case is elaborated through the imaginary of 'freedom from' and 'freedom to' that form, an ethical basis to the varieties of emancipations that groups envisage as leading to their desired community. The narrative employs the mimetic methods of description in order to generate a realist account of interests, actions and events in the context of articulating visions of desired commu-

nities and how to accomplish them through appropriate practices and the deployment of resources.

4. Plays of position, interest and transgression describe the ranges of actions and decisions available to individuals within a given social order that they perceive as impossible to overturn during any envisaged period of time. In a similar vein to the hegemonic strategy, narratives will employ mimetic descriptions of interests and events but in the context of transgressive and oppositional imaginaries where action and change leads to winners and losers without fundamentally altering the social order.

Collecting and constructing the data for the inter-view narrative involves each of the above elements. Writing it up involves opening up the possibilities for reading.

9

From Inter-views to Writing

Can I just take something as read?

The leftovers of research projects were ranged in box files along shelves stacked one above the other around the walls of my office before I moved jobs. Some I sent for storage others I kept with me, now stacked in unopened cardboard boxes. I still have the two or three hundred audio cassettes, the dozen note books, the photos, the news cuttings, the hand transcribed interviews collected during my doctoral research twenty five years ago. They're there somewhere in those boxes. Each new project a new set of box files. Now of course the recordings are digital. I keep telling my students, one hour of recorded interview takes about 5 hours to transcribe. And multiply that by 10 for a video! The piles and piles of data just mount week by week as a project progresses. Working alone means that it becomes impossible to transcribe and analyse all in detail. Working in teams means a large budget that few can get their hands on. I recall a doctoral student I examined once a few years back. He described in detail the coding method he employed based upon Strauss and Corbin (1998). It was exhaustive, a model of the genre. He showed clearly how four hundred categories could be progressively reduced to four. Not the merest hint of living flesh was left in the final discussions of the profession he had studied.

Somewhere between the records of voices, the transcripts, the observational notes, the collection of the documents and artefacts of everyday life and their reduction to the rationally constructed categories of research analysis there is surely a reading that can evoke what it had meant, what it still means, to live, to work, to hope, to laugh, to cry in pain and to hope for a better future? Somewhere in all those records are the sounds, the images of life. How can they be written up?

Today I read in a paper an article written by Zizek (2005) which describes the difficulty of writing critically. He tells an old joke from the ex-German Democratic Republic about an engineer who gets a job in Siberia where all letters are subject to censorship. To circumvent this he and his friends will write in blue if true and red if false. The first letter received, written in blue, states how well supplied all the stores are and how good everything is and ends saying that only red ink is unavailable. So, the moral is: we need to 'invent writing in red ink' if we're to handle critically such words as freedom that are written in the political colours of the powerful, whether these are the voices of fundamentalists, politically correct liberals or those politicians who routinely employ freedom and democracy to justify their actions. If only there were a way to be so unambiguous about truth and falsehood. If only there were such a red ink that could incorruptibly speak the truth about falsehood: 'In order to fight for freedom, we have to be aware of the true contours of our (un)freedom.' But how to write that letter home to our friends about the 'true contours of our (un)freedom'?

(Schostak, reflections on finding a beginning for this chapter . . .)

The letter kills. It lives only in our mouths, the neurones, the glint in the eye, the quickening of the heart beat: its emptiness filled by desire. The sounds, the marks, the concepts function only because they refer to nothing in particular. The fieldwork notes, the recorded sounds and images, the documents, the artefacts are all signifiers sculpted of sound and the physical materials of everyday life. The desire for signification, for meaning, for the presence of an object, a reality that will fill the signifier and the signified with positive contents animates the talk, the writing, the behaviour, the images, the forms created in daily action with others. Each sound, each word, each expression evokes the idea, the mood, the hope for something, or some generalized anxiety about the state of things. Carved in stone, found in the desert, the signs of an unknown language also evoke a desire to fill their forms with meaning, to know something of the world of that language. But meeting another, a stranger, my very existence, the right to my life, my safety, my desire for friendship, for help, or to be left alone is under threat. Language conveys the images, indifferently, of comfort and threat, not just a particular comfort or a particular threat but their *universality*. Through language, desire as the desire for a universal fullness of meaning, of being, is born. However, if language creates this desire for a fullness, it also creates the sense of its current lack, the possibility of the once upon a time existence of plenitude in some past age and thus the hope – or the fear – of its future return to being.

Language offers through its structures the production of meanings that the material world can never fulfil. The image of the perfect love, the perfect home, the perfect cup of coffee, the ideal state of freedom – it never happens. The love, the home, the coffee is there only in its finite, temporary but real aspect with all the attendant faults in amongst the pleasures and pains. The experience is split between the real and the ideal, between presence and absence, between finite and infinite. To reduce all to the signifiers and signifieds of a language is thus to enter a lifeless realm. But only by entering this lifeless realm can individuals meet in communion, think about themselves and their worlds, create knowledge, develop tools and transform the material world about to meet their hopes of fulfilment, their hopes, if any, of reconciliation, community, freedom to live, act and build creatively. Language is both the condition for entrapment and emancipation.

This writing that both entraps and emancipates, kills and creates the desire for life, for things, for worlds is incarnated in each individual who struggles with meanings by which to convey interests, needs, demands, desires, feelings, moods, hopes. Listening and talking are acts of sculpting and being sculpted in order to embody meanings through every sense and upon every surface of the body. This is the extimate relation with language through which both readings and writings take place as indivisible acts. Writing up then becomes an exploration of the possible readings of the research collected data that in turn becomes open to further readings. To read the hieroglyphics of an unknown language discovered in the desert requires a writing of its signifiers upon the sensuous surfaces of the flesh. Without that, their meanings remain utterly exterior. It is this extimate relation, the drawing of an *ext*ernal thing – language – into the most int*imate* relation with thinking, feeling and being that enables both the reading and the writing. Engaging with others during the research process is an extimate process. If it were not, then without direct access to the inner sensations of the other – telepathy – no communication would be possible. The mimetic strategy for narrative case recording defines the process of mimicking the conscious acts of directedness as expressed in language – the intentionality of consciousness as performed in 'looking at', 'moving towards', 'reaching towards', 'grasping something', 'smelling something', 'tasting something' and so on. Each act is a writing, a recording in the sensuous memory of the flesh, the brain. To understand the significance of the acts is a reading continually negotiated, checked in relation to others who provide a verification through assent, responding in expected ways; or, providing correction by responding in unexpected, or undesired ways.

Gradually, there emerges particular ways of talking to produce a sense of the world, a sense of reality, and a sense of what is Right And Wrong, as the master discourse governing a particular view. In Lacanian terms, call this master view S1, the master signifier which cannot be explained because that's the way the great powers of the world operate, or that's the way of Science – that is, there are fundamental demands, ideals, knowledges or sets of rules which may or may not be rational that do not need to be explained, they are the basis for life, the sole justification for doing things this way rather than that way. If the world were perfect such authority would not be needed, rather like Adam and Eve in the Garden of Eden who had no need of knowledge because Paradise is perfect and whole just as it is. Knowledge itself is taboo. And, with knowledge, of course, according to the myth, that wholeness is lost because knowledge divides the subject from the object of knowledge, creates an 'otherness', an otherness that becomes an object of desire, but an object that can never fill the loss of wholeness. Thus with the loss of that paradise, that unity of being, that sense of fullness there comes the desire to get it back, to master the situation, to have it all. But not everyone can have it all. In Hegelian terms there is the struggle that takes place until a master is recognized who through the exercise of power can dominate the others to make them meet the master's every desire. The demands of the master are not to be questioned. Yet, as Hegel tells the story, the subordinate in serving the master get to know the world by reflecting upon it and thus knowledge is created – Slave knowledge. This system of knowledge let us call S2. The role of research is to put S2 into the position of legitimate authority where the arbitrary demands of the master, S1, used to reign – Lacan called this the discourse of the university, it is Hegel's Absolute Reason where the book of the knowledge of everything can be written. Until this point is reached, S2 remains an unconscious potentiality that drives intellectual interests – the desire to *know,* the desire to replace the discourse of the master. As knowledge is developed the power of the expert replaces that of the Hegelian master – the Slave becomes Expert. Through the knowledge of the Sciences the real is to be mastered. But how do we know, at any given time, until that time of Absolute Reason, should it ever come about, that our knowledge is True?

Hysteric like, the student or critical researcher raises questions against the supposed knowledge of the expert, demanding 'but how do you know? Tell me what this *really* means, you're *supposed* to know – but you don't do you.' Lacan saw the role of the hysteric as one who through continual questioning of knowledge, expertise, or the taken for granted, leads to the discovery of new knowledge – in the case of Freud, the questions of his clients led to the production of psychoanalysis itself. Each such discovery is accompanied by an 'enjoyment', a *jouissance,* as Lacan called it, that is much more than just pleasure, it is a kind of explosion, a kind of excess that comes from the transgression of the boundaries or taboos that open up to knowledge, or separate one form of knowledge from another. As boundaries collapse and new vistas open, then there is the sense of some kind of freedom, new ways of thinking, expressing, framing action, engaging with others and creating futures.

Writing is in this sense an hysterical engagement with knowledges about worlds, the ways in which worlds are viewed, the legitimation of those views and the possibilities for action that are either opened or closed, supported or repressed. Rabaté describes the academic discourse that arises in the search for new knowledges as:

> ... the result of the interaction between a divided subject, an always elusive object of desire, and two terms limning the subject's episte-mology: S1, or the master-signifier which will replace the lost object, and S2, unconscious knowledge underwriting the pursuit of intellectual interests. The main signifier S1 provides an ideal or a program while connecting knowledge with its dynamic of hidden 'surplus enjoyment.' These terms make a point which is crucial about Theory as we use it in our scholarship, with the need to find a 'master signifier' as a theme or just a title in a thesis. The master-signifier should not simply mark a territory's difference from all others, but also keep alive some of the initial enjoyment that led to the discovery. Quite often the success of scholarly research will depend upon the horizon of potentialities or the feeling of endless riches generated by a single word chosen as task and field. Knowledge is produced, that is drawn out in some sort of self-education articulating one's libidinal stakes and the unfolding of a chain of words.
>
> (Rabaté 2002: 15–16)

Is there, in the multiple records and collections of artefacts that comprise the research archive – that pile of recordings, images, memories, odds and ends, and notes – 'a single word' that can be chosen as the 'task or field' that opens the data into 'the horizon of potentialities or the feeling of endless riches'? Or is that just the delusion of Theory?

Writing the Paradox

The paradox of writing is that it draws under its analytic and theoretic frames and models the diversity, the differences, the incompleteness, unifying the messiness of the research engagement into a master sig-nifier: a title, a theme, a Theory. A unity of differences is a fragile thing. It is there that a de-constructive writing takes place. Paradox is perhaps unavoidable. It is found in the Hegelian project for a presuppositionless philosophy in which both being and not-being are unified, a paradoxical result of pursuing the Cartesian method of doubt relentlessly (cf. Houl-gate 2005) that echoes still in poststructuralist and postmodern writings. Crudely, if a philosophy is to be presuppositionless then this should be applied just as rigorously to the assumption that something cannot both exist and not exist at the same time. A change in something, for example, implies that something both is and is not identical to its 'self', that is, if it is the same thing that is changing, then the changed 'self' is, however slightly, different from the prior state, yet it remains the 'same' thing. Furthermore, to be defined as an identity depends on defining what it is different from. Hence, the *difference from the identity* is 'contained' conceptually within the concept of the *identity*. These paradoxical plays are not mere wordplay but constitute the conditions for identity, difference, change and the appearance of stability.

In the workplace people's attempts to get to grips with the complex effects of these kinds of paradoxes provide material for de-constructive writing. For example, in trying to make a change take place, everything that one does may simply reinforce no change taking place; or, there maybe counter pressures that negate action taking place. Hence, one may feel both effective and not effective at the same time:

> S   Where I am the type of clients I see, the life of the client is the most important aspect uh. The area I work in is very uh deprived, one of, it's the highest area of social deprivation in in the borough itself, so it's the most important figure key point of uh what, you know how it affects the person's everyday living uh things such as drug and alcohol abuse are very rife, especially with the clients that I deal with um because it's their way of escaping the monotony and the deprivation itself.
>
> (. . .) you find that you you do get frustrated because you're trying hard so hard to do something to help somebody, somebody to do something for themselves and there's all these pressures and issues cropping up that are actually stopping that person from moving on and that you find yourself becoming cynical in a sense that you know, what good am I doing here, what and then you have to then again reflect on (xx) you must be doing something for this client, you've to sit back and think about well what, you know, if you weren't seeing this client what would happen then?
>
> (Phillips, Schostak and Tyler 2000a: 5.5)

This student wanted to make a difference in the real lives of people. To maintain his goal he has to manage his feelings and sense of confidence in the face of uncertainty about the worth of the work and its effectiveness – doing the job for real means not having the certainty of theory or of knowledge as a basis for decision and action. Yet, there has to be a reason to continue, a reconciliation between the desire to be effective and the experience of all the social factors and pressures.

Indeed, for the many voices of the project, doing it for real seemed a uniting theme, a title that could focus the conflictual tensions between the ideal and the real. When the report was published, 'doing it for real' became the sub-title (Phillips, Schostak and Tyler 2000b). This is not to say that a published or formal title is always produced in this way. Even if the phrase 'doing it for real' had not become part of the title, it would still be a key organizing theme, a covert title. This title, if we can call it that, is both constructive and dangerous. In one sense it gathers to itself the sense of each interviewee's focus upon their conception of the 'real' and upon 'doing' as master signifiers as distinct from just theorizing or reflecting. In the doing is the presentiment, not a clear definition, but an anticipation inmixed with a touch of anxiety about there being a task, a job to do, that is surrounded with specific but as yet not familiar, expectations. To do it for real has a sense of falling off the edge of safety, even with support, there is the risk of falling, and failing. Yet, too, there is an exhilaration, a pleasure, a satisfaction. The title opens an horizon of potentialities concerning how the ideas of the real and of doing construct a sense of a world of practice and a sense of becoming a professional and negotiating a place, a subject position in a conflictual field of action for these trainee professionals. As such it becomes an organizing device for writing. Each chapter, each section, each sub-heading elaborates the distinction:

Chapter 1: Educative assessment

Introduction
1.1   Practice curriculum
1.1.1   Transmissive curricula
1.1.2   Self-reflective curricula
1.1.3   Intersubjective curricula
1.1.4   Dialogic curricula
1.2   Assessment voices
1.2.1   The voice of mastery
1.2.2   Self-reflective curricula
1.2.3   Mutual voices: intersubjective curricula
1.2.4   Dialogic curricula
1.3   Summary

At work throughout the opening chapter is a de-constructive strategy. It starts from a description of 'transmissive curricula' placing the focus upon the teacher as the deliverer of a prescribed curriculum rather like delivering the mail. The student is the empty address waiting to be filled by the text. Each section heading displaces the role of student and teacher in the learning process until in the dialogic curriculum the student enters into an active, questioning, researching, relation with the professionals, the patients and others. In this last situation, the views of all are placed into dialogue as a means of exploring what is at stake and what can be done in practice. For such a dialogic relation to occur pre-supposes an openness towards otherness, the articulation of differences and their synthesis into ethically and democratically framed decision making and action. Thus learning is transformed from the rote learning of transmitted theory or knowledge and skills to the engagement of voices and views in a dialogic inter-view. The dialogic curricula opens the field of the real for doing it for real.

The writing strategy that can then follow involves taking each apparent, fixed identity, practice, structure, belief, value, or other category and showing how they can be taken apart. Drawing on discussions like those in Chapters 2, 3 and 4, apparently universal meanings can be analysed in terms of signifiers and signifieds that have no positive contents but are defined differentially in relation to each other in a context that has no centre, no way of unifying all the differences under a total system. This creates an open, ever expanding field of difference where it is not possible to make decisions based upon complete knowledge. Hence, writing can explore the strategies employed by individuals to manage uncertainty. As in Chapter 5, it can be shown through interview accounts that no subject position fully defines the identity, the interests, the needs, the desires of a given individual. Recalling Chapters 6 and 7 where identities are criss-crossed with a range of subject positions there is the potential for hegemonic strategies and explorations of political and (un)ethical (non)decision making and (in)action under conditions of (un)freedom. The writing strategy could focus on ranges of subject positions, under what discourses and communities of practices these are constituted and justified, the interests that are called into play by each, how each are managed by individuals and groups across networks of relationships, how boundaries are formed and traversed, resources manipulated and allocated . . . and so on.

So, in the next chapter of the research report, the theme of doing it for real is further elaborated in the voices and experiences of people adopting particular key assessor roles in clinical areas. They are elaborated around two key extracts from interview transcripts in which subject positions, practices and decisions are explored around the theme of what is supposed to happen and what actually happens. The section headings of the chapter are:

Chapter 2: Context and evidence

Introduction
2.1   The realities of work and clinical practice
2.2   Doing the job
2.2.1   Extract 1 – Managing care and staff
2.2.2   Extract 2 – A bad but typical day
2.2.3   Managing learning
2.3   The problem of role-conflict
2.3.1   The Assessor as supervisor
2.3.2   The Assessor as teacher
2.3.3   The Assessor as subject expert
2.3.4   The Assessor as assessee
2.3.5   The Assessor as carer: putting patients' needs first
2.3.6   The Assessor as carer: one to one support of the patient
2.3.7   The Assessor as carer: dealing with confidential/sensitive issues

The general theme focuses on 'realities' which is further subdivided into the specifics of the job as assessor. As can be seen, the role of assessor is split into 14 subject positions under the theme of 'the problem of role conflict'. Each of these positions is elaborated with interview based material. The remaining nine chapters of the final report further extends the field of differences across a wider range of subject positions (for example, lecturer, mentor, assessee and practitioners across a range of specialist areas), locations (classroom, ward, community), employing a range of mechanisms for learning and assessment (interview, standardized documentation, diaries, portfolios and so on) and justifying their approaches from the standpoints of different philosophies of care and occupational culture. Analyses, interpretations and models of practice are elaborated to present a way of undertaking learning for professionals in practical contexts, that is, doing it for real. The report was later published (Phillips, Schostak and Tyler 2000b) and developed with further funding from the Open University and the English National Board for Nursing, Midwifery and Health Visitors as the research underlying a major course for the professional development of mentoring (Open University 2001) reaching over 2000 Health Care Trusts and Higher Education Institutions.

Getting the title right can have a powerful impact not just for the fortunes of a research project but for the shaping of thought. Its power is poetic even if its phrasing seems literal, even banal. It gathers and condenses a prior range of texts (other interview transcripts, policy documents, and the various artefacts produced in the practices of everyday life) rather in the way that Riffaterre (1978: 25–6) describes the role of what he calls the hypogram. The hypogram acts like a hidden text that provides the underlying sense of another text. That is to say, there is no relationship to a real referent outside the text (1978: 29). What happens is that a key word, a kernel word, provides a range of connotations or presuppositions or relations through puns with other words. Thus, 'A *flute*, for instance, presupposes a flutist, entails an audience, contains semes such as "melodiousness," but also "rusticity," since one kind of flute is Pan's, etc' (Riffaterre 1978: 26) and, of course, why not also the fluted stem of a champagne glass, which then might connote celebration? The possibilities expand but are all related in some way to the kernel word. This kernel may or may not be actually expressed overtly. Thus each of the other words, if they are used in a text refer covertly to the kernel, are organized in relation to it, each word a part that implies the whole, that is the whole semiotic space organized by the kernel. 'Doing it for real' thus refers to no single real instance but refers to accounts about an attitude, an approach, a set of experiences, the feelings, the pleasures, the anxieties that accompany the carrying out of action and dealing with the contingent, unexpected events that take place and give an experience the quality of 'real', not 'play', not 'simulation'. Doing it for real marks a coming of age, a transition point passed from being in the classroom to being in the workplace, a step towards professionality, towards being respected by others who 'do it for real'. Doing it for real, then is about recognition of changed status. However, the status carries impossible demands:

> The theory is very valuable and interesting but nurses are asking for something really to combine the practice with the theory ... something which would match their actual roles much more than just the academic theory.
> (Post reg Assessee – Rheumatology, Masters course, Phillips, Schostak and Tyler 2000a: 6.4)

What is wanted, in terms of 'doing assessment for real' is an impossibility, a combination of the theoretical and the 'real' or the 'actual'. This impossible something is named in the task and the title of the report: doing it for real. The impossibility generates the desire for improved systems, improved professional development, improved resources, better ways of conceptualizing the relation between theory and practice but the gap between the two cannot be sown up, sutured, healed, made whole. Indeed, the danger inherent in giving a title and a task is its impression of closure, its apparent sense of defining the totality of a field, and the sense of the task leading to a definable objective, a solution. It may be that no solution, no closure is possible. That, of course, is the message of poststructuralist thought, well expressed in the deal struck by Derrida with Bennington in the writing of a book about Derrida:

> G.B. would have liked to systematise J.D.'s thought to the point of turning it into an interactive programme, which, in spite of its difficulty, would in principle be accessible to any user. As what is at stake in J.D.'s work is to show how any such system must remain essentially open, this undertaking was doomed to failure from the start ...
> (Bennington and Derrida 1991: 1)

Likewise, the attempt, as initiated by a research grant, to systematize and programatize assessment is doomed to fail. However, in the struggle what is at stake in the attempt can be drawn out, elaborated through all its variations across subject positions, locations, cultures, discourse communities, work contexts and so on. What is at stake requires a close reading of the multiplicities of texts produced and made available in some way to the researcher. The term text is defined as broadly as possible to include any form of inscription, or marking that is defined through its relation to others in a network. A writing presupposes a reading as a reading presupposes a writing. And in the paradox of the text that is never identical to itself is the possibility for emancipation – it proceeds through de-construction.

A writing for emancipation mobilizes resources to exploit the ways in which the apparently complete, solid, self contained melts, fades or recedes as the apparent boundaries separating 'this' from 'that' blur. The result is the generation of a vocabulary forever in movement, changing. There is an inventiveness in this process that in subverting the trans-cendentals and stabilities of formal systems of classifying and reasoning generates a parade of quasi-transcendentals and quasi-stabilities. That is to say, these are vocabularies that resist fixing and freezing into systems. They remind and keep open the gap between representation and the referent, the real, the existential. Rather than an analytic technology, they are an anti-techne.

Constructing the writing resources of the anti-techne therefore involves the exploitation of margins, the porousness of boundaries, the slipperiness of language, the remainders that return to haunt. Engaging with others face-to-face sets in motion a conflict (or an anxiety as to what might happen next) between 'my' view and 'their' view, that is, my way of organizing contents in relation to key (empty) signifiers to (incom-pletely) satisfy desires (or at least hold anxiety at bay) and theirs. The hardest task is to see how the mind gets to be enslaved while feeling free: if some texts were blue and others red as a simple code to say this is true and that is false the task and the field would be easy to define. True and False, like Freedom and Democracy universalize whatever contents are placed within their empty locations. As in the case of Debbie in Chapter 8, being placed into a new context – going into residential care – requires learning to take on new subject positions, handling new ways of behaving, accommodating to new views of the world. For her, the transition involved taking on a new sexual identity and engaging in violence and theft. Maggie, in Chapter 1, also experienced the shock of change when she felt her identity fall away as she felt her family no longer needed her in her old role. Frank in Chapter 7 could not handle the rudeness he experienced in his new job as a teacher and after sleepless nights gave it up. All had views as to what should be and what had been lost. The headteacher in Chapter 7 felt he knew how to develop a sense of identity and community for children from diverse heritage communities. He too had a view of the ideal, knew the right from the wrong. The universalizing signifiers through which they struggled to make sense of their experiences defining what is natural, what is good and bad, were deeply felt. The struggle to write indelibly in a code that marks right from wrong, true from false is not on some strange far off land, but in the everyday, in the street, at home, at work. It is there that the work of emancipation begins, where the ante-techne is to be found, in the displacement of everyday vocabularies.

Displacing Vocabularies

In training to become nurses and midwives, students had to learn how to see the world, a world that etches itself upon their nerves:

> S   Even after being on the wards for eight and a half years as a staffnurse and an EN 'cos I was an EN [enrolled nurse] before that I knew my staff and I knew how to run a ward and manage it. Going out of nursing for 18 months and coming back into the ICU [intensive care unit] environment I felt I knew nothing at all. It was um, noisy, um extremely busy, very active um unfriendly I think at first because it's such a close-knit environment, every-body knows what they're doing, when they're meant to be doing it and you don't want to interrupt anybody and stop them from doing anything because they all seem to be busy as bees sort of with their patients. And you don't want to interrupt that because you feel that you might do something wrong and alarms are going off and you're thinking ooh ooh and it was it was totally nerve wracking.
>
> Int: And how long did it take before you felt less nerve wracked?
>
> S   I'd say now and that's 18 months later [all laugh]. I'm being honest 'cos I've done the course now so I now understand why I'm doing things. I mean I was safe, in my practice um, if I didn't know what I was doing I wouldn't do it. And any results I'd get I'd check, get checked by senior members of staff. But, I mean I still do that now, but I know why I've done it and what I'm looking for and I've, I've analysed it before I go up to them and say this is what I want to do now. (. . .)
>
> (Post registration student in: Phillips, Schostak and Tyler 2000a: 5.3)

The student had been asked to describe what the first day on a ward had felt like. Getting to grips with a world, being able to intervene and take decisions are all major steps. In this case, even having been an experi-enced nurse, the impact of her first day as a student in a new environment was nerve wracking. How did she get to be positioned as a 'know nothing'? Why was there a barrier between her and the 'close-knit environment'? Being 'busy as bees', their locally coded, close attention to the routines and needs of patients excluded her. What was missing, for her, was the understanding of how it all fitted together and 18 months later 'I now understand why' and 'I know why I've done it and what I'm looking for'. But, how does she suppress old ways of seeing so she becomes a know nothing ready to be re-written? Over the months, constant checking with senior staff has re-written ways of seeing and understanding transposing her from ex-staff nurse to know nothing to one who sees and understands and is now free to act as a fellow member of the 'busy as bees' team.

In the extract, the vocabulary itself signals its displacement: 'even after ...', 'I felt I knew nothing', 'you don't want to interrupt', 'you might do something wrong', 'totally nerve wracking'. In her earlier professional career, although not as highly trained, she felt in charge, able to manage staff, control a ward in all its complexity and business. In her new experience as a student, all those certainties had been displaced. There was now a new defining centre to the system of activities, professional knowledge, decision and action. This opens a strategy for writing up: identify potential points of change or transposition as vocabularies are subjected to alternative discourses, trace the sense of displacement, articulate these displacements to identify new possibilities for thinking, acting, being.

Any given interview transcript or other textual source, then, can be approached with such questions as:

1. What are the key or master signifiers being enforced, displaced or potentially open to displacement?
   In the short extract above the signifiers already mentioned can be employed to organize or create major separations between a range of ideas or contents. Thus the 'technical' vocabulary is drawn from the discourses of those who have been recorded, as is common to qualitative research practices. However, the vocabulary does not simply describe – it performs a displacement, that is, it transposes from one signifying system to another, or it removes any sense of a stable centre from which to define what is true, known and good. The category of 'knowing nothing at all' divides a *before*, where she knows how to manage, from an *after* where she feels unable to participate because she has no way of applying her previous knowledge and ways of making decisions and acting. It associates with other signifiers as 'close-knit environment', 'busy as bees' and doing 'something wrong and alarms going off', weaving them together to create a sense of there being a select, purposeful, group of professionals in a state of perpetual professional action that she is as yet unable to join in any helpful, competent, meaningful way. This synthetic weaving offers the prospect of a future state, a kind of promise, of entry into a new, more

professional community of actors. This community offers, then, a new state of stability under which the noisiness, the busy-ness can attain the status of order, capable of being known and understood. There is a before, an in-between and an after. Each state generates topics for writing as the sense of transcendentals or universals collapse to be replaced by provisional quasi-transcendentals employed as transitional props about how to make sense of what is going on until the new transcendentals concerning 'truth', 'knowledge', 'reason', 'right and wrong', 'good and bad', 'justice and injustice' are learnt, understood, internalized as 'reality'.

Choosing a signifier, themes can be organized and elaborated in relation to it. However, which signifiers should be chosen? That depends upon the research agenda, the concerns of the writer and how these are intended to engage with the concerns or agendas of others. In the above case the agenda focused on workplace based learning and how conditions may be improved to support the learning of student nurses and midwives. Hence, the key signifiers were chosen to focus on the people, experiences, practices, discourses, forms of organization and resources involved in the development of students throughout their courses.

2. For each individual, what is the range of subject positions, desires, interests and feelings and how are they managed in relation to a sense of identity?

In the interview extract, there is a range of subject positions: enrolled nurse, student, staff nurse, ICU nurses, senior staff, patients, These can be further placed into the positions of those who know, those who don't know, those who are members of a close-knit environment and those who are not. A given individual, as speaking subject, may occupy and construct or articulate his or her sense of identity through more than one subject position at any one time; and over time these positions occupied and managed may change, hence displacing and modifying the sense of identity. With each position and each change there are associated feelings and interests at stake. According to their needs, desires, interests and feelings individuals may position each other tactically and strategically in order to develop alliances, place others into positions of powerlessness, marginalize them or elevate them into leadership positions, and so on. Thus the dramatis personae, that is, the actors who engage with each other (whether antagonistically, co-operatively, reluctantly, lovingly, hatefully and so on) construct each other into different subject positions for different purposes. As in Diagram 6 of Chapter 6, each subject position articulates a particular view that can be realized through various associated practices and resources. Vocabularies constructed around such subject positions defined only in terms of their difference from each other and from each newly identified difference have the power to displace any sense of a transcendental identity (that is, an identity that remains the same across any context for all time) thus keeping systems open, incompletable. Furthermore subject positions can be articulated into chains of equivalence that bring about changes in the distribution of power across organizations, systems and social life more generally. The description and management of subject positions, the formation – or dissolution – of chains of equivalence, and their impact on identities, the distribution of power, are potential ways of organizing writing under such questions as: What are the feelings and interests associated with each subject position? What feelings are associated with being intersected by a multiplicity of subject positions? How are subject positions managed, frozen or mobilized for action? What kinds of boundaries between subject positions and chains of equivalence are constructed? How are they managed? Each such question or some combination can generate chapters, sections or paragraphs organized to explore the dynamics of a given scene of action such as a classroom, a ward, or indeed a community, a city, a region.

3. What rules or codes govern interpretation, how are decisions made, what can be said or not said, and what actions or practices are enabled, legitimated, prohibited, demonized?

The rules or codes may be identified in the ways in which signifiers are organized into those that are substitutable for each other, those that can be combined to create syntheses of various kinds, the order in which they can be combined and the differences that must be maintained. How individuals, students in the extract, learn to become insiders, able to engage in rule governed action or practices – and thus identify and generate the conditions for transgression – provides a major resource for writing up. When do rules break down and how are decisions made and justified under conditions of incomplete information and knowledge? Drawing on such discussions as those in Chapters 6 and 7, what are the political and ethical implications of the displacement of codes and rules? Discussions of such questions can be organized around the particular experiences of interviewees, drawing out the tensions between their very particularity and the generalizations and the universality of the categories being constructed, employed and exploited to justify decision, practice and action – or their displacement.

4. How are resources organized and allocated?

Resources imply something real, something non-arbitrary, that is required, needed, demanded, desired for the continuance of life and a way of life. What counts as resources for a given dramatis personae? How are they organized in order to meet people's demands, desires and so on? Such questions asked – explicitly or implicitly – during interviews and observations identify how power, knowledge, communication and so on affects the distribution and use of resources. Topics or themes for writing up may focus on what resources are considered to be appropriate, useful, useless; those that are within reach and those out of reach; those that are 'real' and those that are 'fantasy'; the legitimate and the forbidden; the processes of allocation and misallocation – and what happens when stable orders for the management and allocation of resources are displaced. As in some way desirable 'real' (legitimate or taboo) resources become the focus, for example, of struggle, work and appropriation, how they are allocated amongst individuals becomes a key political and ethical question. Those who have and wish to retain power and disproportionate levels of resources will approach the question differently from those who wish to explore emancipatory possibilities. Research and the way it is written up can contribute to either.

5. How is the scene or stage for action conceived and organized as the ground(s) for realization?

The background is not something incidental. It is often unnoticed yet without it, all would fall away. This background includes the materiality that sustains life and the hidden cast whose work is necessary to the maintenance of everyday life. In any given location, say a classroom, the supporting staff, utilities – such as water, electricity, gas – the sets of economic practices and structures, the professional training, the policy makers and so on, are essential to its existence. The ground(s) for action and emancipation(s) include the mix of philosophical, commonsensical, and other values, beliefs and conceptual frameworks which comprise views, or ways of seeing. Writing about how people draw upon – or assume – a given 'ground' in their interviews focuses writing upon 'the true contours of our (un)freedom'. In that sense, it opens the way for the inter-view – as the 'place' of displacement – and the exploration of the pre-suppositionless precondition for any such ground to be either possible or impossible (cf. Gasché 1986, 1999; Laclau and Mouffe 1985; Laclau 1990, 1996; Butler, Laclau and Zizek 2000). Writing then emerges as an articulation of alternative views as a basis for the multiple readings and re-articulations for decision, action and transformation in everyday life. The very possibility of an alternative view sets into process an unstable oscillation, casting a seed of doubt into any transcendental claim a given view might make.

6. How are events and outcomes identified, constructed, brought about?

Interviews can focus – explicitly or implicitly – on how something happens as well as how to make, avoid or prevent something from happening. This focus can generate models or theories that seek to explain how one thing connects to another to produce some desirable or undesirable event or outcome whether expectedly or unexpectedly. Equally, the writing can focus on the mystification or management of impressions of 'truth', 'cause' and 'effect' through which 'explanatory' models are politically employed. In either case, the writing focuses on what is said to 'have to happen' due to particular causes and inter-actions. At this point, there is a kind of return to the master signifier as the cause or the (self) explanatory universal through which particulars are organized to produce desired effects or outcomes. By focusing upon the models employed – implicitly or explicitly – by interviewees a write up can offer alternative readings identifying the processes through which hegemonic strategies are employed to fill desirable empty signifiers with particular contents in order to universalize those contents as formulating 'the True way', 'the Only way', 'the Rational way', 'the professional way', 'the Democratic way', by which to organize every day practices and so on. If, however, there are multiple views then there is no one way, no final way. Rather than there being a single aim for emancipation, there are emancipations, or rather, an unfinishable process of struggle for emancipation(s) from any given view or views. It results in a vocabulary that is always provisional.

The above is not meant to be exhaustive. It cannot be. The only limits are those of time and imagination. The inter-view is a process that radically displaces the ways in which the powerful or the speaking subject centres his or her universe around the 'real ground(s)' upon which decisions are made and actions undertaken. In elaborating the task and field of the project the purpose of writing up is often too easily captured and fixed under a master signifier. Each of these instances, then, provide examples of the creation of temporary vocabularies which act as the resources by which engagements with people, environments and texts can take place. I give them the status only of quasi-stable resources which are open to deconstruction in other readings and for other agendas.

Exit Strategies

When the recording ends, new conversations begin. Not always – but mostly. It is not often that people have the luxury of someone just listening, and of course, was that OK? Was it what you wanted? It is an invitation to continue in some way, perhaps a concern to please, maybe a hint that not everything was said, or a way of providing a last sly spin to what has been said. We have been strangers who have shared a one-sided intimacy – an odd affair. What was it *really* about? Suddenly, perhaps a hidden motive is made known. Can it be recorded? Will I remember it correctly? Can I just switch on again please? What you're saying is so useful it would be a shame not to record it. The game begins again.

There really is no way out. No interview is ever finished. The words recorded find new life in each text written, in each re-reading. The interview only ever exists in those engagements where no final view is possible. So, is it over now, that quest for Enlightenment? What can it now mean to apply free reason across the field of human experience in order to determine:[4]

1. What can I know?
2. What ought I do?
3. What may I hope?
4. What is the human being?

Are Kant's questions now irrelevant to thought about the good society, the life of the human being with others, knowledge of the world – or do they take on a greater urgency?

---

[4] My use of the questions here are endebted to Davis's (2004) discussions of Kant's relationship to contemporary trends in postmodern, poststructuralist theory.

The inter-view, however, does not abandon these questions. Nor does it call any particular answer 'enlightenment'. Rather, the questions act as the hysterical prelude to identifying and representing excluded differences, new knowledges, new ways for social living, new prospects for creativity, excitement, adventure. By continually asking the questions in relation to the data of everyday life new projects are always born. It is not the answer as a finality that is interesting or useful to life, but the question which is always a way out, an exit creating the possibility of the existence of difference. Condensing exit and exist, the inter-view exi(s)ts – a play to emphasize that views can be brought to the crossroads of alternative ways of seeing, creative of new syntheses. Engaging with others, the inter-view is the condition for emancipatory projects. No approach absolves the individual from making decisions. There is no absolute formula to guarantee truth, goodness, utopia. Thus the inter-view only keeps open possibilities, it does not point the way. And decisions have to be made.

The ethics and the politics arising from the inter-view places responsibility with the decisions and the accounts through which forms of action are articulated. There is thus no exit from responsibility. Where responsibility is founded not on a final answer but in relation to otherness, to difference, to openness, to transformation there is always hope for futures that are creative, novel, unique. It is then that emancipatory projects begin. But emancipation is *the* elusive address. For that reason, there are only strategies for emancipation(s) that:

1. disturb apparently foundational statements by revealing the manner in which they were constructed;
2. identify difference in apparently homogeneous structures, entities and categories;
3. exploit ambiguities, puns, contingent associations of all kinds;
4. examine the rhetorical structures through which social action is organized;
5. short-circuit closure by any master or transcendental signifier;
6. identify alternative quasi-transcendentals, quasi-stabilities that evoke or incite or act as lures for desire to engage in action for alternative futures;
7. open spaces for dialogue about alternative views that mutually challenge and mutually mobilize desire for alternative purposes.

The inter-view maps what is at stake in the multiplicity of views that create the everyday fields of struggle. The project is created to represent the different interests of people. What is worth fighting for, arguing for, building, emerges through the inter-view, the dialogue of the views of people who seek recognition and representation of their differences.

References

Abma, T. and Schwandt, T. A. (2005) The Practice and Politics of Sponsored Evaluations, in B. Somekh and C. Lewin (eds) *Research Methods in the Social Sciences*. London, Thousand Oaks and New Delhi: Sage.

ACE Project (1991–1993) Co-Director: John Schostak and Terry Phillips, Assessment of Competence in Nursing and Midwifery Project. Funded by the English National Board for Nursing, Midwifery and Health Visiting.

Ball, S. (1994) Political Interviews and the Politics of Interviewing, in Geoffrey Walford (ed.) *Researching the Powerful in Education*. London: UCL Press.

Barthes, R. (1963) *Sur Racine*. Paris: Seuil, Points edition.

Barthes, R. (1977) *Image, Music, Text*. Essays selected and translated by Stephen Heath. London: Fontana Press.

Bassnett, S. and Trivedi, H. (eds) (1999) *Postcolonial Translation: Theory and Practice*. London and New York: Routledge.

Bataille, G. (1987) *Eroticism* (trans. Mary Dalwood). London and New York: Marion Boyars. Originally published 1957 by Editions de Minuit, Paris, France.

Baugh, B. (2003) *French Hegel. From Surrealism to Postmodernism*. New York and London: Routledge.

Bauman, Z. (2001) *The Individualised Society*. Cambridge: Polity.

Bedford, H., Phillips, T., Robinson, J. and Schostak, J. F. (1994) *Researching Professional Education. Education, Dialogue and Assessment: creating partnership for improving practice*. London: The English National Board for Nursing Midwifery and Health Visiting.

Benner, P. (1984) *From Novice to Expert: Excellence and Power in Clinical Nursing Practice*. California: Addison-Wesley.

Bennington, G. and Derrida, J. (1991) *Jacques Derrida*. Chicago: University of Chicago Press.

Berman, M. (1982) *All That Is Solid Melts Into The Air: The Experience Of Modernity*. New York: Penguin Books.

Bhaskar, R. (1975 and 1978) *A Realist Theory of Science*. Hassocks, Sussex: Harvester Press.

Bourdieu, P. (1993) *La Misère du Monde*. Éditions du Seuil. It was published in

English as *The weight of the world: social suffering in contemporary society* (trans. Priscilla Parkhurst Ferguson et al. 1999). Oxford: Polity.

Butler, J. (1999) *Subjects of Desire. Hegelian reflections in Twentieth-Century France.* New York, Columbia University Press. First published 1987.

Butler, J., Laclau, E. and Zizek, S. (2000) *Contingency, Hegemony, Universality. Contemporary Dialogues on the Left.* London and New York: Verso.

CIEL Project (2004) Collaboration in E-Learning. Report for the Department for Education and Skills, Norwich, Forum Trust Ltd.

Caruth, C. (ed.) (1995) *Trauma. Explorations in Memory.* Baltimore and London: The Johns Hopkins University Press.

Coathup, G. W. (1997) Talking Out: A Search for Empowerment. Unpublished PhD thesis, University of East Anglia, Norwich, England.

Davis, C. (2004) *After PostStructuralism. Reading, Stories and Theory.* London and New York: Routledge.

de Man, P. (1986) The Resistance to Theory, *Theory and History of Literature*, Vol. 33, foreword by Wlad Godzich. Minneapolis: University of Minnesota Press.

Deleuze, G. and Guattari, F. (1987) *A Thousand Plateaus: Capitalism and Schizophrenia* (trans. Brian Massumi). Minneapolis: University of Minnesota Press.

Derrida, J. (1974) *Of Grammatology* (trans. Gayatri Chakravorty Spivak). Baltimore and London: The Johns Hopkins University Press.

Derrida, J. (1990) Force of Law: The 'Mystical Foundation of Authority' (trans. Mary Quaintance), *Cardozo Law Review*, 11(5–6): 921–1045.

Derrida, J. (1992) Force of Law: The 'Mystical Foundation of Authority', in Drucilla Cornell, Michael Rosenfeld and David Gray Carson (eds) *Deconstruction and the Possibility of Justice*. New York and London: Routledge.

Descartes, R. (2001) *Discourse on Method* (trans. R. E. Sutcliffe). Harmondsworth: Penguin Books.

Descombes, V. (1980) *Modern French Philosophy* (trans. L. Scott-Fox and J. M. Harding). Cambridge: Cambridge University Press.

Dilthey, W. (1914–) *Gesammelte Schriften*, 18 vols. Stuttgart: B. G. Teubner (vols 1–12); Göttingen: Vandenhoek and Ruprecht (vols 13–18).

Dreyfus, S. E. (1980) A five stage model of the mental activities involved in directed skill acquisition. Mimeo, US Airforce Office of Scientific Research, Contract No. F49620-79-C-0063, University of California, Berkeley.

Elliott, J. (1991) *Action Research for Educational Change*. Milton Keynes: Open University Press.

Finch, J (1984) 'It's great to have someone to talk to': The Ethics and Politics of Interviewing Women, in C. Bell and H. Roberts (eds) *Social Researching*. London: Routledge & Kegan Paul.

Fink, B. (1995) *The Lacanian Subject. Between Language and Jouissance.* Princeton: Princeton University Press.

Fox, N. F. (2003) *The New Sartre. Explorations in Postmodernism.* New York and London: Continuum.

Freeman, M. D. A. (1983) *The Rights and Wrongs of Children*. London: Francis Pinter.

Freire, P. (1970) *Cultural Action for Freedom*. Harmondsworth: Penguin (published by Penguin 1972).

Freire, P. (1973) *Education: The Practice of Freedom*. London: Writers and Readers Publishing Cooperative.

Gadammer, H.G. (1989) *Truth and Method*, 2nd revised edn. London: Sheed and Ward.

Garfinkel, H. (1967) *Studies in Ethnomethodology*. New York: Prentice-Hall.

Gasché, R. (1986) *The Tain of the Mirror. Derrida and the Philosophy of Reflection*. Cambridge, MA and London: Harvard University Press.

Gasché, R. (1999) *Of Minimal Things. Studies on the Notion of Relation*. Stanford: Stanford University Press.

Geertz, C. (1988) *Works and lives: the anthropologist as author*. Cambridge: Polity.

Gell, A. (1998) *Art and Agency: An Anthropological Theory*. London and New York: Routledge.

Glaser, B.G. and Strauss, A.L. (1964) Awareness Contexts and Social Interaction, *American Sociological Review*, 29: 669-79.

Grosz, E. (1990) *Jacques Lacan. A feminist introduction*. London and New York: Routledge.

Habermas, J. (1987) *The Philosophical Discourse of Modernity*. Cambridge, MA: MIT Press.

Hammersley, M. (ed.) (1984) *The Ethnography of Schooling*. Humberside: Nafferton Books.

Holt, J. (1974) *Escape from Childhood: The Needs and Rights of Children*. Harmondsworth: Pelican.

Houlgate, S. (2005) *An Introduction to Hegel. Freedom, Truth and History*. Oxford: Blackwell.

Howard, R. J. (1982) *Three faces of hermeneutics: an introduction to current theories of understanding*. Berkeley and London: University of California Press.

Hyppolite, J. (1974) *Genesis and Structure of Hegel's Phenomenology of Spirit*. Evanston: Northwestern University Press. Trans. Samuel Cherniak and John Heckman. First published 1946 Editions Montaigne.

Illich, I. (1971) *Deschooling Society*. London: Calder and Boyers.

Jackson, P. W. (1968) *Life in Classrooms*. New York: Holt, Rinehart & Winston.

Johnson, S. (2001) *Emergence. The connected lives of ants, brains, cities and software*. London: Allen Lane, the Penguin Press.

Kohl, H. (1971) *36 Children*. Harmondsworth: Penguin.

Kojève, A. (1969) *Introduction to the Reading of Hegel, Lectures on the Phenomenology of Spirit* (assembled Raymond Queneau, ed. Allan Bloom, trans. James H. Nichols, Jr). Ithaca and London: Cornell University Press. Originally published 1947, Gallimard, Paris.

Kozol, J. (1967) *Death at an Early Age*. New York: Houghton Mifflin.

Kristeva, J. (1984) *Revolution in Poetic Language* (trans. L.S. Roudiez). Columbia University Press: New York.

Labbett, B. (1988) Skillful Neglect, in J. Schostak (ed.) *Breaking into the Curriculum: the impact of information technology on schooling*. London and New York: Methuen.

Labbett, B. (1996) *Personal Principles Of Procedure & The Expert Teacher*. www.enquirylearning.net/ELU/Issues/Education/Ed4.html.

Lacan, J. (1977a) *Écrits. A selection*. London: Tavistock/Routledge.

Lacan, J. (1977b) *The Four Fundamental Concepts of Psyhcho-analysis*. London: The Hogarth Press.

Laclau, E. (1990) *New Reflections of the Revolution of Our Time*. London: Verso.

Laclau, E. (1996) *Emancipation(s)*. London and New York: Verso.

Laclau, E. (2005) *On Populist Reason*. London, New York: Verso.

Laclau, E. and Mouffe, C. (1985) *Hegemony and Socialist Strategy: Towards a Radical Democratic Politics*. London: Verso.

Lyotard, J. F. (1984) The Postmodern Condition: A Report on Knowledge (trans. Geoff Bennington and Brian Massumi, forward Frederic Jameson, in *Theory and History of Literature*, Vol. 10 Manchester: Manchester University Press.

MacDonald, B. (1987) Evaluation and the Control of Education, in R. Murphy and H. Torrance (eds) *Evaluating Education: Issues and Methods*. London: Harper and Row (in association with the Open University); first published 1974 in B. MacDonald and R. Walker (eds) *Innovation, Evaluation, Research and the Problem of Control*. (SAFARI), CARE, UEA, Norwich.

Martinson, R. (1974) What works? Questions and answers about prison reform, *Public Interest*, 35: 22–45.

Mead, G.H. (1934) *Mind, Self and Society*. Chicago: University of Chicago Press.

Milgram, S. (1974) *Obedience to Authority: An Experimental View*. London: Tavistock.

Miller, J. Hillis (2004) Taking up a task: moments of decision in Ernesto Laclau's thought, in S. Critchley and O. Marchant (eds) *Laclau a critical reader*. London and New York: Routledge.

Mouffe, C. (1993) *The Return of the Political*. London and New York: Verso.

Mouffe, C. (ed.) (1996) *Deconstruction and Pragmatism: Simon Critchley, Jacques Derrida, Ernesto Laclau, and Richard Rorty*. London and New York: Routledge.

Neill, A.S. (1973) *Neill, Neill 'Orange Peel': a personal view of ninety years*, revised edn. London: Weidenfeld and Nicholson.

Noffke, S. and Somekh, B. (2005) Action Research in B. Somekh and C. Lewin (eds) *Research Methods in the Social Sciences*. London: Thousand Oaks and New Delhi: Sage.

Norval, A. (1996) *Deconstructing Apartheid Discourse*. London and New York: Verso.

Oakley, A. (1982) Interviewing Women: A Contradiction in terms, in H. Roberts (ed.) *Doing Feminist Research*. London: Routledge.

Open University Course K521, reversioned as K350 (2001) *Assessing Practice in Nursing and Midwifery*.

PANDA Project (1997–1999) Co-Directors: John Schostak and Terry Phillips, 'PANDA' Project, Assessment of Practice at Diploma, Degree and Postgraduate Level in Pre and Post Registration Nursing and Midwifery Education. Funded by the English National Board for Nursing, Midwifery and Health Visiting.

Patrick, J. (1973) *A Glasgow Gang Observed*. London: Methuen.

Pawson, R. and Tilley, N. (1997) *Realistic Evaluation*. London and Thousand Oaks, CA: Sage.

Phillips, T., Schostak, J. and Tyler, J. (2000a) *Practice and Assessment: an evaluation of the assessment of practice at diploma, degree and postgraduate level in pre and post registration nursing and midwifery education*. London: ENB.

Phillips, T. P., Schostak, J. F. and Tyler, J. (2000b) *Practice and Assessment in*

Nursing and Midwifery: doing it for real. Research Reports Series N0. 16, London: ENB.

Pole, C. and Morrison, M. (2003) *Ethnography for Education.* Maidenhead: Open University Press.

Puwar, N. (1997) *Reflections on Interviewing Women MPs.* Sociological Research Online, Vol. 2, no. 1, www.socresonline.org.uk/socresonline/2/1/4.html.

Rabaté, J-M. (2002) *The Future of Theory.* Oxford: Blackwell.

Rancière, J. (1995) *La Mésentente. Politique et philosophie.* Paris: Galilée.

Rancière, J. (2004) *The politics of aesthetics* (with an after word by Slavoj Zizek). London and New York: Continuum.

Richmond, J. (1982) *Becoming our own experts.* Talk Workshop Group, ILEA English Centre, London.

Ricoeur, P. (2004) *The Conflict of Interpretations.* London and New York: Continuum (first published in France 1969).

Riffaterre, M. (1978) *Semiotics of Poetry.* London: Methuen.

Rogoff, I. (1998) Studying visual culture, in N. Mirzoeff (ed.) *The Visual Culture Reader.* London and New York: Routledge.

Rorty, R. (1999) *Philosophy and Social Hope.* Harmondsworth: Penguin Books.

Saussure, F. de (1966) *Course in General Linguistics* (C. Bally and A. Sechehaye, eds. trans. W. Baskin). New York: McGraw-Hill.

Schostak, J. F. (1985) Creating the Narrative Case Record, *Curriculum Perspectives,* 5(1): 7–13.

Schostak, J.F. (1988) Developing More Democratic Modes of Teacher-Pupil Relationships: 'The Early Years Listening and Talking Project'. Conference of the Education Research Network of Northern Ireland at the University of Ulster, November.

Schostak, J. F. (1989) Primary School Policy – the Democratic Way. Conference of the Education Research Network of Northern Ireland at the University of Ulster, November.

Schostak, J. F. (1990) Problem Solving and Educational Action. Conference of the Education Research Network of Northern Ireland at the University of Ulster, November.

Schostak, J. F. (1993) *Dirty Marks: The Education of Self, Media and Popular Culture.* London: Pluto Press.

Schostak, J. F. (1999a) Representing the Cr/eye of the Witness, in A. Massey and G.Walford (eds) *Explorations in Methodology, Studies in Educational Ethnography, Volume 2.* JAI Press: Stanford, Connecticut.

Schostak, J. F. (1999b) Action Research and the Point Instant of Change, *Educational Action Research,* 7(3): 403–20.

Schostak, J.F. (2002) *Understanding, Designing and Conducting Qualitative Research in Education. Framing the Project.* Maidenhead: Open University Press.

Schostak, J. F. and Davis, R. (1990) Report: Alcohol Cultures of Secondary Aged Children, project, funded for one year by AERC.

Schostak, J. F. and Phillips, P. (1997) Evaluation of the assessment of practice at diploma, degree and postgraduate level in pre and post registration nursing and midwifery education, proposal submitted to English National Board for Nursing, Midwifery and Health Visiting.

Schostak, J.F. and Walker, B. (2002) Change to Teaching project, funded by TTA.

Schostak, J.F. and Walker, B. (2003) Extension to Change to Teaching project, funded by TTA.

Schostak, J. F., Schostak, J.R., Piper, H. and Pearce, C. (2004) CAPE UK's 'Of this Planet' – Positive Images Programme. CAPE and the Manchester Metropolitan University.

Schostak, J. R. (2004) *[Ad]dressing Methodologies. Tracing the Self In Significant Slips: Shadow Dancing.*

Schostak, J. R. and Schostak, J.F. (2001) Consultants as Educators – a twelve month study, NANIME Charitable Trust, Norwich, UK.

Schutz, A. (1976) *The Phenomenology of the Social World* (trans. G. Walsh and F. Lehnert). London: Heinemann.

Simons, H. (ed.) (1980) *Towards a Science of the Singular.* Occasional publication, CARE, University of East Anglia, Norwich.

Skinner, B. F. (1953) *Science and Human Behaviour.* New York: Macmillan.

Smith, A. M. (1998) *Laclau and Mouffe. The radical democratic imaginary.* London and New York: Routledge.

Sokal, A. (1996a) Transgressing the boundaries: Towards a transformative hermeneutics of quantum gravity, *Social Text,* 46/47: 217–52.

Sokal, A. (1996b) A physicist experiments with cultural studies, *Lingua Franca* 6(4): 62–4.

Sokal, A. and Bricmont, J. (1997) *Impostures intellectuelles.* Paris: Odile Jacob.

Sokal, A. and Bricmont, J. (1998) *Intellectual Impostures: Postmodern Philosophers' Abuse of Science.* London: Profile Books.

Stark, S., and Torrance, H. (2005) Case Study, in B. Somekh and C. Lewin *Research Methods in the Social Science,* London, Thousand Oaks, New Delhi: Sage.

Stenhouse, L. (1975) *An Introduction to Curriculum Research and Development.* London: Heinemann.

Stenhouse, L. (1984) Library Access and User Education in an Academic Sixth form: an autobiographical account, in R. Burgess (ed.) *The Research Process in Educational Settings: ten case studies.* Lewes: Falmer Press.

Stenhouse, L. (1980) *Library Access and Sixth Form Study (LASS) Project,* UEA, Norwich, www.uea.ac.uk/care/research/sponsors.html.

Strauss, A. and Corbin, J. (1998) *Basics of qualitative research: techniques and procedures for developing grounded theory.* Thousand Oaks, CA and London: Sage.

Talking and Listening Project (1988–9) www.enquirylearning.net/ELU/Issues/Education/archivesEarlyyears.html.

Taylor, C. (1975) *Hegel.* Cambridge: Cambridge University Press.

Torfing, J. (1999) *New Theories of Discourse. Laclau, Mouffe and Zizek.* Oxford.

TYDE Project (1992–1995) Co-directors: John Schostak and Terry Phillips, Evaluation of Three-Year Undergraduate Nursing and Midwifery programmes. Funded by the English National Board for Nursing, Midwifery and Health Visiting.

Zizek, S. (1991) *Looking Awry. An Introduction to Jacques Lacan through Popular Culture.* Cambridge, MA and London: MIT Press.

Zizek, S. (1992) *Enjoy your symptom! Jacques Lacan in Hollywood and out.* London and New York: Routledge.

Name Index

Index

BECOMING A RESEARCHER
A Research Companion for the Social Sciences
Máiréad Dunne, John Pryor and Paul Yates

This innovative book combines what most books separate: research as practical activity and research as intellectual engagement. It clarifies and makes explicit the methodological issues that underlie the journey from initial research idea to the finished report and beyond.

The text moves the researcher logically through the research process and provides insights into methodology through an in-depth discussion of methods. It presents the research process as an engagement with text. This theme moves through the construction of text in the form of data and the deconstruction of text in analysis. Finally the focus moves to the reconstruction of text through the re-presentation of the research in the report. Following through each of these stages in turn, the chapters consider either a practical issue or a group of methods and interrogate the associated methodological concerns. In addition, the book also addresses the rarely explored issues of the researcher as writer and researcher identity as core elements of the research process.

The book provides a range of insights and original perspectives. These successfully combine practical guidance with the invitation to consider the problematic nature of research as social practice. It is an ideal reference for those embarking on research for the first time and provides a new methodological agenda for established researchers.

Contents: *Introduction – Part 1 – Distinguishing Data: Constructing text – The Logic of Enquiry – Talking with people: Interviewing – Knowing with Numbers: Questionnaires – Being There: Observation – Part 2 – Dicing with data: Deconstructing text – Breaking Down Data: Routes to Interpretation – Worrying at Words: Discourse Analysis – Pulverizing Policy: Deconstructing Documents – Part 3 – Data with Destiny: Reconstructing Text – Writing Research: Authoring Text – The Selfish Text: Research and Identity – Methods and Methodology*

208pp   0 335 21394 4 Paperback   0 335 21395 2 Hardback

A HANDBOOK FOR TEACHER RESEARCH
From Design to Implementation

Colin Lankshear and Michele Knobel

"This informative book helped me to understand research in general and to bring focus and clarity to my current research project. The text answers questions and provides guidance and support in a manner that is user-friendly and easy to comprehend ... After reading this book, I feel empowered as a teacher-researcher and would unhesitatingly recommend it to other teacher-researchers, graduate students and educators." – Francesca Crowther, teacher and doctoral student, Nova Scotia, Canada.

This book provides a comprehensive and detailed approach to teacher research as systematic, methodical and informed practice. It identifies five requirements for all kinds of research, and provides clear and accessible guidelines for teachers to use in conducting their own classroom-based studies.

Features:

- A clear definition of teacher research which insists on more than 'stories' and anecdotal 'retrospectives'
- Easy-to-use and widely applicable tools and techniques for collecting and analysing data in qualitative research
- Acknowledges the relevance of quantitative and document-based as well as qualitative forms of inquiry in teacher research
- Accessible and informative discussions of key issues in teacher research, such as interpretation, ethics, and validity.

A Handbook for Teacher Research provides everything the teacher researcher needs in order to conduct good quality practitioner research. It is ideal for upper level undergraduate Education programmes and for postgraduate research, as well as for teacher researchers who conceive and drive their own independent studies.

412pp   0 335 21064 3 Paperback   0 335 21065 1 Hardback

THE MORAL FOUNDATIONS OF EDUCATIONAL RESEARCH
Knowledge, Inquiry and Values

Pat Sikes, Jon Nixon and Wilfred Carr (eds).

"A rallying call for ethical self-awareness ... This is a book for everyone doing educational research." – BJES

The Moral Foundations of Educational Research considers what is distinctive about educational research in comparison with other research in the social sciences. As the contributors all agree that education is always an essentially moral enterprise, discussion about methodology starts, not with the widely endorsed claim that educational research should be 'useful' and 'relevant', but with the attempt to justify and elaborate that claim with reference to its moral foundations. Determining the nature of 'usefulness' and 'relevance' is not simply a matter of focussing on impact and influence but involves a radical re-conceptualisation of the moral and educational significance of what is deemed to be 'useful' and 'relevant'. There is no argument with this emphasis on the generation of 'useful' and 'relevant' knowledge, but it is suggested that educational research requires a fuller and more rounded understanding that takes account of the moral values of those who conduct it. Educational research is grounded, epistemologically, in the moral foundations of educational practice. It is the epistemological and moral purposes underlying the 'usefulness' and 'relevance' of educational research that matter.

Contributors: *Pierre Bourdieu, Peter Clough, Ivor Goodson, Fred Inglis, Gary McCulloch, Jon Nixon, Carrie Paechter, Richard Pring, Pat Sikes, Melanie Walker.*

Contents: *Introduction – Educational research and its histories – Towards a social history of educational research – Living research – thoughts on educational research as moral practice – The virtues and vices of an educational researcher – Against objectivism – the reality of the social fiction – Research as thoughtful practice – On goodness and utility in educational research – Method and morality – practical politics and the science of human affairs – Index.*

192pp   0 335 21046 5 Paperback

WHAT DOES GOOD EDUCATION RESEARCH LOOK LIKE?
Situating a Field and its Practices

Lyn Yates

"a powerful, well informed argument for the importance of pluralism. . . This book will tell young researchers what they need to know about doing educational research; it will encourage experienced researchers to see their own practice in context. It is a profound book that everyone should read." – *Professor Jane Gaskell, Dean, OISE, University of Toronto*

"This brilliant guide to judging educational research examines the most basic questions about research practice that most people think are settled, and reveals them as problematic ... Humorous, sharp, and thoughtful, this readable inquisition explores from differing perspectives 'what does good education research look like' in multiple forms including dissertations, journal articles, and grant proposals." – *Sari Knopp Biklen, Laura and Douglas Meredith Professor, Syracuse University, USA*

This book explains and critically examines some key debates about the quality and value of education research, and shows how it must meet different demands in different places, times and conditions. A major part of the book provides detailed analyses and guidance to different areas in which education research is judged: from academic theses to the press; from highest level competition for prestigious grants to collaborative work with practitioners.

Lyn Yates asks probing questions in six education research arenas – the thesis, the research grant application, the journal article, the consultancy application, book publishing, and the press:

- Who are the judges here?
- What expectations and networks do they bring to the task?
- What are the explicit and implicit criteria for good research in that area?
- What are the common failings?
- What does good research look like?

The book is an indispensable companion to existing textbooks on research methodology. It provides a clear and provocative discourse about the banalities and disorderliness in which education researchers have to operate.

Contents: Acknowledgements – Introduction – Part 1: Political and paradigm disputes, historical change and the field of education – What does good education research look like? Some beginnings and debates – History, fashion and academic research in education – Part 2: Arenas of education research: contexts, genres and the rules of the game – The thesis – Academic journals – Competitive research grants – Commissioned research – Schools, teachers and other practitioner users – Book publishing - The press – Situating research practices – Notes – References – Index

240pp   0 335 21199 2 Paperback   0 335 21247 6 Hardback